COLLECTIVE GOODS, COLLECTIVE FUTURES IN ASIA

How were collective goods provided in the authoritarian developmental states, transitional socialist societies and nascent democracies of twentieth-century Asia? How will the methods of collective goods production change in the new millennium? By whom, for whom, and with what consequences will they be supplied?

Collective Goods, Collective Futures in Asia documents and analyses the contests over the provision of collective goods and examines the impact of their provision on the societies, polities and economies of contemporary East and Southeast Asia. Sargeson's introductory chapter on the conceptualisation and political rationalities of collective goods provision establishes a theoretical framework for ten original, methodologically diverse and empirically rich case studies. Focusing on regional trade and conservation regimes, NGOs, property rights and management institutions regulating access to common pool resources, physical infrastructure, social welfare and urban public space, the contributors to this volume illuminate the new ideologies, actors and arrangements that are producing the collective goods that will shape Asia's future.

This book is essential reading for all those interested in debates about processes of political, economic and social change in Asia, including graduates in disciplines ranging from comparative politics and policy analysis to economics, Asian Studies scholars, foreign aid providers and civil society activists.

Sally Sargeson is a Research Fellow at the Asia Research Centre, Murdoch University, and a Lecturer in Organisational and Labour Studies at the University of Western Australia. She is the author of *Reworking China's Proletariat* and is a regular contributor to scholarly journals and the Australian press.

ASIAN CAPITALISMS
Edited by Richard Robison
Director, Asia Research Centre, Murdoch University, Australia

At the beginning of the twenty-first century capitalism stands triumphant. Yet it has not been the liberal model of free markets, democratic politics, and the rule of law and citizenship that has enjoyed general ascendancy. Within Asia, a range of dirigiste, predatory and authoritarian systems have emerged under the general rubric of Asian capitalism. In this series we seek to explain the political, ideological and social bases of this phenomenon, and to analyse the collision of these systems with the power of global economic markets and highly mobile capital, and their confrontation with emerging domestic, social and political interests. In the context of the Asian financial crisis we ask whether we are witnessing the end of Asian capitalism. Is Asia caught in an inexorable metamorphosis towards liberal capitalism? And what factors are driving the processes of transformation?

LAW, CAPITALISM AND POWER IN ASIA
The Rule of Law and Legal Institutions
Edited by Kanishka Jayasuriya

POLITICS AND MARKETS IN THE WAKE OF THE ASIAN CRISIS
Edited by Richard Robison, Mark Beeson, Kanishka Jayasuriya and Hyuk-Rae Kim

COLLECTIVE GOODS, COLLECTIVE FUTURES IN ASIA
Edited by Sally Sargeson

COLLECTIVE GOODS, COLLECTIVE FUTURES IN ASIA

Edited by Sally Sargeson

Routledge
Taylor & Francis Group

LONDON AND NEW YORK

First published 2002
by Routledge
2 Park Square, Milton Park, Abingdon, Oxon OX14 4RN
52 Vanderbilt Avenue, New York, NY 10017

Routledge is an imprint of the Taylor & Francis Group, an informa business

© 2002 Selection and editorial matter, Sally Sargeson; individual chapters, the
contributors

All rights reserved. No part of this book may be reprinted or reproduced or
utilised in any form or by any electronic, mechanical, or other means, now known
or hereafter invented, including photocopying and recording, or in any
information storage or retrieval system, without permission in writing from the
publishers.

Notice:
Product or corporate names may be trademarks or registered trademarks, and are
used only for identification and explanation without intent to infringe.

British Library Cataloguing in Publication Data
A catalogue record for this book is available from the British Library

Library of Congress Cataloging in Publication Data
Collective goods, collective futures in Asia / edited by Sally Sargeson.
Includes bibliographical references and index
1. Public goods. 2. Asia–Economic policy. 3. Asia–Social Policy. I. Sargeson,
Sally.
HB846.5. C65 2002
306'095–dc21
2002021334

Typeset in Times by Taylor & Francis Books Ltd

ISBN 13: 978-0-415-28444-8 (pbk)

CONTENTS

CONTENTS

CONTRIBUTORS

Sidney Adams is a doctoral candidate at the Asia Research Centre, Murdoch University, Perth.

Mark Beeson is Senior Lecturer in International Political Economy at the University of Queensland, Brisbane.

Chua Beng-Hua is Professor of Sociology at the National University of Singapore.

Hyuk-Rae Kim is Professor of Korean Studies at the Graduate School of International Studies, Yonsei University, Seoul.

Michael Leaf is Associate Professor at the Centre for Human Settlements, University of British Columbia, Vancouver.

John McCarthy is a Research Fellow at the Van Vollenhoven Institute, Leiden.

M. Ramesh is Senior Lecturer in Government at the University of Sydney.

Sally Sargeson is is a Research Fellow at the Asia Research Centre, Murdoch University, and a Lecturer in Organisational and Labour Studies at the University of Western Australia.

Carol Warren is Associate Professor of Asian Studies at Murdoch University, Perth.

Linda Wong is Associate Professor at the Centre for Comparative Management and Social Policy, City University, Hong Kong.

Andrew B. Wyatt is Acting Director of the Australian Mekong Resource Centre, University of Sydney.

Jian Zhang is Lecturer in Politics at the Australian Defence Forces Academy, University of New South Wales, Canberra.

ACKNOWLEDGMENTS

This book is the final volume in the series on the foundations of capitalism in East and Southeast Asia produced by the Asia Research Centre at Murdoch University. Previous volumes in the series comprised a study of legal institutions edited by Kanishka Jayasuriya and an examination of politics and markets edited by Richard Robison, Mark Beeson, Kanishka Jayasuriya and Hyuk-Rae Kim.

We wish to thank the Asia Research Centre at Murdoch University for its financial and administrative support in organising and hosting the conference on 'Shaping Common Futures' that brought together the contributors to this volume in Perth in October 1999. Financial support for the conference and for production of this book also came from the Graduate School of International Studies at Yonsei University, the Australia-Korea Foundation, the Japan Foundation and the Asia-Pacific Confederation of Chambers of Commerce and Industry.

We are grateful to Richard Robison, former Director of the Asia Research Centre, for his encouragement and guidance in formulating the early stages of our research agenda. Every conference depends, for its success, on the enthusiasm and erudition of its participants. In this respect, we particularly wish to thank the many scholars who acted as discussants for the conference papers. Thanks are also due to Del Blakeway, Robert Roche and Sylvia Mead for their organisational skills and administrative assistance, to Roger Frey for editorial advice, and to Craig Fowlie and Heidi Bagtazo, our editors at Routledge, for their suggestions and support.

1

INTRODUCTION

The contested nature of collective goods in East and Southeast Asia

Sally Sargeson

In the last decades of the twentieth century, countries in East and Southeast Asia that had followed so-called 'Asian' models of development attributed much of their rapid economic growth to the fact that they did not rely upon provision of the same collective goods that had been crucial to the rise of Western Europe and North America earlier that century (Dai 1998; Mahathir 1996; Mahathir and Ishihara 1995). Governments in Asia had not been forced by organised labour and electorates experienced in democratic politics to offer guarantees on employment, social security and civil rights. Instead, they cooperated closely with the private sector to minimise regulatory frameworks, taxation and public consumption. Collective goods that were believed to promote economic growth and which enhanced the managerial capacity and power of the state were funded from the public purse. Demands for many other kinds of collective goods, including participatory political structures, income maintenance schemes and environmental safeguards, were ignored or repressed (Ha 1997).

Yet some observers cautioned that ultimately the absence of collective goods would impede growth and generate political, social and environmental problems in the high-performing Asian economies (Robison 1996). Their concerns were amplified during the economic recession that began in the region in 1997. A chorus of voices charged that the initial financial crisis had been triggered, and its impact exacerbated, by the inadequate provision of collective goods. It was claimed that banks and real estate, capital and stock markets suffered from poor regulation. A lack of credible information made prudent investment impossible. Infrastructural deficiencies created production and distribution bottlenecks in the 'second wave' industrialising countries of Indonesia and China. Defective planning, a failure to enforce safety codes and corruption rendered buildings and bridges unsafe even in the earlier industrialisers, Korea and Taiwan. International organisations warned that the region's exclusive health and social security systems could

1

not deal with the impacts of market instability, urbanisation and demographic transition (International Labor Organization 1999; E. Lee 1998; Stiglitz 1998b; World Bank 1998b). There was repeated mention of the inability of legal institutions to safeguard political and human rights, and of security forces' reluctance to quell violence (*Oxford Analytica* 1998: 18 Sept., 9 Oct.). Even organisations like the Asian Development Bank that, at one stage, had endorsed 'Asian' models of development then promoted their neo-liberal reform, now cautioned that the rates of resource extraction in some parts of the region were unsustainable and pollution was adversely affecting human health and productivity (Samson 1998; *Japan Economic Newswire* 1997).

Suddenly, a transformation of the patterns of collective goods provision that had distinguished 'Asian' models of development was on the agenda of policy-making elites and civilian lobby groups. But there was no consensus as to how these patterns of provision should be changed. Policy-makers in US-dominated international forums argued that countries in East and Southeast Asia should adopt a pattern of collective goods provision more akin to that which existed in the Western capitalist democracies. Therefore, Asian governments should conform to rules-based trading, investment and security regimes. They should create more effective regulatory frameworks, transparent institutions, clearly defined property rights and democratic political systems. And they should divest themselves of state-owned enterprises and utilities. New social elites in Asia, on the other hand, pressed for political, institutional and corporate reforms that would grant them more power, and demanded a different mix of public services. Communities reliant upon old production and exchange systems opposed both propositions and lobbied for the revival of what they described as 'traditional' and 'indigenous' collective goods regimes.

Yet the rapid internationalisation, deregulation and then stagnation of Asia's most successful economies had reduced the capacity of governments to provide a wider range of regulatory, infrastructural and welfare goods within their own jurisdictions, much less participate in the provision of collective goods in global and regional arenas. Demands that they cede control to regimes and markets dominated by the North raised concerns about national sovereignty, cultural integrity and economic competitiveness. And the proposal that they democratise and dismantle state ownership threatened the authoritarian foundations of governments and the viability of conglomerates.

How, then, were collective goods to be produced in countries in East and Southeast Asia in the new millennium? For whom, and with what consequences, would collective goods be provided? And what might be learned about collective goods from an examination of debates about their provision in East and Southeast Asia?

Outline of a research agenda

This volume documents and analyses contests over the provision of collective goods in East and Southeast Asia, inquires into the consequences of their provision for the organisation of people and the discursive constitution of the public sphere in countries in the region, and integrates insights gleaned from that study into the theorisation of collective goods. Through methodologically diverse, self-contained case studies that attend to different levels of the geo-political spectrum, the authors examine struggles to create new principles and methods for providing six different kinds of collective goods. Chapters 2 and 3 examine regional trade and conservation regimes. Chapter 4 discusses the formation of non-governmental organisations in Korea. Chapters 5 and 6 analyse changes in the property rights institutions that regulate access to common pool resources in Indonesia and China. Chapter 7 compares the methods of financing physical infrastructure in Laos and Vietnam, and Chapters 8 and 9 examine social welfare reforms in Malaysia, Singapore and China. The planning, creation and use of public space in cities in China, Singapore and Taiwan forms the subject of Chapters 10 and 11. In the light of the case studies, a brief conclusion assesses proposals for the transformation of patterns of collective goods provision that were put forward at the end of the twentieth century.

These disparate case studies advance the following interlinked arguments. First, they correct the view that collective goods have not been provided in East and Southeast Asia. In fact, numerous sorts of collective goods are in evidence in the region. It is the selection, design, method of supply and outcomes of these goods that beg investigation, rather than reasons for their supposed absence.

Second, the case studies show that the provision of collective goods was driven more by the ideological predispositions and interests of ruling elites and influential business constituencies than by any concerted effort on the part of governments to facilitate the expansion of markets. Nevertheless, the discourses that justified political and business leaders' selection of the range, and mechanisms for the supply of collective goods, displayed a shift away from concerns with development and improved living standards toward a focus on enhanced international competitiveness, public sector efficiency and individual responsibility and self-sufficiency.

Third, the outcomes of their efforts were contingent on opportunities opened up by historical coincidence and strategic advantage rather than on the achievement of consensus. Indeed, the case studies demonstrate that consensus on the necessity for, and 'the good' of, specific types of collective goods occurs rarely, because the provision of collective goods that benefits actors at one end of the international political economy, one segment of a national population, or a particular locality, is often to the

3

SALLY SARGESON

disadvantage of others. They might even experience it as a 'public bad'. In this respect, our book iterates what has become something of a common-place among philosophers: 'the good' is unknowable and contestable. We go further, however, in arguing that continuing contestation over 'the good' and over the goals, methods and consequences of supplying collective goods is immanent to the ways in which the public sphere is being expanded and the future is being shaped by peoples in East and Southeast Asia.

It is also important to specify the tasks that this book does not undertake. It does not attempt to survey the vast array of collective goods and the different modes of their production in the many countries of East and Southeast Asia. Nor is it intended to offer a typology and a set of cross-country comparisons of a particular category of collective goods, a role that has been performed admirably by several other volumes, including the companion books in this series that centre on legal institutions, political structures and market regulations. And, in focusing on collective goods politics 'on the ground' in Asia, this book does not directly engage with the immense volume of public choice and game-theoretic literature on the subject of collective goods.

This introduction defines collective goods, describes the ideologically inscribed discourses that have explained transformations in the provision of collective goods in East and Southeast Asia, and draws together lines of inquiry that are pursued, with differing degrees of emphasis, in the following chapters. It is useful to begin by defining collective goods for a number of reasons, not least of which is that the subject has been studied by scholars working within different disciplinary traditions. In particular, it is necessary to examine critically the assumptions of rational individual interest and utility maximisation that commonly inform analyses of collective action problems. These assumptions help to explain why collective goods are not always provided even where they appear to be of crucial importance as, for example, in Asian countries ostensibly bent on economic development. However, they do not acknowledge that pre-existing *collectively* produced assets, values, organisations, institutions and technologies shape interests and ideas of utility, and may help to overcome the impediments to the provision of public and collective goods.

The major part of this introduction focuses, therefore, on causality and consequence. In this inquiry, Rose and Miller's (1992) agenda for investigating political rationalities serves as a useful analytical tool. Political rationalities specify the objectives that collective goods serve, the organisations entrusted with their supply, and the subjectivity of their recipients. It will be argued that post-colonial governments in East and Southeast Asia discursively represented the provision of collective goods, first in terms of state-directed development, and then in the individualising vocabulary of neo-liberalism. However, the decisions as to which goods should be provided

4

often reflected the preferences of political elites, government agencies and influential social coalitions. It is hardly surprising, then, that the consequences of collective goods provision were often economically sub-optimal.

Moreover, the collective goods provided often failed to achieve outcomes promised by legitimating appeals to 'the common good', 'the public good', 'the public interest' or 'the national interest'. Nor did those goods accommodate the demands of international organisations, the aims of new domestic political forces, or address growing concerns about environmental degradation, the viability of local cultures and social equity. While the resulting debates, conflicts and efforts to develop new approaches to collective goods provision are expanding the public sphere in East and Southeast Asia, the public sphere itself has become a key site for the propagation of neo-liberal ideologies.

On collective goods: definitive attributes and contested assumptions

Types of goods

Goods, according to Cerny's (1995: 598) narrow definition, are roughly synonymous with assets. Foldvary's (1994: 11) use of the term denotes facilities, assets and intangible institutions, services and systems involved in production and exchange. Both definitions highlight the economic utility of goods. In that respect, they resonate with the neoclassical economists' proposition that the greater good is served by the maximisation of a society's total income and wealth. That, in turn is achieved through the most rational organisation of resources, production and distribution. At the point known in the economic literature as Pareto optimality, it becomes impossible to provide goods that will improve the welfare of any individual without negatively affecting the welfare of others.

But goods are not provided just to meet objective economic 'needs' or to maximise utility. Benjamin writes that 'goods are whatever satisfy wants; wants are whatever needs humans perceive as necessary or desirable to fulfill' (1980: 8). Benjamin emphasises that people's wants will be shaped by cultural traditions and social interaction. Their collective wants will be pursued through debate, intrigue or conflict, as well as by voluntary transactions (1980: 11–12). This interpretation of goods points to the fluid, socially constructed and politically contested nature of human needs and desires. In keeping with the recommendations of philosophers such as Robert Olson (1967; see also Galston 1991), Benjamin also draws a subtle distinction between instrumental or intermediate goods (the goods produced as the means to achieve a desired end) and intrinsic goods ('the good' that is the end desired from the provision of instrumental goods). To cite an example, an efficient urban sewerage system, an instrumental good, helps achieve the intrinsic good of public health.

Most scholars of the category of goods described as collective goods employ a definition that hinges upon a specific form of property relation that combines rights associated with ideal types of private and public goods. Pure private goods are produced by and allocated through markets. They are excludable and legally can only be consumed or transferred to others with the consent of their owners. The private good is of limited utility to all but its owner. Neo-classical economists consider this property relation to be the most likely to result in Pareto optimality because, as all costs and benefits are established by markets and borne or captured by individual owners, there is an incentive for those owners to achieve efficiencies (Taylor 1982).

At the polar extreme, pure public goods are indivisible, owned by no-one and accessible to all (Samuelson 1954). Public goods are non-rivalrous in consumption. That means that their use by some people will not detract from the quantity or quality of the good available to others (Foldvary 1994). The benefits and costs of providing public goods are externalised. In other words, they are passed on to non-producers and even to people that might not want to consume the good. By way of illustration, an international convention to control greenhouse gas emissions is a global public good whose provision has been opposed by certain governments and industries. The absence of individual property rights and market mechanisms in the production, distribution and consumption of public goods is thought to render these goods susceptible to under-supply and over-consumption. To refer to the illustration offered above, although everyone wants stable climatic conditions and clean air, not everyone is prepared to sign a convention limiting greenhouse gas emissions. For these reasons, public goods are generally considered to be economically sub-optimal.

As De Bruin (1991: 307–8; see also Benjamin 1980: 11) observes, very few goods wholly fulfil the criteria of purely private or purely public goods. Instead, as the case studies in this book illustrate, many goods fall somewhere between these extremes.

Three features of collective goods

Collective goods are distinguished by some degree of joint supply and use. Although parts of the production and distribution process may be undertaken for profit by individuals, the goods generally are produced through a cooperative effort and are not priced by markets (Meyer 1996; Pass and Lewis 1993: 73). In Chapter 8 of this volume, Ramesh explains variations in the provision and financing of public, collective and private goods. Some collective goods, including quarantine and juridical systems, are funded and maintained wholly with public revenue dispensed by national governments. Physical infrastructure, such as the transport and power-generating projects examined by Wyatt in Chapter 7, may be financed by governments, private financiers, banks and international financial institutions, and constructed by private consortiums. Still other collective goods are produced voluntarily by groups of states, organisations or generations of people committed to ideological or political ideals or in the performance of customary practices. Relevant examples include the liberal trade regime mentioned in Chapter 2 by Beeson, the non-governmental organisations (hereafter, NGOs) that have fostered democratisation in Korea, studied in Chapter 4 by Kim, and the customary rights, or *adat*, that Warren and McCarthy in Chapter 5 argue once regulated villagers' access to Indonesian forests. An even broader interpretation of the concept of a collective good as a product of joint supply, applied by Leaf and by Chua in the concluding case studies in this book, are the urban public spaces that are created by all of a city's inhabitants.

A second feature of collective goods is that they exhibit differing degrees of non-excludability. Some collective goods are wholly non-excludable because logistically it is difficult to divide up the good or shut anyone out. For example, every boat within sight of a lighthouse has access to the signals it provides. Exclusion would require that boats be forbidden to enter the area in which the lighthouse operates. However, many collective goods are divisible and some degree of exclusion is possible. These goods may be made available only for the legitimate use of the members of a bounded population or group. For that reason, they are sometimes referred to as 'impure public goods' or 'club goods' (Reisman 1990; Hanson 1978; Buchanan 1965). Trade regimes are club goods that reduce transaction costs between member states, while not offering the same advantages to non-members. The village collective enterprises analysed by Zhang (Chapter 6) and the government-funded welfare systems examined in this volume by Ramesh (Chapter 8) and Wong (Chapter 9) benefit only those people that meet selected criteria such as village residence, citizenship, age and employment status.

Collective goods also possess differing degrees of non-rivalry. Consider, for example, that the signatories to an international trade or environmental protection convention are not disadvantaged by the participation of other states. Similarly, the enjoyment by one person of the icons of a shared heritage – such as the 228 monuments built by governments in Taiwan (Chua, Chapter 11) and the local temples constructed by civil associations in Quanzhou (Leaf, Chapter 10) – does not reduce the utility of those icons to other beneficiaries of that heritage. In other cases, however, the good may be depleted through congestion and subtraction. An irrigation system serves as a case in point, because the extraction of water by people upstream reduces the amount of water available to consumers downstream.

In exhibiting rivalry in consumption, collective goods such as irrigation systems resemble common pool resources (McKay and Acheson 1990; Ostrom 1990; Berkes and Farvar 1989). Yet naturally occurring common pool resources, like the southern bluefin tuna examined by Adams in Chapter 3, are not collective goods. Sell and Son (1997; see also Ostrom *et al.* 1999; Berkes and Farvar 1989: 9) draw a useful distinction between the two by pointing out that the creation or maintenance of collective goods *demands a joint contribution* from states, organisations, communities or individuals, whereas common pool resources may occur independently of human intervention. However, their maintenance *requires people to restrain themselves from taking* from the pool. When overcrowding or excessive extraction from a common pool resource occurs, there is an incentive to design regimes, rules or agencies to enforce restraint on the part of resource users. That is, there is a reason to devise organisational or institutional forms of collective goods. Adams' case study provides a case in point. Australian fisheries scientists lobbied for the formation of the Commission on the Conservation of Southern Bluefin Tuna – a collective good – because they were concerned about stock depletion. But these sorts of organisational and institutional restraints are not always created. Why?

Collective action problems

As collective goods are jointly supplied and, to some degree, are non-excludable, it is difficult to allocate the costs and benefits of their provision among individual producers. Scholars who accept the Hobbesian assumptions of Mancur Olson (1965) argue that as each individual's contribution toward the supply of a collective good outweighs the benefit they personally can expect to derive from it, and as non-contributors also might benefit from its provision, rational, utility-maximising individuals will shirk from contributing to its production and consume more of the good than they helped to produce (Taylor and Singleton 1993). To this proposition, realist scholars add the caveat that actors may refuse to cooperate in the provision of a collective good unless they believe they will gain more from its supply than their competitors (Snidal 1991). Thus other features that sometimes are used to define collective goods are that, like public goods, they are susceptible to the collective action problems of free riding, under-supply and over-consumption (Taylor 1987).

In much of the literature on collective goods provision, assumptions of rational self-interest and utility maximisation have been used to account for the behaviour not only of individuals, but also of firms, bureaucracies, states and regional organisations. This line of reasoning is evident in several chapters of this book. Wyatt, for example, argues that in pursuit of private profits, international investors and engineering corporations involved in the construction of infrastructure in Vietnam and Laos left governments of those countries bearing unacceptably high levels of risk. Adams explains the depletion of the southern bluefin tuna partly by referring to the desire of competing fishing industries to maximise their harvests. Zhang argues persuasively that the absence of clearly specified, individual property rights in collective enterprises in rural China encouraged excessive extraction of revenue by local governments and officials and loafing – a form of free riding – by local employees. A similar argument is developed by Beeson to account for the reluctance of governments in East and Southeast Asia to participate in a liberal trade regime and force their corporations to observe the rules of that regime. Beeson points out that this can be understood as an attempt by these export-oriented countries to free ride on the benefits created by a deregulated environment, while persisting in the protectionism and state direction of credit that underpinned their export competitiveness.

However, while the inadequate and inappropriate provision of collective goods often occurs because of self-interest and utility maximisation, there nevertheless are compelling reasons why we should be cautious about incorporating the potential for collective action problems into a definition of collective goods. For one thing, if self-interest and utility-maximisation are assumed to be universal motives, then in the absence of coercion or the offer of inducements, there seems to be no plausible explanation as to why people would cooperate to produce collective goods from which they stand to gain little (Schmidtz 1991; Hume 1951). In fact, as Weintraub (1997) remarks, such assumptions simply make many instances of collective goods provision incomprehensible. Nevertheless, as the case studies in this book testify, in the absence of a dominant power, or even in the face of repression and at considerable personal cost, where people repeatedly interact they do manage to overcome collective action problems and supply collective goods. Jane Mansbridge observes that on occasion they even appear eager to do so: 'Human beings derive great satisfaction from acting on principle, making commitments to others, and taking part in co-operative endeavours' (1998: 3).

Second, assessments of self-interest and utility are not made in an historical, institutional, cultural and social vacuum. The knowledges, organisations, institutions and technologies that inform our calculations of self-interest actually are the outcomes of prior collective actions, as North (1990) reminds us. In other words, methodological assumptions of rational self-interest and utility maximisation tend to overlook the fact that collective actions have created the enormously complex systems of incentives and constraints within which individual choices are made.

Finally, although these assumptions inform many elegant models and retrospective analyses of collective action situations, they actually are of little use in helping to predict the outcomes of contemporary efforts to provide collective goods. In the absence of complete, accurate and commonly held information, individuals, firms, and even powerful governments and international agencies, miscalculate what might be in their interest and likely to maximise their gains. They ignore relevant information. They are influenced by ideologies, subjective beliefs and irrational fears. They sacrifice significant long-term benefits for the sake of trivial, but immediate, returns. Such 'errors' of rational judgement can result in new configurations of power and interest and, ultimately, generate new demands for collective goods.

Let me illustrate the import of these arguments before returning to our definition of collective goods. One pertinent example of a collective good that has shaped the contemporary rationale of self-interest is the set of private property institutions that are central to the operation of capitalist markets. Peter Miller (1994; see also Douglass 1980; Polanyi 1945) has shown that the unencumbered, alienable individual property rights that figure in the literature on collective goods both as economically optimal type and as behavioural rationale were the creation of seventeenth and eighteenth-century European governments keen to restrain predatory rulers, replenish their coffers and address the concerns of an increasingly influential bourgeoisie. Certain instances of possessive, individualistic behaviour might best be viewed as responses to collectively produced policies and property institutions, rather than as reflections of an innate human characteristic that gives rise to a definitive problem in the provision of collective goods (Hampsher-Monk 1996; Macpherson 1978).

This is exemplified in counterpoint in this volume by case studies of changing property institutions in China and Indonesia. Zhang writes that the creation of rural collective ownership by the Communist Party of China between the late 1940s and early 1950s was intended to disenfranchise as well as dispossess local gentry. In the 1990s, the effort to privatise suburban village enterprises was driven by villagers, wary of officials' abuse of power and eager to benefit from urbanisation and economic growth. Local officials refused to dismantle the collective ownership of enterprises because they wanted to achieve economies of scale, protect their personal shareholdings and pass accumulated assets on to future generations of villagers. In contrast, privatisation that was promoted by officials met with resistance in Indonesian villages. McCarthy and Warren argue that a World-Bank-funded programme to allocate land titles to individuals to facilitate plantation agriculture and resource extraction was judged by villagers to deny the community's *adat* and members' religious, social and economic rights. In these locations, radically different responses were precipitated by dissatisfaction with collective property rights institutions.

With those concerns in mind, the authors of this book employ a minimalist definition of collective goods that centres on their three attributes of joint supply, non-excludability and non-rivalry. We are acutely aware, however, that collective goods satisfy shared ideals, wants and needs, as well as economic functions; that it often is difficult to elicit sufficient contributions toward the provision of collective goods; and that the design, methods of supply, and scope and results of their distribution are contentious issues. The research agenda suggested by these simple insights involves an investigation of the vocabularies and voices that give prominence to certain sets of wants, needs and desires. What makes their provision seem necessary to groups of people? What agencies are given the task of allocating collective goods? And how, and with what consequences, are conflicting demands for collective goods resolved?

The political rationalities of collective goods in East and Southeast Asia

Rose and Miller's (1992) schema for analysing political rationalities provides a useful tool with which to approach the task before us. Larner describes political rationalities as the 'discursive field through which the ends and means of government are articulated' (1997: 13).

Drawing on the case studies presented in this volume, this section sketches the changing morality and principles that have legitimated the exercise of power, the aims of government and the distribution of tasks and programmes for providing collective goods, and the ways in which these programmes have been represented discursively to make them 'thinkable' and, hence, do-able in countries in Asia in the last few decades of the twentieth century. To simplify this task, though at the risk of generalising about disparate, internally differentiated societies, I employ the broad categorisation of states set out by Beeson and Robison (2000: 10–14). Beeson and Robison distinguish between the 'developmental' states of East Asia (Japan, Korea, Taiwan, Singapore), the socialist countries of China, Vietnam and Laos, and the quasi-'predatory' oligarchic state, Indonesia. This broad-brush overview of political rationalities illuminates a shift in approaches to collective goods provision, particularly apparent in the former two categories of country, from provision by authoritarian governments committed to development, toward provision by globalised markets and individual consumers.

Neither the Hobbesian authoritarian state nor the Smithian 'invisible hand' of the market, however, has demonstrated the capacity to produce the instrumental goods that fulfil aspirations for intrinsic goods. Invocations of 'the common good', 'the public good' or 'the national interest', serve as touchstones in the political rationalities that popularise provision of collective goods. Projecting a vision of 'the common good' that will motivate, organise and legitimate efforts to provide collective goods is a hegemonic project (Mansbridge 1998). Drawing on Gramsci's use of the term, this means that agents and media of socialisation instil elite values and goals in members of the population such that they accept and express those values and goals as their own. As Downing and Thigpen concede in an essay on liberal notions of 'the common good', this hegemonic project is *politically* defined and executed' (1993: 1052; see also Stretton and Orchard 1994; Galston 1991). It also is politically contested by those who play no part in defining 'the common good', or who have no stake in its realisation.

SALLY SARGESON

The rationale of development and collective goods provision

Cerny hypothesises that nation-states emerged in Europe, in part, as organisational forms for providing those public goods required by expanding capitalist markets (1995: 598). In the post-colonial societies of East and Southeast Asia, a cadre of new political leaders also viewed the provision of public and collective goods in instrumental terms. However, as will be shown, their priority was not to create political structures and collective goods that would support markets, but rather to organise both markets and collective goods to serve their nationalist, developmental goals and their party and personal interests.

National sovereignty, development and improved living standards figured as the core components of the vision of 'the common good' enunciated by the modernising leaders of Asia. Economic growth, achieved by rapid industrialisation and the export of resources and manufactures, was viewed as a means to realise that vision. An ideology of development detached and prioritised the 'needs' of the economy over political and social issues in the developmental states of East Asia. Development of the productive forces was central to socialist modernisation in China, Vietnam and Laos. Equally, in Indonesia, Chalmers writes that development

> became an ideology in the strongest sense of the term, describing the purpose of political activity, the methods used to achieve that goal, the attitudes which public figures should express, as well as serving as an effective ideological weapon against opponents of the regime.
>
> (Chalmers 1997: 3)

In the developmental and, to a lesser extent, socialist states, throughout much of the last half of the twentieth century a small, relatively independent, unified cohort of politicians and bureaucrats dominated the planning agencies that directed high-growth economies. Organs such as Japan's Ministry of International Trade and Industry, the Economic Development Board of Singapore, the Economic Planning Board and Ministry of Finance of Korea, the Council for Economic Planning and Industrial Development Bureau in Taiwan and China's State Planning Commission channelled credit into selected industries and those areas of physical infrastructure, such as railways and telecommunications, that were deemed to be crucial to the achievement of pre-determined growth targets.

To borrow a term used by Jayasuriya (1998) and Cotton (2000), through the 'enterprise associations' that were created by these powerful government agencies, political leaders and civil servants collaborated with, and coordinated, domestic businesses to increase their share of export markets. In this volume, for example, Adams suggests that competition between Japan's tuna cooperatives and the major trading houses of Mitsubishi, Mitsui and

C. Itoh, was moderated, access to other countries' inshore fisheries secured and the national fishing effort maximised through the intervention of the Ministry of Forestry and Fishing.

Populations, tabulated in ethnic, occupational, class, gender and even residential categories, became the object of a new disciplinary pedagogy, designed to instil in them the notion that patriotism and self-worth could be measured by productivity. In the generously funded school systems in the developmental states, productivism was promoted through the now-familiar discourse of 'Asian' cultural values: nationalism, collectivism, close family relations, deference to authority, thrift and a strong work ethic (Kapur 1996; Mahathir and Ishihara 1995). Schools in the socialist states propagated the 'proletarian' values of nationalism, class solidarity, love of labour and self-sufficiency. The hierarchical, personalised relations that marked business and work cultures were replicated in a relationship of authoritarian paternalism between state and citizen. This is clearly illustrated in the chapter by Leaf, who describes Chinese state-owned work units, with their brief to permanently employ, remunerate, house and provide social security and healthcare for urban residents, as 'mechanisms for the ideologically driven integration of state and society'.

Conversely, planners neglected institutions, infrastructure and services that were considered to be unimportant to the growth of the economy or the stability of ruling regimes. Civic associations, labour organisations and activities that were not controlled by the government or devoted to improving productivity were carefully monitored or repressed (Deyo 1989; Sargeson 1999). Recommendations on urban planning, industrial health and safety and environmental protection that planners judged might impede business were ignored.

The exclusive decision-making structures, 'guided' export drive, rapid rates of accumulation, carefully structured corporatism and investment in education that were represented as characteristic features of the high-performing Asian economies were lauded as aspects of a transferable development paradigm by national leaders and international agencies (Mahathir 1996; World Bank 1994a). Globally and locally, these discursive representations were intended to legitimate the operation of authoritarian governments and explain their limited, selective disbursement of collective goods.

Scholars who have looked beyond these legitimating representations find, however, that political considerations, as well as a commitment to economic development, motivated the provision of many collective goods in the developmental and socialist states (Kwon 1997; Crone 1993). A case in point is provided by public housing. Housing for ordinary people, channelled through organisations like the Housing Development Board in Singapore and China's state-owned enterprises and government departments, helped to contain wage demands and repress industrial unrest during phases of rapid industrialisation and urbanisation. Yet vastly more generous housing entitlements, together with comprehensive medical entitlements and pensions, were supplied to civil servants and military personnel in order to motivate them and elicit their loyalty toward ruling regimes. In Chapter 11 of this volume, Chua suggests that even the 'greening' of Singapore was viewed by Lee Kuan Yew not only as a lure to investors, but also as a canny political tactic.

Where collective goods served no strategic, political or economic purpose, provision was limited. Workers in Korea and Taiwan protested that their wages and working and living conditions failed to keep pace with productivity gains and the growth in GDP. In churches, night schools and at cultural events organised by their employers, they mobilised to press for improved political and economic rights, as well as specific collective goods.

Even welfare goods were not distributed on the basis of need in many of the developmental states and socialist states. This was explained by government spokespeople as evidence of Asian people's preference for intra-community and intra-kin reciprocity (*Far Eastern Economic Review* 1998; *China Daily* 1998; Goodman and Peng 1996). Indeed, requests for public assistance were said to betray a failure on the part of those groups to meet their 'traditional' responsibilities and perform their 'customary' functions. However, some 'traditions' of welfare and 'customary' roles that supposedly obviated the necessity for public welfare provision actually were necessitated by legislation and discriminatory policies. Nowhere is this more apparent than in governments' expectations that women's 'private' lives would serve 'the national interest'. In Singapore, for example, married women's provision of care to the elderly, disabled and young was underpinned by laws that made adults responsible for the upkeep and supervision of lineal relatives and policies that channelled public housing and family subsidies through male employees (Chua 1996a). Unmarried mothers – considered a needy group in most societies – were ineligible for public housing.

Beholden to the interests of immensely powerful coalitions comprising political, military and business leaders, the capacity of the Indonesian state to supply collective goods that would promote growth and win popular support for the ruling regime was markedly weaker. Nevertheless, there too, organs within the state controlled domestic investment. In order to facilitate exploitation, production and export that purportedly was in 'the national interest', key sectors of the economy were monopolised. In their poignant study of the destruction of customary regimes, McCarthy and Warren describe the usurpation by state ministries of the rights that once regulated Indonesian villagers' access to land, minerals and forests (see chapter 5).

The contradiction between the claim that Indonesia's economic growth was a national developmental venture, and the growing reality of appropriation and accumulation by a small cohort comprising leaders' families and their cronies, was superficially resolved by representation of the nation as an organic whole, articulated by the hierarchical, functionally differentiated roles that were attributed to idealised images of the 'traditional' family and village community (Chalmers 1997; Bowen 1986). The validity of that representation was called into question by the fact that women, farmers and people living in the outer provinces did not proportionately share in the benefits of growth (Dirkse *et al.* 1993). Activists called for social security provisions for urban employees, particularly in the private and informal sectors. Protests against regional and rural/urban disparities grew, and provincial separatist movements increased in strength.

Certainly, the centralised polities, close links between bureaucracies and business, and instrumental design of collective goods that characterised countries in East and Southeast Asia facilitated rapid industrialisation, the expansion of exports and accumulation of wealth. Selected areas of physical and social infrastructure were well funded from the public purse. Basic healthcare and primary education improved markedly. As several authors in this volume demonstrate, state intervention in those areas was cost-effective and had positive consequences for living standards, and for equity and cohesion among the populations of beneficiaries.

However, international agencies pressed governments in the region to dismantle their pro-active trade and industry policies. Property rights, media, judicial systems and banking suffered from government intervention. Most people were excluded from participating in political and corporate decision-making. These organisational and institutional limitations of government exacerbated their relatively weak fiscal foundations. Consequently, even had governments been willing to supply collective goods that served the goals and interests of 'marginal' groups, it is unlikely that they would have had the capacity to do so. Residual social security systems continued to exclude large numbers of people (Cox 1998). Civil rights were heavily circumscribed. And in many parts of the region, the natural environment was treated by planners and businesses as an exploitable, exportable resource and a sink into which the wastes of cities and industries could be emptied.

The neo-liberal turn in collective goods provision

Whereas collective goods provision was justified in terms of the ideology of development in much of East and Southeast Asia up until the mid-1980s, by the end of the century political rationalities in the developmental and transitional socialist states displayed decidedly neo-liberal features. The role and aim of government was legitimated in a quest to attain, and retain, a national competitive edge in markets dominated by the US.

National competitiveness was pursued, first, by the privatisation of many public and collective goods. This reduced government expenditure and the tax 'burden' of firms and salary earners. Privatisation also established a mechanism to eliminate free riding, under-supply, over-consumption and externalities, as owners would produce and consume only those goods required and would internalise all costs and reflect them in pricing (*Interpress Service* 1997; Schmidtz 1991). Second, improved public sector efficiency was sought through deregulation. Independent, rational individuals were to satisfy their wants through consumption from public and private producers competing in unconstrained markets. Third, new legislation bestowed on individuals property, contractual and civil rights and allowed the formation of participatory associations. In what Burchell (1996) has described as a 'responsibilising' method of governance, an increasingly individualised citizenry began to be granted, or to assume the 'freedom' and technical capacity to provide for itself.

What was the impetus for these changes? And how did neo-liberal approaches to the provision of collective goods in East and Southeast Asia affect the roles of governments, non-governmental organisations and communities and the emergence of a public sphere?

In explaining the neo-liberal turn in the provision of collective goods, there has been a good deal of debate as to the relative causal importance of political and economic factors at different levels of scale. Numerous scholars have pointed to increased international economic interaction as a key force in exporting neo-liberal political rationalities. Certainly, higher order economic governance structures proliferated throughout the 1990s (Reinicke 1998). Susan Strange (1995) hypothesised that these regimes were necessitated by the growth of global financial transactions, commerce and communication, an increase in the incidence of cross-border externalities and the declining capacity of nation-states to supply collective goods that could reduce transaction costs and compensate for social dislocations and disadvantage. Conversely, neo-liberal theorists assert that the pressures and opportunities presented by global markets aligned the norms and goals of international organisations, states, corporations and civil society, and created a consensual basis for cooperation (Kaul *et al.* 1999; De-Shalit 1997). Realist scholars, on the other hand, look for instances of inter-state competition over strategic power and market share to explain the new trend. Hence they view neo-liberal reforms in Asia as a capitulation to demands by the dominant state in the international order, the US, that governments in the region relinquish precisely those mercantilist measures and public policies that had been instrumental in expanding their economies.

These debates are reflected in the contributions to this volume. Beeson argues that the economic crisis of 1997 provided an historic opportunity for hegemonic international organisations to pressure governments in Asia to comply with regimes designed to achieve US strategic and trade goals. IMF loan packages offered to Thailand, Korea and Indonesia initiated fundamental changes not only in economic relations, but also in the exercise of political power (Beeson and Robison 2000; Bello 1999). The conclusions reached in the case studies on Indonesia by McCarthy and Warren, and on

16

Vietnam and Laos by Wyatt, lend qualified support to Beeson's argument. At a time when the governments of those countries lacked investment capital, international aid agencies promoted schemes to allocate land titles and forest concessions to individuals and to introduce private foreign investment into transport and energy sectors. The schemes increased regional trade and guaranteed profits for entrepreneurial farmers and foreign firms at the expense of dispossessing local peoples and impoverishing governments.

Adams rejects the proposition that the neo-liberal turn in collective goods provision is evidence of growing international interaction, mutual understanding and policy convergence. In his analysis of the reasons for the formation of the Commission on the Conservation of Southern Bluefin Tuna, he argues that the Commission was formed not because of the achievement of consensus among participants, but rather because of the *conflicting* agendas of the signatory states and increasing contestation within Japanese society over what was in 'the national interest'. Furthermore, policy-makers in Japan feared that unless they agreed to participate in the Commission, Australia might exclude Japanese boats from its lucrative fishing grounds and global environmental activist groups might win support for even more stringent regulation of fishing activities. The apparent unity of interests in Australia was largely an artifact of the dominance of scientists and bureaucrats and the marginalisation of the fishing industry in the policy-making process. In other words, the most politically influential voices within the country that enjoyed a strategic advantage prevailed.

Hence the case studies by Beeson and Adams provide limited support for realist explanations of the neo-liberal turn in collective goods provision. But as both authors point out, realist theory is unable to account for the ideological and structural changes that shaped particular constellations of domestic interest and influenced policy design.

It is a key contention of this book that the prior provision of collective goods changes coalitions of power and interest within nation-states and provides new social forces with the means with which to intervene in the policy process. In many countries in East and Southeast Asia, the most outspoken critics of the old patterns of collective goods provision comprised the very groups that either had been beneficiaries of states' restricted, selective disbursement of collective goods, or had been disadvantaged by their provision. And their tools of resistance comprised collectively supplied organisations, institutions and communications technologies. Within the offices of the old bureaucracies, recipients of national scholarships that had funded degrees in Chicago business schools promoted privatisation and deregulation. Bold members of the Indonesian judiciary applied new codes of civil and administrative law to denounce government incompetence, repression and corruption (Bourchier 1999). Workers in Korea mobilised support for campaigns to demand welfare rights at night schools. In Singapore, middle-class professionals expressed their dissatisfaction at their governments' self-interested revision of their national history by attending public meetings and penning letters of complaint to newspapers and internet sites. And indigenous peoples were morally supported in their battles against dam builders and legally represented in global arbitration forums by NGOs like the International Rivers Network (Mayer 1996).

Nowhere are the domestic origins of neo-liberal reform more apparent than in Korea. Linda Weiss' (1998; 2000) studies of the progressive dismantling of Korea's economic planning apparatus by bureaucrats in the Ministry of Finance throughout the 1990s illustrate how reformist agencies within the state voluntarily relinquished their planning capacity. In this volume, Kim traces that history from a different standpoint. He suggests that the state's devolution of a range of governance functions resulted from growing tensions over inequitable social welfare coverage in the 1980s. The government responded by amending constitutional acts relating to welfare and relaxing restrictions on the formation of civil organisations. Taking advantage of this new political space, NGOs began to intervene in the design of political institutions, legislation and public policy. Using the vocabulary of citizens' and shareholders' rights, they encouraged people to request disclosure of public and corporate budgets. The promulgation of legislation on freedom of information and improved access to the judicial system facilitated the auditing of government departments, banks and conglomerates, or *chaebol*. Media coverage and the staging of mass rallies allowed these 'publics-in-formation' to articulate their objections to the disbursement of public monies to political leaders and their cronies. In short, Korean NGOs began to establish the preconditions for a mode of governance in which the individual-as-citizen would embrace their responsibility not only to manage themselves, but also to oversee the activities of governments and businesses.

The theme of efforts by reformers within governments to privatise collective goods, increase competition among providers and individualise social rights, is developed by Ramesh and by Wong in their studies of welfare goods. In the 1980s and 1990s, governments in Malaysia, Singapore and China shuffled responsibility for urban employment, social security, health, education and housing from their departments and state-owned enterprises to private employment agencies, insurance firms, schools, real estate corporations, philanthropic associations and, ultimately, individuals. Issues that once had justified the existence of extensive state bureaucracies became the province of individual risk management and market transactions. On the one hand, government spokespersons and state media proclaimed that these reforms were made inevitable by the exigencies of globalisation and shortfalls in government revenue and state enterprise profits. On the other hand, the reforms were depicted in a positive light. Market financing and provision would bestow a new range of freedoms, opportunities and choices on the entrepreneurial providers and client-consumers of services. Benevolent citizens would supply a minimal safety net for those incapable of taking care of themselves.

Ramesh argues that many of these reforms were economically sub-optimal, and resulted in greater deprivation of the poor. This was particularly apparent in China, where per capita income was much lower than in Malaysia and Singapore and rapid liberalisation of the economy resulted in increased unemployment. Despite the adverse consequences of individual-ising social rights, however, Wong argues that the Chinese government still had the power to define what was in 'the common good' and to determine which authorities would produce collective goods. Indeed, the paradox that China's transitional socialist government was able to go further in privatising welfare services than many of its counterparts in wealthy, social democratic societies might best be explained by reference to its ability to suppress debate about collective goals and methods.

However, the chapters by Zhang and by Leaf suggest that China's central government might not always possess the ability to determine which collec-tive goods are provided and how they are to be financed and supplied, much less manipulate the desires of its subjects and impose an authoritative defini-tion of 'the common good'. The divergence between their conclusions and that of Wong cautions against simple generalisations about the causes and consequences of collective goods provision, even within a single authori-tarian state. In Zhang's case study of property rights reform in a suburban village, attempts to privatise the collective assets that funded villagers' social security were driven not by a state keen to divest itself of expensive welfare burdens, but by the interests of wealthy villagers defined *in opposition to* the interests of local officials in particular, and the central government in general (see also Sargeson and Zhang 1999). So long as they remain unre-solved, Zhang concludes that struggles between residents and local governments over control of collective property will result in less than optimum economic outcomes. Perhaps of greater significance, though, is the possibility that these struggles will lead to the diminution of assets available to fund collective goods for future generations of villagers.

Leaf's study of the creation of public space in the city of Quanzhou presents a more sanguine view of the complex interactions and processes that have propelled the neo-liberal turn in East and Southeast Asia. Informed and partly funded by overseas Chinese associations, residents of the city did not adhere to the central government's modernist aesthetic, homogenising planning goals and hierarchical, bureaucratic procedures. Instead, in their construction of self-built housing and collaboration to upgrade infrastructure and restore temples, they created culturally diverse public spaces and expanded the autonomy and organisational capacities of local civil associations. Along with other contributions in this volume, Leaf's paper reminds us that a neo-liberal political rationality is not simply a method of rule developed by international agencies and state authorities and imposed on a passive citizenry. Rather, it is hegemonic. Neo-liberal under-standings of governmentality are internalised, exercised as 'self-rule' by empowered, responsible, individual citizens and expressed in their creation of local organisations, institutions, social security systems and the shared built environment.

In contrast to the relatively comprehensive adoption of neo-liberal approaches to collective goods provision in the developmental and transi-tional socialist states, efforts at implementing neo-liberalism in Indonesia were piecemeal and ineffective. Debates over the aims and methods of providing specific types of collective goods were muffled by bigger conver-sations, as political parties, military factions and activist groups struggled to gain support for their visions of 'the nation', 'the national interest', democracy and equity. Much of their campaigning hinged on what Higgott (2000: 261) has termed 'the politics of resentment', or domestic reactions against the dictates of the IMF and Western creditors and perceived threats to national sovereignty and integrity. Political parties thrown, for the first time, into electoral competition made common cause with beleaguered government departments, state industries, workers and irate consumers to oppose proposals by economic reformers to privatise public utilities and withdraw subsidies for fuel and foodstuffs. Key public institutions, including the army and Jamsostek, the state-owned social insurance company, lost legitimacy. The devolution of fiscal responsibility to regional administrations further undermined the ability of reformers in the central government to build coalitions in support of neo-liberal programmes for collective goods provision.

But while the capacity of the centre to fund and supply collective goods was weakened, it was not compensated for by the development of greater capacity at regional and local levels or the by empowerment of individual citizens. Consequently, as Warren and McCarthy demonstrate, the commons became a site of intense competition. International organisations promoting privatisation, local bureaucrats engaged in rent-seeking, corporations eager to secure access to cheap natural resources, and indigenous villagers and immigrant groups, all vied to assert their rights to control land, waterways, forests and fisheries.

Given these temporal changes and the discrepancies between Indonesia and the countries to its north, is it possible to generalise about the outcomes of collective goods provision in East and Southeast Asia? Two common themes are evident. The visions of 'the common good', 'the national interest' and 'the public good' that have legitimated the provision of instru-mental goods have been manipulated to serve the goals and interests of the political elites that have dominated these countries. Yet our case studies also demonstrate that even among people who, at any particular time, subscribed to hegemonic conceptions of 'the common good', there were disagreements as to which instrumental goods should be provided, and how they should be financed and supplied. The definition of what constituted a public 'bad' was also sensitive to differences in geo-political scale, ideological inclination, class, gender and ethnicity. The resulting debates and conflicts precipitated changes in the political rationalities of collective goods provision.

What is also made clear by the case studies in this book is that throughout the 1990s the provision of organisational and institutional collective goods increased while the accessibility of many infrastructural and welfare goods decreased. Civil associations multiplied. Availing themselves of new legal institutions and media, those associations extracted and consolidated certain political and social entitlements for large populations. However, the elimination of encompassing customary rights and the allocation of individual property rights had negative consequences for welfare, intergenerational equity and environmental sustainability in several countries. Privatisation and the individualisation of social policy produced a greater array of welfare goods, but increased their cost and reduced their availability. And, without an initial levelling of the playing field and the creation of a redistributive mechanism to compensate the poor, neo-liberal rationalities of collective goods provision increased inequalities of opportunity, assets and consumption (E. Lee 1998; World Bank 1998b; *Bangkok Post* 1998: 2 July). That, in turn, undermined altruism and trust.

These contrary trends have important implications for the emergence of, and interactions in, the public sphere in East and Southeast Asia. As these implications are examined in several of the following chapters, it is necessary first to establish what we mean by the term 'public sphere'.

Collective goods and the public sphere

We follow Habermas (1989) and Calhoun (1998) in conceptualising the public sphere as that realm in which people define themselves as 'publics' through ongoing communication, definition and negotiation over their shared concerns. The public sphere is created in the course of open, participatory debates over an enormous range of issues – including such macro-concerns as the exercise of political authority, human, civil and labour rights, distributive justice and group identity, and micro-issues such as urban development, transport proposals and educational curricula. Definitions of 'the common good' and 'the national interest', together with local visions of 'the public good', continually are invented, contested and reinvented in the public sphere. The selection and method of providing collective goods also provides an important focus for the conversations that give rise to, and take place in, the public sphere.

Indeed, it is to engage with precisely those issues that many people come together as 'publics'. But there is another way in which 'publics' come into being. As Chua eloquently explains in this volume, 'publics' are not only the products of the negotiations they conduct over the provision of collective

21

goods, but they are also rhetorical devices used in the course of those nego-tiations. Invocation of 'the public', like reference to 'the common good', allows government leaders, group spokespersons and activists to lay claim to some degree of popular legitimacy in lobbying for provision of particular collective goods.

One of the strengths of this volume is to elucidate the powerful ideolog-ical discourses that inflect contemporary efforts to provide collective goods in East and Southeast Asia. As the developmental, socialist and nationalist ideologies that have flowed from the centres of power in the region ebb, new neo-liberal political rationalities are shaping contestation over collective goods, spawning new 'publics' and reconfiguring the public sphere in at least two distinct ways.

On the one hand, groups of people are developing the organisational and institutional resources with which to communicate about issues of common concern and to intervene in debates over international, national and local problems and policies. The diverse goals, tools and composition of these groups are testimony to the ability of collective goods to inspire and facili-tate cooperative actions. We read in this volume, for example, that at different levels of the geo-political scale, 'publics' are being created to chal-lenge monistic conceptions of the Indonesian nation. Shifting the boundaries between beneficiaries and non-beneficiaries of state employment and social security schemes in China has fostered a sense of solidarity among newly excluded workers. Village committees and city authorities in Quanzhou have collaborated in the construction of drains and roads in order to press higher level governments for provision of another collective good – the expansion of the municipal limits. The media in Taibei helped to broaden the scope and composition of 'publics' through its reporting of the demolition of squatter settlements and the creation of city parks. In sum, actions over collective goods provision are opening up a more inclusive, dynamic public sphere in East and Southeast Asia.

Simultaneously, however, the members of these new 'publics' are appealed to in the mean-spirited vocabulary of individual self-interest. 'The good' of collective goods, they are told, must be measured according to the criteria of economic utility. Governments calculate precisely the costs and benefits they will incur in the short term due to participation in the produc-tion of collective goods that promise immense global and intergenerational advantages, such as conventions on the prohibition of biological weapons and the conservation of watersheds. To offset reductions in government expenditure, citizens are promised lower tax burdens, opportunities for personal enrichment and greater consumer choice. They respond by pursuing their interests as individual taxpayers, shareholders, clients and consumers. The production and supply of residual public and collective goods is tendered to profit-driven providers. Those who access and benefit from the welfare goods supplied are drawn into 'responsibility' contracts that stipulate stringent terms and penalties so as to protect the interests of the taxpayer. Other goods, including policing and medical care, are supplied to consumers on a user-pays basis. Thus 'publics' becoming individualised, and debates over 'the common good' in the public sphere are couched in – and in opposition to – the hegemonic discourses of neo-liberalism.

Conclusion

The primary aim of this chapter has been to define collective goods and point out the pitfalls of integrating the potential for collective action problems into a definition of collective goods. While not disputing the ubiquity of those problems, it is in the methods used in their resolution that we choose to identify the characteristic features of collective goods: that is, joint supply, and some degree of non-excludability and non-rivalry.

Some of the findings of the following case studies directly challenge triumphalist claims that contemporary neo-liberal models of collective goods provision are superior to the developmental models that preceded them. But it is not our aim to champion any specific mode of provision. Indeed, just as this book offers a timely reminder that no simple set of innate human characteristics has created the collective action problems that people in the region confront in their endeavours to provide collective goods for the twenty-first century, it also warns that collective action problems cannot be resolved simply by reinforcing authoritarian national political structures or by democratisation and the deregulation of markets.

This introduction has also been concerned to trace the changing political rationalities of collective goods provision in East and Southeast Asia. Notwithstanding the fact that the aims, methods and discourses for collective goods provision often have been engineered by elites, we argue that those aims, methods and discourses have always been contested by groups that have benefitted or been excluded from, and disadvantaged by, the distribution of goods. One of the reasons why collective goods are politically divisive is that they draw boundaries between beneficiaries and non-beneficiaries. However, in identifying the factors that have prompted changes in patterns of collective goods provision, we have looked beyond the self-interest of distributional coalitions to investigate the impact of interactions between governments in the region, and international regimes and organisations. We have traced the popularisation of a neo-liberal ideology of collective goods provision, and highlighted the agency of various domestic social forces in promoting aspects of that ideology. And we have discussed how open deliberation over issues of common concern has consolidated the identities and demands of new 'publics' and served to enlarge the public sphere.

Although international agencies, governments, private providers and groups of individuals undoubtedly will continue to play an important role in collective goods provision, so too will new kinds of 'publics' serve as a source of changing visions of 'the good' and of the instrumental goods designed to meet their aspirations. But even if the ideas of 'the good' pursued by these 'publics' prove to be more individualised than they were in the past, the complex cultural, ideological, political and institutional genealogies of these societies mean that patterns of collective goods provision in East and Southeast Asia are unlikely to replicate the models of provision found in the Western capitalist democracies.

THE CONSTRUCTION OF INTERNATIONAL REGIMES IN EAST ASIA

Coercion, consensus and collective goods

Mark Beeson

It has become commonplace to observe that we live in an increasingly interconnected, not to say global era. While it is necessary to treat undifferentiated notions of 'globalisation' with some caution, international economic interaction in particular has clearly been accelerating. In such circumstances, the external environment within which international commerce occurs has become an increasingly important influence on both the activities of private economic actors and the more general domestic affairs of nations. The conduct of economic activity, both internationally and domestically, is increasingly guided by specific regimes, or influential rules and norms that help shape private sector and state behaviour in line with particular goals and objectives. While such regimes might seem a clear example of an international collective good, in that they are intended to reduce 'transaction costs' by providing a stable framework within which international commerce can occur, I suggest that their construction is necessarily a deeply political exercise, which inevitably helps to entrench a specific normative vision of the way such activities should occur.

For this reason the crisis that began in East Asia in 1997 was not simply a problem of short-term crisis management, but a more enduring challenge to the durability and – perhaps more significantly in the longer term – the legitimacy of state-led models of economic development. Profound national or systemic crises are moments when existing orders are subjected to intense scrutiny and opportunities exist for fundamental change (Gourevitch 1986). The crisis had the effect of focusing attention on both the supposed shortcomings of Asian forms of capitalism and on the overarching international system of which they were a part. Consequently, while much effort was expended on trying to rectify the immediate difficulties of individual economies and to generate 'appropriate' longer term domestic responses to the crisis, it is important to recognise that this was to be achieved by linking such efforts to a wider international framework.

Reform in East Asia has been closely associated with and driven by external agencies, authorities and actors intent on encouraging the domestic adoption of a wider, internationally influential agenda of neo-liberal regulatory reform.

The greatest historical significance of the crisis, therefore, may be that it marked a concerted attempt to construct or impose a market-centred regime within East Asia, at both the domestic and regional levels. If successful, such reforms would effectively snuff out what has hitherto been a viable and – especially from the perspective of local political elites – attractive alternative model of economic organisation. Seen in this light, therefore, the construction and content of the overarching framework within which future international economic relations are conducted becomes an issue of primary importance. The sort of international regime that emerges in the aftermath of the crisis will profoundly influence the course of regional economic development and political relations at both the intra- and inter-regional levels. It is an opportune moment, therefore, to look at the way such a regime may be constructed and the principles it may embody.

The principal intention of this chapter is to examine the theory and practice of regime formation, and to consider the role of specific regimes as potential mechanisms for the provision of collective goods. I begin by examining regime theory and linking it to notions of collective goods. An important distinction is made here between realist and Gramscian notions of hegemony in the construction of international orders. I argue that while these perspectives are predicated upon very different assumptions about the way the world works, they both offer important insights about the development of the contemporary international political economy in East Asia. In the final section of the chapter I examine recent events in the region in more detail, and consider their implications for the future of international relations more generally.

Regime theory and the construction of international economic orders

The international economic system in the post-war period can be characterised broadly as an 'open', liberal, and increasingly global order. Even those countries like Japan, which have often employed mercantilist strategies that privilege national economic development, have been able to take advantage of the collective good of an international economic order, replete with rules, dispute resolution mechanisms, and transnational regulatory authorities intended to reduce transaction costs and generally maintain economic stability. In short, the international political economy has developed a number of features – especially the existence of behaviour-shaping rules and norms – which may be described as constituting an international regime.

Although the definition – not to say the operation – of regimes is contentious, the various theoretical perspectives that attempt to make sense of international economic cooperation are especially relevant for two principal reasons: first, at a moment when a new international economic order is being actively constructed in East Asia, regime theory can help us understand contemporary events. Second, such an analysis is an important test of the utility of the various theoretical perspectives themselves, yielding surprising results and a potentially important synthesis of perspectives.

Some definitional clarification

Before embarking on such an exploration, however, it is important to try and clarify a number of the key concepts that will be employed in subsequent discussion. In this regard, deciding quite what a regime actually is, and how it is distinguished from other abstract conceptualisations like 'institutions' or 'organisations', is an initial difficulty. The most celebrated and frequently cited definition of regimes was developed by Stephen Krasner (1983: 2), who suggested that regimes are 'sets of implicit or explicit principles, norms, rules, and decision-making procedures around which actors' expectations converge in a given area of international relations'. A number of points are worth noting about this formulation at the outset: in this conception, regimes are not simply confined to rule-based systems and dependent on the application or threat of sanctions for their success. There is also an important element of socialisation or learning implicit in this definition. In other words, inter-state behaviour may not be dependent solely on the application of overt 'structural' power,[1] but may also be a function of more subtle ideational processes, in which particular norms or social practices that are primarily associated with the most powerful nation of a specific era are adopted by nominally independent actors (Ikenberry and Kupchan 1990).

Although a number of writers use the terms 'regime' and 'institution' more or less interchangeably, there are a number of – albeit somewhat Jesuitical – distinctions that may be made between them. One of the most useful ways of distinguishing between and employing these two terms is by recognising that the rules, values and practices of an enduring regime, be it the international trading system or the emerging regimes for managing global climate change, may be institutionalised. At its broadest, therefore, a *regime* is what Oran Young (1994: 26) calls 'a governance system intended to deal with a ... limited set of issues or a single issue area', while an *institution* is 'a set of rules or conventions (both formal and informal) that define a social practice, assign roles to individual participants in the practice, and guide interactions amongst the occupants of those roles'. Put differently, a regime is the overarching framework that guides or informs activity in a particular issue area, whereas institutions are an expression or condensation of this impulse at the level of specific political, economic and social practice.[2] Finally, *organisations* may be distinguished from both regimes and institutions because of their essentially material nature, the existence of specific personnel, budgets and legal standing (Young 1994: 26).

With this conceptual ground-clearing accomplished, it is now possible to consider the way regimes have been treated within a number of highly influential schools of thought. While there are some major disagreements between these broadly conceived positions, each has important insights. Indeed, as the international political economy continues to change and evolve, a number of these perspectives may be given renewed life and relevance. This is especially clear in the case of realist models of international relations.

Realist and liberal theories of hegemonic stability

Unlike the majority of the contributions to this volume, the primary focus of analysis here is not the nation-state or the domestic arena, but the international system within which individual states are embedded. Even to describe this external environment as a 'system', however, suggests an initial assumption about the character of this sphere that is at odds with the dominant tradition of realist international scholarship. Realist understandings of inter-state relations are predicated upon the assumption that such relations are essentially anarchic. International relations are an endless struggle for survival in which sovereign states attempt to maintain their own integrity and seek to advance their own interests in competition with rival states. Importantly, states are, according to realists, more interested in *relative* than absolute gains. In other words, states would rather forego gains that they might derive from cooperative actions if rivals are likely to receive a greater advantage (Greico 1988).

Given such an essentially pessimistic view of the world, the prospects for international cooperation might seem remote. If states are fundamentally antagonistic, potentially hostile, and inevitably suspicious, how are they to overcome collective action problems and provide the sort of predictable, rule-based economic environment that seems essential in an era of greater economic integration? For realists, the crucial factor that allows the creation of an enduring regime within which to manage international interactions is power. The leading or 'hegemonic' power of a particular era is able to use its position to impose a specific international order from which it expects to be the principal beneficiary (Gilpin 1987). At moments of great crisis, especially after an international war that consolidates the position of a new hegemonic power, the rising hegemon is presented with especially propitious circumstances in which to shape the new order. I shall explore the implications of this position in more detail in the second section which considers the specific East Asian situation, but let me outline the argument in advance:

the passing of the Cold War and the economic problems experienced by East Asia presented the US with an historic opportunity by which to reshape elements of the international system.

Before considering the specifics of the realist position and its implications for regime creation, it is important and instructive to contrast it with what is alternatively known as the 'liberal', 'liberal-institutionalist' or – most confusingly of all – the 'neo-liberal' position.[3] While the liberal model shares a number of key assumptions with realism, there are also major differences between these perspectives, particularly regarding the operation of regimes. Liberals, like realists, consider states to be the key actors in the international system, and make similar assumptions about their sovereign, unitary status and their inherent rationality. Where liberals depart from realists is in their optimism about the possibilities for cooperative inter-state behaviour, particularly in overcoming cases of 'market failure'. Put differently – and despite a strong normative commitment to the operation and encouragement of market processes – liberals recognise that there are occasions when markets cannot provide key public goods and that it is ultimately incumbent upon states to cooperate and ensure their provision (Keohane 1995). Like realists, liberals consider that a hegemonic power can play a critical role in coordinating or guiding the actions of states, but unlike realists, liberals see hegemons as essentially benign (Little 1997).

To understand why liberals might take such a view of the actions of powerful states, it is necessary to briefly retrace the origins and development of the 'hegemonic stability thesis' that assumed such a prominent position in international relations theory during the 1970s and 1980s. The most influential initial formulation of the hegemonic stability thesis, albeit not in precisely those terms, was developed by Charles Kindleberger. In Kindleberger's seminal analysis of the Great Depression, he argued that economic collapse had occurred during the 1930s because no state was willing or able to play the role of systemic stabiliser. Kindleberger (1973: 28) argued that

> the international economic and monetary system needs leadership, a country which is prepared, consciously or unconsciously, under some system of rules that it has internalised, to set standards of conduct for other countries; and to seek to get others to follow them.

Without a powerful nation prepared to act as a stabiliser and underpin, or if necessary impose, a specific international order replete with essential public goods like a stable currency regime, counter-cyclical lending and open markets, then the international system was always at risk of collapsing into beggar-thy-neighbour insularity and protectionism. The success of Pax Brittanica in the nineteenth century and Pax Americana in the late twentieth century, when seen in this light, was a consequence of the emergence of two nations that had the capacity and the preparedness to act as a systemic stabiliser.

This schema has been subjected to some powerful and persuasive critiques. The most obvious potential failing of the hegemonic stability thesis is its inability to account for the continuing existence of an open international economic order at a time when the US's status as a hegemonic power is commonly taken to have been significantly diminished (see for example Kennedy 1988). Two points merit consideration in response to this criticism. First, Snidal (1985) has persuasively argued that international cooperation is not only possible in the absence of a dominant power, but may actually be encouraged as 'secondary' powers actively cooperate to provide collective goods. Second, as Susan Strange (1987) pointed out more than a decade ago, and as recent events in East Asia seem to confirm, it is debatable just how diminished the US actually is. In other words, not only does the US still seem able to exert a preponderant influence over international affairs, but the continuance of a broadly liberal international economic system may not be solely dependent on the existence of a hegemonic power that is prepared to underwrite the common good. This opens up the possibility that the US may be able to exploit its highly favourable position to pursue relatively narrow 'national interests' without jeopardising the entire international system.

These issues will be explored in more detail in the specific context of East Asia. Before this, however, it is important to consider a very different perspective on the notion of hegemony which, while not generally concerned with regime construction and maintenance *per se*, nevertheless provides an invaluable adjunct to this discussion.

Gramscian conceptions of hegemony

One of the most enduring criticisms of both liberal and (especially) realist conceptions of the international system and the sorts of regimes that emerge to govern it is that it is overwhelmingly state-centric. Because states are seen as the central actors in determining the shape of the international system, less attention is paid to other actors and the complex historical interactions between economic and political forces that increasingly transcend national boundaries. Gramscian conceptions of hegemony, by contrast, provide a more broadly based account of the sorts of economic and political developments that characterise and help to constitute the contemporary international order. Importantly, they also offer a way of conceptualising the often ambiguous status of the leading hegemonic power in an era when the autonomy of the most powerful nation is often constrained, and in which the very articulation of 'the national interest' is increasingly problematised by processes of globalisation and the concomitant blurring of political boundaries and economic identities (Beeson 2000a).

Although scholars utilising a Gramscian-derived theoretical framework have shown little enthusiasm for, or interest in, the concept of regimes, nevertheless, such a framework offers some important insights that can help us to understand their creation and persistence (Gale 1998). The Gramscian conception of hegemony pays far more attention to the broader, historically specific, socially embedded political and economic bases of particular 'world orders'. In this conception, most influentially and completely formulated by Robert Cox (1987: 7), hegemony is

> more than the dominance of a single world power. It means the dominance of a particular kind where the dominant state creates an order based ideologically on a broad measure of consent, functioning according to general principles that in fact ensure the continuing supremacy of the leading state or states and the leading social classes but at the same time offer some measure or prospect of satisfaction to the less powerful. In such an order, production in particular countries becomes connected through the mechanisms of the world economy and linked into world systems of production. ... An incipient world society grows up around the inter-state system, and states themselves become internationalised in that their mechanisms and policies become adjusted to the rhythm of the world order.

In this formulation, the international rise to prominence of market-centred neo-liberal ideas and practices can be understood as something more than simply an expression of the will of the dominant power of an era. Rather, the sources and expression of social power are more complex, diffuse and increasingly transnationalised, making them simultaneously more and less powerful. On the one hand, as the sovereignty and autonomy of the state has been steadily undermined by the challenges from 'above' and 'below', which have encouraged a leakage of state authority to a range of trans- and sub-national actors, the capacity of even the most powerful states to shape domestic, let alone international, outcomes has diminished (Strange 1996). On the other hand, the Gramscian perspective reminds us that processes of social learning, institutional embedding and a general consolidation of the constellation of social and political practices associated with what Gill (1995) calls a 'market civilisation', simultaneously 'naturalise' the existent order and make alternatives much more difficult to realise. In other words, despite the apparent decline in the position of even the most powerful states, hegemony or the maintenance of a wider, historically specific geo-political order is not dependent on the existence of a single preponderant power to underpin it. In Agnew and Corbridge's (1995: 17) pithy formulation, 'there is always hegemony, but there are not always hegemons'.

Despite the general disinterest in, or repudiation of, the regime concept by critical theorists, Gale (1998: 275) perceptively points out that regimes may be conceived of as 'instances of institutionalised hegemony'. Particular regimes are an expression of complex processes of political contestation, social learning and changes in the overall environment that generate specific governance strategies and instrumentalities. This does not mean, it should be emphasised, that the student of regimes is implicitly advocating or approving specific regimes as functional or necessary responses to particular collective action dilemmas. On the contrary – and despite regime theory's highly US-centric antecedents – taking regimes seriously not only provides important insights into the maintenance of particular world orders, but may even provide the critical tools with which to challenge the existent order.

Regime theory: an overview

Gramscian theory alerts us to the necessity of developing a more broadly based conceptual framework that encompasses both state and non-state actors, as well as the less tangible aspects of ideational interaction that are implicated in the development of the specific rationalities associated with a particular world order. In this regard, the conscious or unconscious recon-figuration of what Cox (1987: 25) calls the dominant 'interpretative structures of thought and mental rules for making decisions' is central to the post-crisis developmental trajectory in East Asia, where a very different political rationality to that of the Anglo-American economic orthodoxy has predominated hitherto (Beeson and Jayasuriya 1998). However, even while we remain cognisant of the larger, world-historical backdrop within which the crisis and its management has unfolded, it is still necessary to try and map the precise way the new post-crisis international economic regime has developed.

In order to try and understand the way in which a new post-crisis interna-tional regime is emerging, it is useful to distinguish between different levels of analysis (Buzan 1995). At the broadest level there is a generalised impulse toward *some* form of cooperation as a consequence of the increased interna-tional economic integration associated with processes of globalisation. As Cerny (1995) points out, nation-states are simply incapable of supplying the sorts of collective goods that are associated with transnationalised economic processes, dependent as they are on the maintenance of a predictable, regu-lated international commercial framework that transcends state boundaries and competencies. In this new environment where states are no longer neces-sarily the most influential agents of change in the international system, and in which authority over agenda-setting, rule-making, norm promotion and regulation are increasingly shared with non-state actors, the entire basis of collective action is fundamentally altered (Mayer *et al.* 1993). In such circumstances, resolving collective action dilemmas involves a complex dialectic between states (and their concomitant domestic political forces), the international sphere (which includes both transnationally organised or externally oriented private economic actors) and an increasingly influential layer of non-state or inter-governmental organisations that occupy a pivotal place in the emergent, multi-layered structures of international governance (Held *et al.* 1999). Put differently, regime formation and maintenance is dependent on an evolving, multi-level interplay between national and transnational forces, state and non-state actors and an open-ended debate about what might be the most appropriate forms of economic governance in an era of globalisation.

The important point to emphasise here is that while there may be identifiable systemic 'needs' that flow from an open international economic order, there is no inevitability about the precise form the resolution of this collective action dilemma will take. Although the highly influential brand of liberal regime theory promulgated by the likes of Robert Keohane (1984) is shot through with the assumptions of a particular form of 'Western' rationality that has its genesis in public choice theory,[4] even orthodox variants of regime theory remind us that this is not necessarily the result of any inherent rationality or teleology. Oran Young (1983), for example, usefully distinguishes between regimes that are self-generating, negotiated or imposed. The latter two categories suggest that not only are the precise contours of any regime unpredictable in advance, non-teleological, and thus the subject of contestation, but that they might be unwillingly embraced by some of the participants. Simply put, in some circumstance weaker states – or private sector actors, for that matter – may have little choice other than to accept the overarching logic of the dominant regime with all its associated rules and norms, rather than risk either being excluded from a perceived benefit of regime membership or being subjected to punitive sanctions. This is an especially important consideration in an era of intensifying economic competition, for as Hollingsworth and Boyer (1997: 38, emphasis added) note, 'powerful countries can create regimes that favor their firms and sectors *and that encourage competitor nations to alter their productive systems in the image of those of the hegemonic country'*.

This is clearly a consideration of central importance in attempting to understand the way the US attempted to influence the management of the East Asian economic crisis. As we shall see, the US and key inter-governmental agencies like the International Monetary Fund (IMF) hoped to reconfigure East Asian economic and political practices in keeping with the overarching logic of the post-war liberal international order. An examination of the circumstances in which US hegemony was consolidated reveals a complex picture in which the US's ability to exploit its dominance has been constrained by the strategic imperatives of the Cold War or, more recently, by the changing and contradictory nature of hegemonic power in the contemporary era. The key question is whether the US will be able to take advantage of the changed circumstances in East Asia to consolidate a regime that more closely reflects US economic and political goals.

Economic regimes in post-crisis East Asia

Although the immediate trauma of the crisis has abated, its impact continues to be felt in the construction of a post-crisis regulatory regime. It is already possible to identify some of the most important factors which have helped to shape this new environment. Indeed, identifying the key issues and players during and in the wake of the crisis is not a difficult challenge, for there has been a coordinated and self-conscious attempt to impose or ensure adherence to a distinctive neo-liberal, market-centred economic order in the region. To appreciate the significance of this development it is necessary to place these events in an appropriate historical context.

East Asia and the post-war international order

Of late, discussion of 'the international order' and its constitutive institutions has tended to focus overwhelmingly on economic regimes. This is hardly surprising. The conventional wisdom, amongst all but the most diehard realists at least (see for example Mearsheimer 1990), is that there has been a major shift in the relative importance of 'low' as opposed to 'high' politics. In other words, there has been a secular shift from geo-politics to geo-economics in the priorities of individual nation-states (Luttwak 1990). Although this remains a powerful argument – especially following the Cold War's end – it is also important to remember that things were not always so: it was precisely the former privileging of broader strategic concerns that permitted the existence of, and in many cases actively encouraged, nationally based economic regimes that bore little resemblance to the sorts of neo-liberal orthodoxy that are currently being encouraged in the region. The diminution of this strategic imperative has allowed the US to change its own calculus of national advantage and attempt to create a transnational regime in East Asia designed to further its own interests, especially economic ones.

During the Cold War the US was intent on developing an international system that was at once dynamic economically and secure strategically. Without the highly contingent strategic imperative the Cold War fostered, and the concomitant perceived need to keep client states in the 'Western' camp, it is safe to assume that US hegemony might have taken a very different, and possibly less 'benign' form. Indeed, it is important to remember that under 'normal' circumstances there are powerful incentives for hegemonic states to exploit their position economically (Conybeare 1987). However, the preoccupation with grand strategy and the perceived necessity of wedding client states to the capitalist camp meant that the US was prepared to overlook a range of political and economic practices that it might have found unpalatable in other, less ideologically charged circumstances. As a consequence, frequently undemocratic, authoritarian political leaderships, and highly mercantilist economic practices that were often associated with unaccountable political elites were tolerated, if not actively encouraged. This permissive environment evaporated in the face of the US's own more aggressive and unilateral approach to economic issues (Bhagwati and Patrick 1990).

Consequently, at the centre of the reform packages that emerged in the wake of the crisis, particularly from organisations like the US-dominated IMF (Pauly 1997), was a concerted attempt to systematically reconfigure the economic structures and political relationships that are synonymous with the so-called 'developmental state'. Although the central characteristics of this model are by now comparatively well known,[5] they merit brief repetition as they have been the subject of so much criticism.

The developmental state was pioneered by Japan with the intention of accelerating the process of industrialisation and 'catching up' with the established industrialised countries. Crucially, this goal was to be achieved by relying predominantly on the efforts of state planners, rather than market forces as occurred – theoretically, at least – in countries like the US. By employing a range of trade and industry policies that were designed to encourage domestic economic actors, a number of East Asian governments attempted to develop a national presence in a range of industries that were considered to be prerequisites for an advanced industrial economy. A couple of aspects of the developmental state model were especially important and have been the target of much regulatory reform in the wake of the crisis. First, the East Asian model was generally dependent on very close, collaborative relationships between government – or more accurately in most cases, elements of the bureaucracy – and business. This capacity of 'the state' to effectively direct the course of economic development by communicating with, and if necessary coercing, local business has been taken to be a key element of the economic rise to prominence of East Asia, and as central to what had, until recently at least, been the region's relative success when compared with the Anglo-American economies (see for example Weiss 1998).

The other aspect of the developmental model that emerged in Northeast Asia and that flouted Western economic orthodoxy was the provision of so-called 'directed credit', in which East Asia's extremely high domestic savings were channelled to targeted industries deemed worthy of support by political elites. There are a number of reasons why this approach to the provision of credit is significant in the context of the crisis. First, and the source of the most criticism from outside the region, was the suspicion that such preferential relationships inevitably encouraged corruption and non-transparent economic practices (Lane *et al.* 1999). In this perspective, close relations between business and government inevitably led to 'crony capitalism' and reckless, economically unsustainable investment patterns. It is not necessary to accept the logic of this argument to acknowledge its importance in legitimating the highly interventionist role adopted by the IMF in systematically attempting to restructure domestic economies across East Asia. A second perspective on the question of credit provision sheds a less benign light on such reformist pressures: even the World Bank (1993: 288) has acknowledged that the use of directed credit was an important and successful element of the developmental experience which conferred significant competitive advantages on a number of East Asian economies.[6] It needs to be stressed, therefore, that the crisis offered the opportunity to restrict, if not abolish, what has been a key element of the rise and competitive position of a number of East Asian states by establishing a regime that actively discourages such practices (Gills 2000).

Theorising the new economic order in East Asia

It is worth emphasising just what has changed between pre- and post-crisis Asia. In this regard, it is in some ways misleading to speak of a 'new' economic order, for East Asia has always been part of the overarching global system that was established at Bretton Woods.[7] Indeed, it was precisely the existence of this international order and the existence of open markets – especially in North America – that allowed the East Asian states to develop in the way and at the speed they did. The highly successful policies of export-oriented industrialisation that distinguished East Asia from Latin America (Gereffi and Wyman 1990), for example, would simply not have been possible without the international institutional infrastructure that characterised the Bretton Woods regime. What is different is that the US, with the active support of a number of key inter-governmental organisations like the IMF, has been able to pursue policies designed to ensure much closer compliance with the spirit and practice of that liberal economic regime. Put simply, the US has had a – possibly unique – opportunity to encourage or insist upon the adoption of the sorts of economic practices of which it approves.

To put this in the language of collective goods theory, the US – freed from the strategic and ideological constraints that characterised the Cold War period – is able to spearhead a process designed to resolve the 'free rider' problem in East Asia.[8] No longer will the nations of East Asia be able to take advantage of the comparatively open markets of North America without a reciprocal opening of their domestic economies. Nor will they be able to direct capital to privileged economic actors at 'unfair' or non-market determined prices. On the contrary, the envisaged economic regime in East Asia is designed to ensure compliance with a wider international agenda of neo-liberal reform in which the market, rather than the state, will be the ultimate determinant of competitive advantage. What is of greatest significance here is not whether such reforms are intrinsically more 'efficient' than the state-led model that has prevailed in East Asia hitherto. The most important question for the purposes of this chapter is how well existent theories of international relations and regimes help us to understand the emergent economic order in East Asia, whatever its underlying logic may be.

In this regard, the state-centric focus of realist theory has a number of weaknesses but some surprising strengths. Clearly the realist perspective is strikingly deficient in its ability to account for the often highly complex and contradictory domestic sources of state behaviour (Milner 1997), or the increasingly important transnational relationships between key political and economic actors that help to shape national and intergovernmental policies (Held *et al.* 1999; Mann 1997). This is an especially important consideration in the context of inter-state contestation in post-crisis Asia. Not only are there multiple influences on the construction of US policy toward Asia making the idea of a single national interest or position problematic, but as Risse-Kappen (1995: 6) points out, transnational forces may have a profound impact on the integrity of states, especially where – as in East Asia – the state has customarily assumed a dominant role in national affairs:

> the more the state dominates the domestic structure, the more diffi-cult it should be for transnational actors to penetrate the social and political systems of the 'target' country. Once they overcome this hurdle in the state-dominated systems, though, their policy impact might be profound.

It is precisely in this situation that a number of the currently or formerly authoritarian governments of East Asia found themselves. Not only was the legitimacy of the governments in countries like Thailand and South Korea seriously undermined by the dramatic decline in their economic positions, but the comprehensive nature of the reform packages that were pressed upon them by organisations like the IMF were designed to systematically transform existent patterns of state/business relations (Beeson 1999a). While realist theory may have little to say about the way such domestic struggles are realised within the context of a global political economy that is simultaneously undermining state authority and dissolving national economic borders, it does remind us of the potential importance of residual hegemonic power. The crisis presented the most powerful country in the world with the opportunity of forceably imposing an economic regime centred on market mechanisms on the vulnerable countries of the region (Bello 1998).

This blatant use of economic and political leverage in the context of post-crisis regime construction provides a particular challenge to much liberal theory. Clearly, the idea that East Asia's emergent economic order is the

product of an inherently rational learning process in pursuit of some technically optimal, positive-sum end point looks increasingly implausible. Indeed,
the inaffectuality of the principal organisation charged with encouraging
such a process of collaborative, market-centred reform – the Asia Pacific
Economic Cooperation (APEC) forum – is testimony to the shortcomings of
much liberal theory (Beeson 1999a). Certainly, liberal theory has been able
to account more effectively for some of the domestic and transnational influences on state policy, but it is invariably imbued with a number of normative
and theoretical assumptions, especially about the US and its role in the
world, that undermine both its credibility and its capacity to explain contemporary events, particularly in an Asian context (Johnson and Keehn 1994).

Overall, the neo-Gramscian theoretical framework potentially provides
one of the most comprehensive and sophisticated accounts of regime formation and maintenance – despite a general lack of interest in regimes amongst
scholars working within the area. On the one hand this perspective has the
strengths of the realist perspective, as it continues to take the notion of state
power in pursuit of national goals seriously (Carfuny 1990). On the other,
the Gramscian perspective links this to, and provides a more plausible
account of, the ideological or normative dimensions of transnational
economic governance and restructuring; one which helps us to understand
how neo-liberalism may become the constititionalised template for future
economic development (Gill 1992). Indeed, the Gramscian-derived perspective marks a significant advance on the dominant liberal model, as this latter
perspective generally continues to place regime change in a voluntarist,
rational choice framework that pays insufficient attention to long-term
structural change.

The apparent dominance of the neo-liberal model notwithstanding, a
number of scholars have suggested that its influence is on the decline as the
'Washington consensus' unravels and resistance to market-centred reform
gathers strength in the region (Jayasuriya and Rosser 1999). While there is
clearly something in this, it is revealing that the country in East Asia that
has been at the forefront of attempts to resist the rising tide of neo-liberal
reform – Malaysia – has 'voluntarily' abandoned its experiment with capital
controls, despite continuing and widely held reservations about the stability
and impact of the international financial system (see Beeson 2000b).
Significantly, even in Malaysia domestic political alliances and economic
orientations have been altered by the crisis, making further economic
reforms more likely despite reservations about their efficacy (Stubbs 2000).
Indeed, it is noteworthy and revealing that although there was intense debate
about the durability of the 'international financial architecture' in the immediate aftermath of the crisis, and clear evidence of its role in precipitating
the crisis in the first place (Winters 2000), little of substance was done.
Given a recent region-wide recovery it is even less likely that significant
reform of the international financial system will be enacted.

This situation is suggestive of both the difficulty of supplanting an entrenched economic regime that is supported by powerful transnational interests and – paradoxically – of the limits of US hegemony. Even if elements of the US's policy-making elite wished to re-regulate the international financial system in the interests of long-term global stability, they would clearly face a difficult challenge. Not only are there 'technical' issues which are increasingly regulated and determined by private sector experts, but there are interests both within key agencies like the US Treasury and amongst the controllers of mobile financial capital who would vigorously oppose any move to wind back the autonomy of the financial sector.[9] In short, in the absence of a crisis which had an unambiguously negative impact on US interests – especially at the domestic level – it is difficult to see the US seriously pursuing reform. Without US support, a major transformation of the international economic system is unlikely if not impossible. US hegemony may be constrained, but it remains the defining element of the existing order, and an essential component of any possible alternative.

Concluding remarks

Underlying changes in the organisation of economic activity, particularly the transnationalisation of productive processes and the growing power, mobility and political influence of financial capital, mean that new patterns of political-economic relations are emerging both within and across national borders. In such an environment, where structural changes in the international economy open up new opportunities for domestically based actors to access global markets, we need to recognise that even countries with little historical enthusiasm for neo-liberalism, like Japan or Korea, were experiencing significant transformations of domestic relations and a diminution of state capacities even before the crisis (Leyshon 1994; Woo-Cumings 1997). In other words, even without the intervention of the US and the IMF it is conceivable that there would have been increasing domestic pressure for further economic liberalisation. The principal significance of external intervention in the crisis, therefore, has been to consolidate a process that was already in train.

The ultimate measure of the durability of this new economic regime will be the extent to which neo-liberal norms and practices – which are already embedded in the wider international economic system – become part of the internal institutional architecture and domestic social practices of the region. However, even if market mechanisms increasingly become the dominant determinants of economic outcomes and a critical part of the resolution of transnational collective action dilemmas in the region, this may prove only a transitory phase. For one of the key contradictions or shortcomings of the market mechanism is that 'if not contained [it] will erode all traditional institutional arrangements ... [and] bring about its own destruction' (Boyer and Hollingsworth 1997: 447). Put differently, the impo-sition of a new market-, rather than state-centred economic regime in East Asia may unleash precisely the sorts of social 'double-movement' that Polanyi (1957) identified as such a central component of the erosion of laissez-faire capitalism in nineteenth-century Britain – at a time when it was experiencing a similar, fundamental economic and social transformation.

The resolution of East Asia's collective goods dilemmas will, therefore, ultimately be dependent upon the actions of East Asians themselves. The generation of political elites that oversaw the spectacular transformation of the region under the auspices of authoritarian rule may be swept aside, as the full impact of the changes being unleashed by a combination of struc-tural transformation and external intervention take hold. However, it cannot be assumed that this will lead to either the consolidation of neo-liberalism or liberal democracy, for that matter. As a number of the other contributors to this volume make clear, the states of East Asia face a range of problems that may not be resolvable via market forces nor ameliorated by democratic expression. Under such circumstances the creation and maintenance of a trans-regional economic order may be shaped by a more complex array of factors than most existent theoretical models would have us believe.

Notes

1 Susan Strange's (1994: 24–32) influential formulation suggests that there are four elements to 'structural' power, involving the capacity to exercise control over the spheres of security, knowledge, finance and production.

2 For a more detailed discussion of institutional theory and practice and its rele-vance in East Asia, see Beeson (2002).

3 In what follows I shall reserve the term 'neo-liberal' for that brand of economic policy that is associated with the so-called 'Washington consensus' that advo-cates small government and privatisation, trade and financial liberalisation, and a general privileging of market mechanisms as the most appropriate and efficient determinants of economic outcomes.

4 For one of the most influential accounts in this regard, see Buchanan and Tullock (1965).

5 On the development state, see Chalmers Johnson's (1982) seminal work. On its adoption elsewhere, see Wade (1990). For a contemporary evaluation in the wake of the crisis, see Woo-Cumings (1999).

6 In this context it is important to distinguish between the states of Northeast Asia where credit provision – for a long time at least – appeared to more closely reflect the ideals of enlightened state planning, and Southeast Asia, where the role of the state was a good deal more predatory (see Beeson and Robison 2000).

7 Of course, world systems theorists would argue that East Asia has been locked into and shaped by capitalist expansion for a good deal longer than that. See Arrighi (1998).

8 The free rider problem is, of course, a major obstacle to the provision of collec-tive goods, particularly for larger groups of actors. The seminal discussion is provided by Mancur Olson (1965).

9 On the increasing power of the private sector in regulatory issues, see Underhill (1995).

3

THE INTERNATIONAL MANAGEMENT OF SOUTHERN BLUEFIN TUNA

Consensus, conflict and communication over a common pool resource

Sidney Adams

The Southern Bluefin Tuna (SBT) has been described as the 'Porsche of the sea'. SBT can swim at speeds of up to 70km/h[1] and an adult bluefin can attract $100,000 on the sashimi market in Japan (Wigan 1997: 149). This makes SBT the most commercially lucrative of all tuna and pelagic species. SBT spawn in Indonesian waters and migrate throughout Australian, New Zealand and South African territorial waters. Outside these national boundaries the freedom of the high seas governs the harvesting of fish and other oceanic resources. No single state or international governing body has jurisdictional sovereignty to manage the stock or arbitrate competing claims to the fishery.

As a result of continuous fishing pressure from both Japan and Australia, since the late 1960s SBT stocks have been seriously over-exploited. Japan's catch effort peaked at 78,000 tonnes in 1961 and has rapidly declined since that time (Caton 1991: 350). Australia's catch effort increased from the early 1950s, reaching a peak of 16,843 tonnes in 1981 (Crough 1987: 16). Both countries unilaterally imposed management restrictions on their fishing fleets in order to reduce the impact of fishing on the resource during the 1970s and early 1980s (Caton *et al.* 1990: 2–3). However, trilateral scientific meetings between Australia, Japan and New Zealand that were held annually from 1982 confirmed that the decline of the stock had continued. By 1988, scientific delegates were unanimous that parental stocks had been reduced to less than 25 per cent of their unexploited levels ('Report of the Seventh Meeting of Australian, Japanese, and New Zealand Scientists on Southern Bluefin Tuna' 1988: 44).

Yet despite having agreed on the extent of the decline in stock levels, there were serious conflicts over the allocation of catch levels between the

41

principal fishing nations: Australia, Japan and New Zealand. The failure, in 1984, to reach an agreement on a suitable catch level resulted in Japanese vessels being prohibited from fishing prime SBT grounds in Australian territorial waters. Further strain between the two countries was precipitated by Australia's attempts to reduce the global harvest of SBT in 1988 and 1989. In the mid-1990s, Japan's proposal that it increase its overall catch through an experimental fishing campaign met with staunch opposition from both Australia and New Zealand. In 1995 Japan called for an extra 6,000 tonnes (CCSBT 1995) and in 1996 and 1997 it requested an extra 3,000 tonnes (see CCSBT 1996; 1997). These tensions climaxed in 1998 when Japan unilaterally took an extra 1,400 tonnes of the fish. Australia and New Zealand consequently banned Japanese vessels from fishing in their territorial waters (Horden 1998a). The following year, an additional 2,000 tonnes of quota was taken by Japanese vessels, prompting Australia and New Zealand to take Japan to the Law of Sea tribunal (*Guardian Weekly* 1999).

Allegations of illegal and excessive fishing effort have further complicated relations. Since 1990, Japanese vessels have been fined and impounded on several occasions in retaliation for over-fishing and/or falsifying catch records. In December 1996, for example, forty Japanese vessels were caught illegally fishing SBT after the closure of the official fishing season (CCSBT 1997: 2–4). The incident heightened suspicion that Japan was unwilling to regulate its catch. Japanese fishermen have not been the only culprits caught over-fishing the stock (Stevens 1996: 367–9). Korean vessels allegedly have been working alongside their Japanese counterparts and helping them to disguise their excess catch. Taiwanese fishing vessels have taken increased quotas, and the catch of SBT in Indonesian territorial waters also has been growing.[2] While the extent of illegal, excessive fishing is unknown, the likelihood that this is exacerbating the pressure on an already depleted stock raised concerns about the possibility of achieving sustainable levels of harvest (CCSBT 1996: 3).

Conflicts over their respective rates of SBT exploitation continued to flare, despite the fact that restrictions on the catch had been implemented by the early 1980s. In 1983, Australia, Japan and New Zealand agreed to prevent any further growth in catches, implementing restrictions of 20,000 tonnes, 29,000 tonnes and 1,000 tonnes respectively. By 1985, Japan had agreed to further reduce its catch to 23,150 tonnes. However, by 1988 major restrictions in the catch were imposed. In that year, global quotas were reduced to 15,500 tonnes, with a final quota reduction to 11,750 tonnes in 1989. That final allocation gave Australia a quota of 5,265 tonnes, Japan 6,065 tonnes and New Zealand 420 tonnes (Neave 1995: 19). Throughout the 1990s, this remained the official international quota. In 1994, signatories to this voluntary agreement formed the Commission for the Conservation for Southern Bluefin Tuna (CCSBT). The stated objective of the CCSBT is 'the conservation and optimum utilization' of SBT (CCSBT 1994: 2). A more specific and ambitious objective has been enunciated by the scientific committee of the CCSBT; that is, to restore the parental stock to 1980 levels by the year 2020 (CCSBT 1994: annex one, 2).

This international regime appears to present something of a paradox. Ongoing disagreements over the rates of exploitation of the fish stocks are at odds with the unanimous agreement to regulate catch levels that was reached in 1985. This puzzle goes to the heart of debates concerning the regulation of global common pool resources. Does the CCSBT represent the emergence of a fundamental consensus between the principal players in the fishery? Alternatively, is the international regime itself the site of tensions between different and competing interests, each with their own policy agenda for the fishery? If that is the case, who are those interests? Why was an agreement on global catch levels reached between parties with conflicting agendas? Or is the CCSBT simply a coincidental outcome of efforts to facilitate communication and mutual understanding among all interested parties?

Theorising the CCSBT

In the context of the increasing incidence and complexity of transborder problems in the 1980s and 1990s, the capacity of international regimes to promote cooperation among states has emerged as an important focus of inquiry (Haggard and Simmons 1987; Keohane 1982; Milner 1992). Three influential theoretical approaches yield different answers to this inquiry: 'liberal regime theory' or 'liberal institutionalism', 'realist' analyses of international relations, and the theorisation of 'epistemic communities'. The explanatory power of these theoretical approaches is considered by Mark Beeson in the preceding chapter. However, it is worth specifying briefly how each of these might have the potential to unravel the apparent paradox of the concurrent formation and operation of the CCSBT and ongoing conflict between Australia and Japan over the fishing of SBT.

Liberal regime theorists look to international regimes as evidence of a growing functional reciprocity that is shaping inter-state and global interaction. Increased levels of interaction and the need to solve collective action problems in order to achieve optimum utility and efficiency are believed to be drawing state actors into webs of interdependence (Keohane and Nye 1977: 8). International regimes represent the convergence of actors' expectations about the benefits of cooperation, as they allow them to reduce transaction costs, exchange scientific data and agree on the 'rules' of the game (Keohane 1982).

That optimistic assessment of the potential for international regimes to resolve global collective goods problems is contested by realists, who view power differentials and security concerns as the primary determinants of inter-state relations (Greico 1988: 488). Hegemonic states provide leadership and coordinate the resolution of international collective action problems with a view to advancing their own interests (Viotti and Kauppi 1993: 15). Thus international regimes are epi-phenomenal to the power configurations of the international system (Young 1994: 30).

Does either perspective provide an adequate account of the dynamics of regime formation in the case of the SBT fishery? Liberal regime theorists explicate the creation of international regimes by referring to utility and efficiency. However, utility and efficiency have quite different meanings for the various parties involved in this regime. Fishermen define their utility and efficiency as the maximisation of access to stocks. Environmental groups claim that utility and efficiency imply the maintenance of bio-diversity. Scientists identify the application of their findings and recommendations to the management of the SBT as measures of utility and efficiency, while for governments, it means the resolution of conflict between user groups and interested constituencies. At present, the CCSBT does not appear to improve utility and efficiency for any of these parties. On the other hand, realists' interpretation of regime formation as the result of intervention by a hegemon, and of conflict as the outcome of an imbalance of power, proves to be of little explanatory value in a situation where there is no hegemonic state. Despite Japan's economic might, it was Australia that took the lead in forming the SBT regime in the 1980s. Conflict continues even though the balance of power has not changed.

To understand the factors giving rise to these apparent contradictions, I shall argue that it is necessary to investigate the ways in which different alliances of actors are producing competing conceptions of 'the national interest' and shaping policies on the SBT in Australia and Japan. The link between ideology, policy and political and social interests has been a critical focus of the literature on 'epistemic communities' (Hass 1992). An epistemic community is defined as a community that claims expertise on a specific issue and actively seeks to advance its knowledge claims so as to achieve policy outcomes consistent with its ideological orientation (Hasenclever *et al.* 1996: 209). Therefore, governments, international and non-governmental organisations and international regimes are all foci for lobbying by competing epistemic communities. This definition invites a potentially fruitful analysis of the particular configurations of actors and knowledges that contribute to competing conceptions of 'the national interest'.

However, the literature on epistemic communities fails to explain how interests and knowledge interact with power (Haggard and Simmons 1987: 512). That lacuna may be filled by employing a Gramscian conception of hegemony that links the different capacities of actors to the social origins of the state (Gill 1997: 1993). This concept of hegemony encompasses a consensual definition of power that has both structural and ideational dimensions. Structurally, statehood produces unique configurations of alliances between the state and sections of civil society. Ideationally, the economic and political structures of a hegemonic state are legitimated in·the commonsense frameworks, values and norms of daily life. The exercise of power becomes embedded in the fabric of nationhood and the culture of everyday life. The concept of hegemony helps us to investigate the structural and ideational traits that reflect the dominance of particular sets of interest in the design of fishing policies in Japan and Australia.

Both the Australian and Japanese fishing policy communities express 'ideal types' of the different political rationalities that have emerged from historically contingent state forms (Weiss 1998). The Japanese fishing paradigm reflects a profoundly commercial orientation. Developmental goals and commercial interests have been embedded in the nation-state, government policy and civil society (Johnson 1982). In stark contrast, the fishing policy in Australia reflects a concern to quarantine the state from commercial interests and achieve conservation goals. It is the political capacity of the state to maintain that separation and pursue those goals that is the remarkable feature of this particular instance of policy design. This is because on other issues relating to the environment, Australian government policy has served as a conduit for powerful commercial interests.[3]

Yet the CCSBT is more than the site of a clash between different state forms. For Robert Cox, relations between states and international society are influenced by the interplay of hegemony in economic, political and ideational realms at different levels (Cox 1981: 138–41). Powerful states internationalise the interests of dominant domestic classes. Convergence in all three realms at national and international levels represents a tacit consensus around historically contingent forms of capital that have been made prominent in international society.

In the CCSBT regime, continuing conflict over catch levels is an overt expression of the tensions between policy-makers and epistemic communities that are influenced by different constellations of domestic interest, are characterised by distinct political rationalities and pursue incompatible goals. The agreement on quotas, far from resulting from a convergence of actors' expectations at the negotiating table, is linked to the competing agendas of alliances of actors in the two countries.

This paper will draw on these theoretical insights to trace the origin and influence on national governments and on the formation and operation of the CCSBT of fishery institutions, industry interests and policy communities in Australia and Japan. Analysis of these particular configurations of knowledge, interest and power reveals not only unique state forms and institutional and policy environments, but also sharply contrasting visions of 'the national interest'.[4] While recognition of those dissimilarities motivated the formation of the CCSBT and has propelled continued negotiation within it, nevertheless the differences continue to impede cooperative management and conservation of the SBT. This case study highlights problems and possibilities facing international cooperation over other global common pool resources.

Conflicting political economies of fishing policy

Australia

The embedded assumption underpinning fishing management policy in Australia is that it is necessary to protect fish stocks from over-fishing. This reflects the views of the groups that construct and implement government policy and, in more general terms, vocal groups in civil society. There are two dimensions to this form of hegemony. The first is the political capacity of the state to determine management policy over the commercial sector; the second is the commonality of the goals of state and civil society.

The Australian government's capacity to regulate its commercial fleet has its origins in the marginal role that the fishing industry has played in the economic, social and cultural life of the country. Up to the 1950s, the fishing industry was a cottage industry servicing local markets. It was only in the 1960s and 1970s that fishing fleets began to increase in size in response to growing domestic and international demand (Hardmen 1963). As a result, instances of political lobbying are largely confined to local sectoral representations. For example, the Tuna Boat Owners Association of Australia (TBOAA) based in Adelaide is the main representative of Australian SBT fishers. At a national level, the National Fishing Industry Council serves as an advisory body to the federal government. As a result of this limited state and national coordination of industry interests, SBT industry officials argue that the only political leverage that the industry exerts *vis-à-vis* the federal government is that it is a fairly large employer in a marginal electorate.[5]

Policy is thus determined almost independently of industry, through an extensive inter-departmental process of soliciting scientific and management advice from organisations whose prime goal is stock protection. Key scientific departments involved in policy input include the Commonwealth Scientific Industrial Research Organisation (CSIRO) in Hobart and the Bureau of Resource Science based in Canberra. Management policy in most domestic fisheries is developed by the Australian Fisheries Management Authority. However, due to the migratory proclivities of the SBT, policy relating to the stock is also the responsibility of the Fisheries and Aquaculture Branch within the Department of Agriculture, Fisheries and Forestry. Industry is consulted on the formulation of government policy only through a Management Advisory Committee that has been established by the federal government.

Commercial interests are further marginalised by the strong symmetry between the state's agenda and the goals of vocal environmental groups that are concerned with fishery issues. While it is difficult to quantify the direct political impact of these groups on policy, it is clear that through the media, educational forums, exhibitions and protest spectacles, they elicit strong community support for proposals that promise to ensure species conservation.

The degree to which the government enjoys relative autonomy in policy design is evident in the ease with which it regulated the industry and reduced the significant over-capacity that had developed in the fishery by the early 1980s. Despite opposition from the fishery, the size of the fleet was reduced by 60 per cent in 1984. This was an initial effect of the implementation of Individual Transferable Quotas (ITQs) in the fishery. ITQs regulated fleet capacity according to quota levels set by the state. However, they also created a more secure fishing environment, because they transferred legal rights to harvest a proportion of the total allowable catch to fishers who purchased quotas. The integrity of the system has been underpinned by a strong capacity to enforce compliance. This contrasts with other quota systems that have been introduced in fisheries throughout the world, where the implementation of simple quotas has paradoxically increased capacity as individual fishers attempt to maximise their access to a limited amount of stock. It is also contrary to the experience of many European governments in which reducing the fishing capacity of politically powerful fishing industries has been more problematic. (Horden 1998b).

As a result of the reduction in the total allowable catch and sale of ITQs, at the end of the 1980s Australia's SBT fishers were forced to radically adjust their fishing effort. From historically having been an inshore fishery targeting juvenile fish, the harvest of larger offshore fish was considered by members of the industry to be the only way to achieve viable returns. Fishing for mature fish, however, required the purchase of larger, more seaworthy vessels equipped with purpose-made gear and the acquisition of knowledge about new grounds. The industry was simply caught between the heavy financial debts that had been incurred through the purchase of ITQs and new equipment, and its inability to achieve immediate returns on quota. Many tuna fishers turned to skipjack fishing in the South Pacific. This proved to be a financial disaster, as the Australian operators were unable to compete against the heavily subsidised Japanese, Korean and US fleets operating in the region.

The transformation to 'high value' fishing occurred without subsidisation. The Australian government views subsidies as a source of unnatural distortion in production and consumption activities. In the absence of subsidies, however, much of the Australian offshore industry went into receivership by 1992. While many governments concur with their Australian counterpart that subsidies distort market signals, few enjoy a comparable level of political autonomy and the consequent capacity to reduce or eliminate subsidies to influential industries struggling in the face of international competition.

Indeed, it was only because of an injection of Japanese capital into Australia's tuna industry that the fishery revived. In 1988, joint venture arrangements were established between Australian and Japanese industry.

This involved the leasing of Australian quota to Japanese industry. The amount of quota leased to the Japanese tuna fishery increased until, in 1993, it comprised 2,824 tonnes. In 1995, arrangements regarding the lease of quota were suspended. Another component of the joint venture arrangements was the investment of Japanese capital in the development of aquaculture in Port Lincoln. By the end of the decade, aquaculture comprised the mainstay of fishing activities in Port Lincoln and the Australian fishery had switched to 'high value' fishing.

In part, Japan's investment in the Australian industry can be interpreted as one instance of a global trend. After the 1970s, Japan lost many traditional fishing grounds due to coastal nations around the world extending their national sovereignty from 12 to 200 nautical miles in an effort to achieve greater regulation of the world's oceans. Joint ventures were adopted as a strategy to maintain Japanese vessels' access to traditional fishing grounds (Bergin and Haward 1996a: 123–30). They also offered a means of gaining political allies where Japanese fishing activities had been subjected to much scrutiny and criticism, particularly from increasingly vocal environmental movements. This strategy certainly succeeded in the Australian SBT fishery, where those remaining in the industry became keen apologists for Japanese fishing interests.[6] However, as explained below, in relation to the SBT fishery, Japanese investment in aquaculture was due also to the strategic location of the Australian industry.

The struggle to maintain the commercial viability of the country's tuna fishery has received little attention, much less sympathy, in the broader Australian community. Indeed, tacit consensus exists in the community that the fishing of SBT is an environmental issue that goes to the heart of the broad 'national interest'. This has been fully internalised by Australia's political leaders. By way of illustration, in 1988 the former Prime Minister Bob Hawke proposed that a moratorium be placed on tuna fishing (*Australian Fisheries* 1989: 10). Well publicised protests by Greenpeace have fostered the view that the fishing of SBT is antithetical to 'the national interest'. In February 1998 the Greenpeace flagship actively sought to disrupt fishing activity in the Great Australian Bight in an attempt to highlight the decline in stocks. Despite the fact that SBT fishers felt aggrieved over the illegality of this action, they felt powerless to contest Greenpeace's protest because they recognised that the organisation occupied the high moral ground and enjoyed strong community support among ordinary Australians.[7]

In short, Australian policy on SBT is largely informed by expert organisations whose prime goal is stock protection. The government possessed the capacity to refuse to subsidise an industry that was struggling in the face of intense competition, and force it to finance its transformation through downsizing, overseas investment and a diversification of activities. Its ability to do so was partly a consequence of the fact that there is a consensus between state and civil society on policies and management strategies relating to the SBT.

Japan

The Japanese government's response to overcapitalisation in the Japanese fishing fleet was the direct antithesis of that of the Australian government. This response reflected very different configurations of power and the predominance of commercial interests in the policy milieu. Appreciating the origins of these commercial interests is critical to an appreciation of Japan's policy goals and the dynamics shaping the international management of the SBT.

The commercial orientation of Japan's policy toward the SBT is shaped by structural and ideational factors. The interests of the tuna industry are deeply entrenched in the design of fishing policy. Moreover, trading houses that wield considerable political influence have become active in the international trade of tuna and other fish products. Both are legacies of the nationalist, developmental commitment of the modern Japanese state that embeds commercial interests in its policy commitments.

The centrality of industry concerns has its origins in the creation of the Diet in 1890. The Diet served as a conduit for the recognition of both rural[8] and small business interests (Pempel and Tsunekawa 1979: 252). The rural sector was critical in funding the growth of Japan's industrialisation (Smith 1988). The export of fish products, together with tea and silk, was particularly important in earning foreign exchange, while revenue from land tax and excise tax on soybean sauce, tobacco and other basic consumer goods were important sources of government revenue (ABARE 1988: 272; Pempel and Tsunekawa 1979: 248). The primary industry sector has also been a significant employer, with almost half the population working in the sector up until 1945 (Fujinami 1987: 57).

The importance of the fishing industry is reflected in political representation, and in its links with government and civil society. Rural and semi-rural constituencies comprise 20 per cent of the total population of voters, but decide up to 30 per cent of the total number of seats in the Japanese Diet (George 1981: 413). Tuna interests are represented directly in the Diet from the regions of Kochi and Miyagi, where the industry is a large employer. However, throughout regional Japan the industry's political clout is underpinned by its economic importance (Bergin and Haward 1996a: 61). The state has also developed extensive networks of publicly funded research organisations and financial services devoted to the industry (Borgstrom 1964: 256–265). Moreover, since the early to mid-1970s the nexus between the state and the fishing industry has been strengthened informally by the appointment of retired bureaucrats from key ministries to positions in the industry. Extensive links also exist between market wholesalers and the industry

SIDNEY ADAMS

(Ashenden and Kitson 1987: 112–18). This historical legacy has also helped to popularise the interests of the fishing sector throughout the bureaucracy, as well as in civil society. Hence, the entrenchment of fishing interests in the Japanese state contrasts markedly with the Australian situation.

The political centrality of the fishing industry is particularly apparent in the institutional forms and content of the debate over management of the SBT. The state, represented by the Fisheries Agency within the Ministry of Agriculture, Forestry and Fisheries (MAFF), is lobbied by five tuna organisations for favourable treatment with respect to boat licences and fishing grounds. The key tuna organisations are Nikkatsuren (National Offshore Japanese Tuna Fisheries Cooperative Associations), Kinkatsukyo (National Offshore Tuna Fisheries Association) and Enkatsukyo (National Tuna Fishery Association). There are also two industry associations representing purse seine operators: Kaimaki (Overseas Purse Seine Fishery Association) and Kaimaki (Federation of North Pacific District Purse Seine Cooperative Associations of Japan).

Problems began to confront Japan's SBT fishery in the 1970s. Rising labour and fuel costs had sharply reduced profitability of the overcapitalised fleet (Weber 1997). Moreover, difficulties of obtaining adequate catches resulted from a reduction in tuna stocks and the loss of traditional fishing grounds through the movement to enclose and regulate the oceans.

Of greater significance than the tuna industry's responses to these domestic and international challenges, however, is that the Japanese state became actively involved in reconfiguring the domestic fleet into a commercially viable industry. The Japanese government provided aid and development assistance to Pacific coastal states, and paid access fees to their fishing grounds on behalf of Japanese operators (Weber 1997: 125–6). It imposed tariffs on imported fishery products, despite international pressure to open its domestic market (Pempel and Tsunekawa 1979: 261). National laws were changed to allow for the hiring of cheaper crews (Owen and Troedson 1993: 9–10). A range of subsidies was introduced to compensate for rising fuel costs, offset the costs of fishing further afield, assist in the construction of more fuel-efficient vessels and encourage the downsizing and restructuring of the fleet. From 1976 to 1987, state subsidies and industry compensation eased the removal of 524 tuna and skipjack vessels (Bergin and Haward 1996a: 108). This resulted in a significant restructuring of the fleet throughout regional Japan, but most particularly in the politically sensitive prefectures from Wayakama and Shizuoka to Miyagi.

Trading house companies have exerted a strong effect both on the domestic tuna industry and the government's policy toward the fishing industry. Trading companies are unique institutions that have grown out of Japan's resource dependence. The process of national industrialisation, inaugurated by Japan's forced incorporation into the world trading system in the early Meiji period, was spearheaded by trading houses (Yoshino and Lifson

50

1986). During the 1960s trading houses developed an interest in the international tuna trade in response to the boom in domestic demand for the product (Comitini 1987). The major trading house groups involved in the tuna trade include Mitsubishi Corporation, Mitsui and Co., C. Itoh and Co. and Marubeni Corporation (Comitini 1987: 5).

Within a decade, the trading houses' appetite for fish products had become almost insatiable and they had begun to operate in direct competition with the Japanese SBT industry. Trading companies developed links with Korean and Taiwanese tuna fleets through providing subsidies to build new boats, and paying in advance for the purchase of catch. Imports of tuna from both Korea and Taiwan expanded rapidly, undermining market prices being earned by Japan's tuna fleet. This generated significant conflict between the fishery and Japanese trading houses. As early as 1975, the industry campaigned for a boycott on fish imported by the trading houses from Korean vessels (Owen and Troedson 1993: 7). Competition between the industry and trading houses to maximise their access to tuna further reinforced the commercial orientation and dynamism of the Japanese policy milieu.

This Gramsciian reading of the links between the Japanese state, the fishing industry, trading houses and policies relating to SBT, requires a note of caution. While industry interests have dominated the formulation of policy, this does not mean that environmental interest groups or the broader Japanese population have not been concerned with species conservation. A growing body of literature is emerging that documents the extensive environmental activism that occurred in Japan in the post-1945 period, and which increased in incidence and organisational capacity in the 1990s (Broadbent 1998; Macken 1981; Tsura 1999). However, at this historical juncture, environmentalists have not yet influenced fishing policy and management. The commercial concerns of the fishing industry are clearly of paramount importance in the framing of government policy on SBT.

It is clear that different configurations of power and interest construct antithetical policy environments in Australia and Japan. Within Australia, fishery bureaucrats and scientists whose aim is conservation have taken a stock approach to the management of fisheries. Their advice is easily incorporated into government policy because their goals are supported by active, well organised environmental groups, and the fishing industry is in a weak position both economically and politically. This is in direct contrast to Japan, where policy formulation and management approaches are determined by the struggle of the fishing industry and trading houses to ensure their access to stocks, market share and maximum profits. At present, opponents of the industry enjoy little political influence.

The conflicting aims and contrasting institutional environments that interact in the CCSBT help explain why, to this date, international management of the resource has been so vexed. But, given these conflicting national interests, political structures and alliances and policy goals, how and why was the CCSBT ever established? Is it possible that a consensus might emerge between Australia and Japan in the near future? It is to these critical questions that our analysis will now turn.

The CCSBT: conflict, cooperation or communication?

From 1982, the Australian government began to urge New Zealand and Japan to place a global ceiling on the catch of SBT. Having secured the agreement of the other nations to specify catch quotas in 1985, Australia then campaigned to convert the voluntary trilateral agreement on quotas into a formal international management regime. This occurred with the signing of the Convention for the Conservation of Southern Bluefin Tuna in May 1993 and its ratification by the three countries one year later. This created the formal international regime, the CCSBT.

Article 3 of the Convention document contains explicit provisions to set mandatory quota levels and allocate quota among the signatories. Article 9 establishes the scientific committee as an advisory body to the CCSBT, thereby conferring on fishery scientists a pivotal role in policy design and management (CCSBT 1994). Since May 1994, the parties to the CCSBT have met annually. A scientific meeting precedes the formal management meeting. Within the CCSBT a subcommittee, called the Ecologically Related Species Working Group, has been formed to examine ways of regulating the bycatch of non-tuna fish species and birds. The first meeting of the group was convened in Wellington in December 1995. By the close of the third commission meeting in February 1997 it was recommended that the parties to the Convention collect data concerning the incidental catch of seabirds, promote the use of bird-catch mitigation devices such as tori poles, and test the economic viability of night setting of longlines in SBT fishing operations (CCSBT 1997).

This regime clearly is a projection of the Australian government's aim of regulating the international catch of SBT to conserve the species. However, as the foregoing analysis has illuminated, the conservation of stocks is not the principal goal of Japanese policy. Quite the contrary: the Japanese government operates as a conduit for fishing industry interests, keen to maximise their access to stocks. Why, then, did Japan assent to the Australian proposals?

Australia's geographical position was critical in gaining Japan's agreement to quotas. It is in close proximity to fishing grounds for juvenile SBT, provides port facilities for the Japanese fleet, and its fishing zone is home to quality SBT product. Despite the dramatic reduction in overall quota levels during the mid-to-late 1980s, Japan was unable to fish its quota allocation because of the declining availability of stock on the high seas (Caton *et al.* 1990: 1). In order to remain commercially viable, operators were forced to fish closer to the Australian fishing zone as the greater cost in fuel, bait and steaming time was simply negated by declining returns. The overall importance of the Australian fishing zone to Japan's southern hemisphere fishing campaign can be seen by the linkage of agreement on SBT quotas to Japan's access to Australian waters (Harwood 1996: 179–85).

Australia also had leverage because of the migratory pattern of the stock.[9] Most juvenile SBT swim in Australian territorial waters. Moreover, because juveniles swim in large surface aggregations, they are easy to catch in large quantities. Adults, on the other hand, swim at great depths and in smaller numbers in the high seas. This gives Australian industry a significant strategic advantage in the fishery, as excessive harvesting of juveniles could significantly undermine the movement of stock to the high seas. Of particular concern to Japan were Australia's purse seine vessels. Purse seines have the capacity to harvest large schools of fish during any one fishing session. When the Australian government called for a dramatic reduction in quota levels in the late 1980s, Japan feared that a rejection might prompt a reprisal from Australian industry in the form of depletion of the stock. Discussions with Australian industry during this time reveal that Japan was particularly concerned that Australia discharge its purse seine fleet in exchange for Japanese acceptance of reduced quotas and investment in South Australia's aquaculture.

Growing international environmental concern further spurred Japan to consider protecting its commercial interests through a quota agreement with Australia and New Zealand. In the early 1990s, northern bluefin tuna and SBT were both nominated for listing on the Convention on International Trade in Endangered Species (CITES). Although neither was eventually listed, the potential for future listing encouraged regulation of the catch (Bergin 1994: 139).[10] In short, Japan agreed to quotas in the fishery precisely because it offered a means of securing access to stock and commercial advantages for its fleet, rather than because it concurred with Australia and New Zealand over the necessity to conserve stock.

Even though the formation of the CCSBT is a consequence of one party utilising geo-political leverage and the other making strategic accommodations, it nevertheless might be the case that the CCSBT could facilitate greater cooperation or achievement of consensus in the future. However, the way annual negotiations are currently conducted does not augur well for improved cooperation, much less consensus. Despite their agreement to regulate catch, the different approaches of the two countries to the issue of stock management are vividly illustrated by the composition of the national delegations that meet at the negotiating table. The Australian government delegation is comprised only of government officials, and it acts as an autonomous entity. Australian industry representatives and environmental groups only have observer status at these international meetings. In contrast, while the MAFF formally acts on behalf of the Japanese government, extensive consultation occurs between industry and government representatives both before and during the annual negotiations (Bergin and Haward 1996a: 6). Thus the CCSBT negotiations become the site of repeated conflicts over the allocation of quota.

Increased fishing of SBT by unregulated fisheries and trading house involvement in the international trade of tuna also point to a less than optimistic conclusion to this inquiry. Korea and Taiwan both have an explicitly commercial approach to the management of fish stocks (Bergin and Haward 1996b). Both countries have advocated that quota allocations be significantly increased in the future, a suggestion that has received a cool reception from Commission members, especially Australia and New Zealand (see CCSBT 1996: 3). The growing catch within Indonesia's territorial waters poses a particularly intractable problem. It appears unlikely that in the foreseeable future Indonesia will have the will or the funds to train personnel and acquire the infrastructure to adequately police fishing activity in the spawning grounds south of Java (CCSBT 1996). Japanese trading houses also harvest and market tuna outside the formal CCSBT framework. Product coming into the Japanese market overrides restrictions put in place both by the CCSBT and the Japanese Fisheries Agency because trading house activities come under the aegis of the powerful Ministry of International Trade and Industry (MITI).

These obstacles notwithstanding, it is indisputable that the CCSBT has slowed the rate of decline of the SBT by allowing greater scrutiny of the catch effort of all parties fishing the resource. Similarly, through the work of the Ecologically Related Species Working Group and the installation of bird-catch mitigation devices on Japanese and Australian vessels, there has been a reduction in the level of bird mortality associated with tuna fishing. The CCSBT has also played an important role in facilitating communication and collaborative work between Australian and Japanese fishery scientists, and their data on the stock's migratory behaviour and reproductive potential is an important resource in the annual CCSBT negotiations on quota levels.

It is not inconceivable therefore, that in the long term the CCSBT could evolve into a site of 'institutional learning'. In the light of the foregoing analysis, this is most likely to occur through the adjustment of Japanese policy toward Australia and New Zealand's normative goals. One possible catalyst for such a shift is the apparently insurmountable set of problems confronting Japan's tuna fleet, prompting a reappraisal by the state of the wisdom of continuing to subsidise the industry. Structural tensions between the state and industry have become increasingly apparent through the winding back of subsidies to industry in the 1990s (Bergin and Haward 1996a: 107–10) The fishery's efforts to resist the withdrawal of state subsidies might be undermined by the increasingly popular morality of environmentalism. This could facilitate the formation of new alliances between politicians, sympathetic bureaucrats and environmental groups. Indeed, anecdotal evidence suggests that such new alliances are being forged. In the 1990s, Japan's civil service began to recruit a new generation of bureaucrats less closely aligned with industry, avowedly liberal in political and economic orientation and internationalist in outlook.[11] A normative shift towards more environmental concerns could also transform the activities of the trading house groups. Growing consumer boycotts and activism towards unregulated tuna imports could pressure the trading houses to regulate imports of tuna. Similar tensions are also apparent in Korea's tuna sector, and there too, of course, political structures are changing and the environmental movement is becoming stronger. This gradual change in the environment in which policy is designed in Japan could create greater synergy and links between scientific communities, and policy goals and management strategies more in keeping with Australian and New Zealand objectives.

Conclusion

The foregoing analysis has demonstrated that the apparent paradox of Australia and Japan continuing to engage in low-level conflicts over the fishing of SBT, despite having agreed to impose quotas on catch levels, is explicable, first, in the light of conflicting domestic interests, political rationalities and institutional configurations. Second, it is understandable because of the leverage exercised by one party and the strategic considerations of the other.

Government policy in Australia is informed by scientific and management input that aims to protect tuna stocks. This is reinforced by the common goals pursued by the state and environmental groups, and by the historically marginal position of Australia's fishing industry. Japan's policy environment is almost the antithesis of that in Australia. The influence of the fishing industry in Japan originates in the developmental ethos of the modern Japanese state and the disproportionate representation of regional fishing electorates. Government policy aims to protect the tuna industry rather than the stocks. Japan's acceptance of reduced quota levels was prompted by a concern that its fleet might be denied access to Australian territorial waters if Australian government aims, Australian SBT fishers and Australian and international environmental groups were not accommodated in the early 1990s.

Liberal regime theory does not appear to have a great deal of explanatory value in the context of this case study of the formation and rather vexed operation of the CCSBT. Increased international interaction and a desire to resolve an important transborder collective action problem have not yet resulted in ideational and policy convergence, much less consensus. Nor was the regulatory regime a consequence of the flexing of muscle by a self-serving hegemon, as realists suppose, even though Australia's exploitation of its geographical location as a point of leverage in its negotiations with Japan does lend qualified support to the realist position.

In combination with the realist account, application of a modified Gramscian framework does provide important insights into the factors that determine the success of efforts to establish and make effective international regimes such as the CCSBT. It is indisputable that to succeed, the political and economic interests of key national players – Japan's tuna industry and the environmental lobby in Australia – must be accommodated. However, the composition of players and their interests are always in flux. Moreover, this case study demonstrates that the formation of international regimes is affected by changing domestic political alliances, legitimating discourses, policies and institutions. As the example of international environmental groups nominating the SBT for a CITES listing suggests, those changes might be prompted by the action or interaction of agents at different levels of geo-political scale. The lesson is clear: in the long term, there are no advantages to be gained by making concessions only to those who are powerful in the present.

A cursory glance at the international management of other global common pool resources underscores these conclusions. There is no uncontested notion of 'the common good'. Despite their avowed commitment to sustainability and conservation in the case of the SBT, Australia and New Zealand's stance on other global resource dilemmas are almost identical to Japan's position on tuna fishing. Under pressure from powerful resources, industry and rural lobbyists, the Australian government has campaigned actively for higher emission levels of greenhouse gases despite international efforts to reduce emissions. Similarly, the New Zealand government has actively defended its commercial fishery's interests in taking higher catches of orange roughy, a stock that straddles Australian and New Zealand territorial waters, in opposition to Australian efforts to reduce fishing pressure on a declining resource. The achievement of any sort of international consensus – be it on the SBT, greenhouse gases or the orange roughy – requires much more than the resolution of procedural or technical differences or the creation of a new international regulatory regime. It awaits the construction of a political mechanism for addressing the interests, normative assumptions, goals and policy preferences of a wide variety of domestic as well as international actors, now and in the future.

Notes

1 See *Science For Sustainability*, CSIRO division of fisheries fact sheet on SBT called 'On the tuna trail'.
2 The take of SBT within Indonesian territorial waters is a complex mix of both local subsistence fishing effort, and domestic and international commercial fishing activity. The take of SBT in the western Indian Ocean region principally forms a bycatch to the target species of bigeye and yellowfin tuna in this region.

3 For instance, despite opposition from indigenous groups, environmental NGOs and many members of Australian and international communities, the Australian government has been a strong supporter and advocate of corporations that have sought to mine uranium in the world-heritage-listed Kakadu National Park in the Northern Territory.

4 The paper will focus principally on Australia and Japan. These countries have been the main nations harvesting the resource. Due to the importance of the Australian Fishing Zone (AFZ) to Japan's fishing strategy, international negotiations have been primarily between Australia and the Japanese. To date New Zealand, Korea, Taiwan and Indonesia have had a marginal role in the fishery.

5 Information obtained in interview with industry representatives and fishermen in February 1998.

6 *Ibid.*

7 *Ibid.*

8 Discussion of the fishing sector will include the agricultural sector in Japan. Together, these constitute 'rural interests'.

9 Information obtained from interviews with the SBT industry during February 1998.

10 A CITES listing has two levels. A listing on Appendix 1 prohibits the commercial trade in a species. Listing on Appendix 2 requires significant regulation requirements, such as export permits from the country of origin (Tsamenyi and McIlgorm 1995: 8–9).

11 These generational shifts in Japan's bureaucracy were described in interviews with an academic based in Australia who has devoted over ten years of research to Japan's tuna fleet and its policy environment.

4

NGOs IN PURSUIT OF 'THE PUBLIC GOOD' IN SOUTH KOREA[1]

Hyuk-Rae Kim

In the last few decades of the twentieth century, the global community witnessed the growing impact of non-governmental organisations (NGOs) in local, national and international spheres (Boli and Thomas 1997; Ghils 1992; Price 1999). This was evident in their increasing involvement in a range of issues relating to human rights, gay rights and citizens' rights, anti-corruption, the environment, gender, health, disaster relief, grassroots development and consumer protection. NGOs actively shaped perceptions of what was in 'the public interest' and organised people and events to pursue those interests through providing goods and services. But NGOs' activities extended well beyond their not-for-profit provision of goods and services to include the development of governance institutions (Clark 1991; Commission on Global Governance 1995; Korten 1990; Wolch 1990). In many instances, they played the role of policy entrepreneurs. For example, they proposed and assisted in the implementation of policies, and formed organisations dedicated to the protection of public interests by monitoring government and business activities (Fisher 1998; Kim 2000a; McCarthy *et al.* 1992; Salamon and Anheier 1994; Weiss and Gordenker 1996; Wuthnow 1991).

Until the late 1980s, NGOs were suppressed in South Korea (hereafter Korea) under the policies of the military authoritarian regime. It was only after the turning point of the 'Democratic Movement' in 1987 that NGOs began to flourish. Korea's democratic transition was characterised by the decentralisation and deregulation of government activities. Many functions formerly the responsibility of parts of the bureaucracy were taken over by NGOs. As a consequence, NGOs increased in number, their activities and ideological orientations became more diverse and they exercised greater political influence. Furthermore, NGOs based on local communities and local issues proliferated, and they enjoyed greater autonomy and power.

Throughout the 1990s, the emergence of NGOs in particular, and civil society more generally, profoundly modified the political landscape in Korea. The dominance of the major political parties and politicians in the political life of the nation, and the prioritisation of state and business interests in determining 'the public interest', was challenged with increasing frequency and effectiveness. NGOs questioned whether popular sovereignty actually was exercised by granting citizens one-time voting rights during an election period. They complained that because of the exclusivity of elite networks and the close collusion between the state and business, the rights of citizens and small shareholders were frequently ignored and sometimes even suppressed.

But after the onset of the financial crisis in 1997, the Small Shareholders' Rights Campaign instigated by the People's Solidarity for Participatory Democracy (PSPD) began to draw attention to the rights of small shareholders that had been overshadowed by the arbitrary power of large-scale businesses. Then, in the sixteenth parliamentary election for Assembly members in 2000, over 1,000 civic organisations formed a coalition called the Citizens' Alliance for General Election 2000 (CAGE) for the purpose of eradicating corrupt politics and restoring sovereignty to the citizens. CAGE generated such diverse activities as the anti-nomination movement, the anti-regionalism campaign and the negative campaign against 'blacklisted' politicians. Despite legal challenges to its right to intervene in an election campaign, CAGE successfully ousted fifty-nine out of eighty-six 'blacklisted' candidates. CAGE, together with other NGOs, established a new benchmark in the decentralisation of governance functions and in the consolidation of participatory democracy (Kim 2001a). Thus NGOs have established the institutional and organisational basis for protecting the rights of small shareholders in business, and for achieving popular sovereignty in the political arena.

This chapter argues that both the state and the market fail to provide public and collective goods and services, and to establish proper governance in reference to the provision of those goods. NGOs may satisfy the demands for public and collective goods and services that are unresolved by markets and governments. Hence this chapter investigates Korean NGOs both as collective goods in their own right, and as important providers of public and collective goods. Second, the chapter provides an historical overview of the development of NGOs in Korea as a basis for examining the shifting relationship between Korea's state and civil society. Third, the chapter investigates the role of NGOs both as institutional alternatives and as policy entrepreneurs in the pursuit of intrinsic goods; most particularly, 'the public good' of citizens' sovereignty and small shareholders' rights.

The case study centres on three major NGOs and their activities in pursuit of 'the public good': the PSPD and its Small Shareholders' Rights Campaign, the Citizens' Coalition for Economic Justice (CCEJ) and its Fair Election Campaign and, finally, CAGE's campaign to eliminate corruption and encourage democratic participation in the political system. While differing in many aspects, these NGOs are similar in that they are organisational forms of collective goods that have been created to allow and regulate citizen participation in both the political and business arenas. Even though they are far from representative of the majority of Korean NGOs, they are forerunners in undertaking collective action in pursuit of political aims. An investigation of these organisations helps to identify the conditions that are shaping the development of Korean NGOs and their roles as public institutions and alternative providers of collective goods and services, and contributes to a broader understanding of the forces propelling democratic transition in Korea. It also illuminates the complex social interactions that contribute toward the creation of what Rose (1996) labels a 'responsibilising' mode of governance. And finally, it provides a topical illustrations of how NGOs influence popular notions of what sorts of collective goods are for 'the public good'.

The emergence of NGOs for the provision of public and collective goods

Generally, NGOs are defined as private voluntary associations that are not part of government or business, that are freely formed by private citizens and that are not motivated by profit (Anheier and Seibel 1990; Bennet 1980; Kim 1997; United Nations 1980; Willets 1982). Substantial characteristics of NGOs can be inferred from this definition. First, NGOs are formal organisations. They have the explicit objective of achieving certain goals within a framework of rules that govern the relations among the members of the organisation and that outline the duties of each member (Blau and Scott 1962: 5; Etzioni 1961; Kim 2000a). Second, NGOs are private non-profit organisations that differentiate themselves from governments and for-profit organisations (Salamon and Anheier 1994; Kim 1997). However, in recent years, there is more evidence of increasing collaboration between governments and NGOs – especially in providing public and collective goods – and the boundaries of these functions are becoming blurred. Third, NGOs create ideas of voluntarism and networks of civil engagement designed to produce notions of trust that facilitate social cooperation. In consequence, they help to enlarge the political commons where state and civil society interact. In sum, NGOs are non-state actors that are private in form, but public in character and non-profit-oriented in their objectives and activities (Anheier and Seibel 1990; Kim 2000a; McCarthy et al. 1992; Powell 1987; Powell and Clemens 1998; Salamon 1995; Salamon and Anheier 1994; Weiss and Gordenker 1996).

Around the globe, there is an increasing awareness that the forces of globalisation have created situations where governments alone cannot cope with public issues, thus leaving a growing space for NGOs to fill.[2] This recognition of governments' limits coincides with a decline in the budgetary capacity of states and a loss of confidence in the ability of states to provide adequate political forums and appropriate public policies, goods and services (Risse-Kappen 1995; Rosenau and Czempiel 1992; Salamon and Anheier 1994; Weiss and Gordenker 1996; Wuthnow 1991).

On the one hand, governments have responded to these new demands and their budgetary constraints by devolving responsibility for the provision of what were formerly considered to be wholly public services to quasi-autonomous organisations. They have also encouraged individuals to take care of themselves, as illustrated in this volume by Wong's chapter on the individualisation of social rights in China. On the other hand, NGOs are themselves collective goods that have been created voluntarily by citizens to serve as organisational vehicles for the pursuit of specific public purposes. The growth of the NGO sector is itself a proof that the kind of public realm that the government is either unwilling to create or unable to handle, is rapidly expanding. At the same time, as Rose (1996) observes, new strategies for governing 'at a distance' and modes of creating a 'responsible' society that organises and regulates itself are being devised. These dual movements reposition not just the functional roles of governments and NGOs in the provision of public and collective goods and services, but also their relative political power. This repositioning is of historic significance in the case of countries such as Korea, because it modifies the model of authoritarian governance that has long characterised the developmental states in East Asia.

It has become something of a commonplace to suggest that public and collective goods entail the existence of collective action problems (Olson 1965). These concepts, and the wisdom of linking them, are discussed at length in the introductory chapter of this volume. But ideas about the dynamics of collective action problems are particularly relevant to the argument presented here about the role of NGOs in compensating for the failure of states and markets to provide adequate public and collective goods. For that reason, they merit repetition. A public good is one that, once provided, cannot feasibly be withheld from any member of a society (Calhoun 1998; Mansbridge 1998).[3] If goods are public, it always benefits each individual to consume those goods without paying for them, that is, to free ride on others' provision of those goods. Similarly, the concept also entails both positive and negative externality problems that are associated with a more general category of 'market failures'. Externalities, whether positive or negative,[4] render markets inefficient in providing goods that are not owned by anyone, but can be used by anybody. The provision of public goods through the market virtually ensures that they are in short supply since few consumers pay voluntarily for products they could obtain without having to pay (Weisbrod 1977). With market demand low, producers create less of these goods and services than the public really wants.

The presence of externalities or market failures justifies government intervention. Indeed, it is a critical function of government to identify those areas in which the market fails, and to meet demand. However, governments cannot anticipate all of the public and collective goods that are desired by their citizens. They produce only that range and quantity of public and collective goods that they are ideologically predisposed to supply or that satisfy crucial political constituencies. In addition, as Zhang's chapter in this volume illustrates, governments' provision of public and collective goods might primarily reflect their own interests, and not be for the good of the immediate public. Inevitably, this leaves some demands unfulfilled by both the market and the government.

There is, therefore, a functional logic to the emergence of NGOs as the providers of goods that are under-supplied by both the market and the government (Salamon 1987; 1995; Weisbrod 1977). It is to meet demands for a range of public and collective goods, including forums for participation in political and economic processes, that these organisations are created.

However, there are inherent limitations on NGOs that in many respects are similar to the limitations of government as a mechanism for providing public goods (Salamon 1995). For example, the transaction costs involved in the provision of public and collective goods, including the costs of mobilising voluntary action, tend to be high. NGOs have a tendency to focus on a single issue and only to attend to the interests of their members. They thus pay insufficient attention to the interests of other 'publics'. Furthermore, NGOs as providers of public and collective goods tend to be incapable of generating resources on a scale that is both adequate and reliable enough to cope with problems involved in the financing and supply of many goods and services. In part, this is a reflection of the free rider problem that frequently occurs with public and collective goods. So long as sole reliance is placed on a system of voluntary contributions, it is likely that the resources made available will be less than those needed to produce public and collective goods on a scale that society considers optimal (Powell and Clemens 1998; Steinberg 1987; Weisbrod 1977). Thus the NGO sector, despite its advantages in terms of creating a meaningful sense of participation, social obligation and legitimacy, has serious drawbacks as a generator of resources and provider of public and collective goods (Salamon 1987; 1995).

In consequence, alternative routes involving civilian co-optation and collaboration, as well as a division of labour between the state and NGOs in the provision of public and collective goods (Smillie and Helmich 1993), have to be sought. In certain cases, it might be appropriate for the state to specialise in the authorisation and financing of services, and to delegate responsibility for their delivery to NGOs. However, as the following case studies of Korean NGOs' initiation and monitoring of state and business activities demonstrate, under many circumstances it is crucial that NGOs retain their autonomy from the state in order to protect their organisational integrity.

The state and NGOs in South Korea

Korea, since its liberation from Japanese colonial rule in 1945, has pursued two major national projects: economic development and political democratisation. The rapid economic growth that resulted from the implementation of seven consecutive five-year economic plans from the early 1960s to 1997 led to the recognition of Korea as a model of East Asian capitalist development (Kim 2000b). As Beeson observes in Chapter 2 in this volume, the state's direction of savings and investment was a determining force in this economic development. At the same time, however, the state's repression and restriction of basic democratic rights impeded the growth of civil society (Kim 2000c). The central government's bureaucracy maintained a virtual monopoly on decision-making authority and jurisdiction over all public issues. The government's monopoly over the design and supply of many public goods was symptomatic of this authoritarian system of state-centric governance (Kim 2000a; 2001b). It is therefore not surprising that in this context, many working-class and civil movements were characterised by their anti-government and anti-corporate positions.

In the 1980s, student activists directly challenged the government's claim that the demands of economic development necessitated that democracy be postponed. At the same time, workers charged that deepening regional and sectoral imbalances and growing distributive inequities required a clear policy response. The Korean government consequently began to establish the legislative foundations for a social welfare system that it hoped would mitigate the growing social conflict caused by directed economic growth. In the constitutional amendments that attended the new welfare provisions, it was stipulated that the state had a duty to secure the welfare of its citizens.[5] The expanded social role of government and the associated legal changes provided new opportunities for NGOs to form, and to extend the scope and scale of their activities and play a more active part in the design of public institutions and the implementation of government policy.

NGOs built upon those early gains in the 1990s. In part, this was a consequence of their own role in articulating demands for an expansion of the political arena through establishing rights to association and access to information. In January 1994, the regulation that required the registration of civil organisations was somewhat relaxed to allow organisations to register after they were formed (*Dong-A Ilbo* 1996; E. Lee 1998). With the complete abolition of the law in 1996, citizens could more easily organise themselves without being subjected to government authorisation. The appointment of civil organisations' board members no longer needed to be authorised, nor could the government annul appointments at random. In addition, for-profit activities could now be carried out without prior consent from, or registration by, the government (Office for Government Coordination 1998). Furthermore, after struggling with requests from citizens and NGOs for two years, the government finally promulgated the Information Disclosure Law in January 1998. This law aimed to ensure the transparency and account-ability of government by granting individuals access to the information of government agencies, including the legislature and the judiciary. Also, this law provided a legal basis for the filing of suits against government bureau-cracies that refused to disclose requested data or information. If the law was to be observed, it would ensure that the operations of the government would be laid open for scrutiny by citizens.

In this respect, the Information Disclosure Law became the embodiment of popular sovereignty because it granted to citizens the right to monitor whatever occurred in the public sector, thereby reversing, in principle if not always in practice, the direction of surveillance and relations of authority and obligation. Since 1998, NGOs have referred to the Law and requested data that would allow them to watch over government activities. In the main, the results have been disappointing, as the government offices nomi-nated frequently have devised ways and excuses to avoid the release of data that may subject them to public criticism. Nevertheless, court orders for access to information are increasingly being applied for by NGOs. For example, the PSPD's Open Information Working Group has requested data from various ministries, and filed complaints on the grounds of the Information Disclosure Law when denied access to the requested informa-tion. As the result of one such action, the National Tax Administration was ordered by the court to furnish the data it previously had refused to disclose.

Furthermore, in response to President Kim's proclamation of the devel-opment of civil society as one of his main policies, in 1999 the ruling party passed legislation that enhanced the institutional status and financial struc-ture of NGOs. This law provided NGOs with free lease of an office, diverse tax favours and free postal rates. It also included tax exemption on contribu-tions to NGOs' activities. For the support of NGOs, the Ministry of Government Administration and Home Affairs has also set up the NGO Cooperation Division to provide administrative backup for the execution of the legislation. The Division is responsible for devising policies in support of NGOs, and for the execution of the annual budget which includes 15 billion won set aside as subsidies for NGOs (*Dong-A Ilbo* 1999).

These legislative and institutional changes were conducive to growth in the number of NGOs and the scope and scale of their activities. A particu-larly large number of NGOs were established in the decade between 1987 and 1996, as opposed to both the numbers of NGOs established in the previous period, and all other types of civil organisations established after 1987 (Kim 1997).[6] Of 730 NGOs surveyed in 1996, only 24.2 per cent had been created during the Park and Chun eras, between the early 1960s and the mid-1980s, while the great majority had been formed after the mid-1980s. Nevertheless, despite the rise in numbers, most NGOs in Korea are small in size. This can be inferred through the number of full-time employees. Of the organisations surveyed, 37.1 per cent reported between two and five full-time employees, and 85.2 per cent employed ten or fewer full-time employees. The small number of employees in each NGO also indicates their lack of organisational capacity to manage large projects, develop technical skills, offer career paths for valued employees and pursue long-term strategic planning.

The sharp rise in the number of NGOs founded since 1987 also verifies that the establishment of NGOs is highly correlated to the process of political democratisation (Kim 1997). An analysis of the historical pattern of establishment shows that the democratic movement opened up a socio-political space in which NGOs could emerge, expand their organisational capacities and extend the scope of their public and political activities into such spheres as environmental issues, citizens' rights, anti-corruption, human and gender rights, and welfare. In particular, the nation's leading civil organisations, the PSPD and the CCEJ, which were formed after the 1987 democratisation movement, extensively participated in the political process. Since their formation, they have played important roles as policy initiators and monitors of government and business activities, thereby assisting in consolidating and extending the gains of the original democracy movement.

Korean NGOs in pursuit of 'the public good'

NGOs that claim to represent public interests have been recognised by the government and mass media as repositories of diverse, creative and expert human resources that have the capacity and obligation to present solutions to public issues.[7] In fact, the government has stated that one of its aims is to foster a democracy in which the citizens and NGOs directly participate in governance. In this regard, the PSPD, CCEJ and CAGE have played exemplary roles in instigating institutional reform and creating opportunities for citizens to exercise their sovereignty in politics, and exercise their rights as small shareholders in business.

The PSPD[8] is a non-profit civic organisation with the objective:

> to check the state's power by engaging the voluntary participation of citizens from all classes and sectors, suggesting concrete policies and alternative solutions, and building a society of participatory democracy in which freedom, human rights and welfare are fully realised by citizen action.
>
> (PSPD 1999)

The organisation was launched in 1994 with 200 members. By the year 2000 membership had increased to around 5,000. There are about forty full-time employees and some 200 volunteer activists working for the organisation. The PSPD is composed of nine major action bodies, each specialising in an area of concern,[9] as well as five affiliated organisations, twelve citizen circles, a policy-formation committee and a citizens' committee.

In the PSPD,[10] the action bodies are the real driving forces of efforts to create and enforce citizens' rights, primarily through the launching of public campaigns and the revision of law and litigation. These action bodies have been involved in various kinds of campaigns that popularise a notion of 'the public good' that centres on the right of citizens to demand transparency in political and economic governance. These include: the Watch Campaign Against the National Assembly, the Watch Campaign Against the Judiciary, the Transparent Society Campaign, the Minimum Social Welfare Campaign, the Small Shareholders' Rights Campaign and the Restoration of Citizens' Rights Campaign. In this section, I will focus on the campaign that has attracted most attention from the media, as well as considerable public support: the Small Shareholders' Rights Campaign.

The PSPD's Participatory Economy Committee launched the Small Shareholders' Rights Campaign in 1997 with the aims of protecting the rights of minority shareholders that had been granted by commercial and securities exchange laws, and increasing the transparency of corporate management. The ultimate objective was to reform a corporate governance environment that was characterised by over-diversification, excessive debt, insider trading and inheritance of ownership. Thus, while many of the aims of the campaign coincided with those of some of the austerity reform measures prescribed by the International Monetary Fund (IMF) after the onset of the 1997 financial crisis, the PSPD's campaign predated the IMF's initiative.

The Small Shareholders' Rights Campaign utilised a strategy of mobilising small shareholders to act as a unified group in possession of substantial equity, and thereby protect themselves against the arbitrary business management practices of the *chaebols*. In March 1997, the campaign received much public attention when the Korea First Bank's annual stockholders' meeting was held twice, after a lawsuit to annul the first ended in victory for the PSPD. The PSPD brought legal actions challenging the procedural breaches and validity of the resolutions made at the annual shareholders' meeting. The Seoul District Court found that there had been procedural errors and accepted the small shareholders' petition to cancel resolutions passed at the meeting. The court also pointed out the responsibilities of the former president and directors at the First Bank and ordered them to pay 40 billion won (approximately US$28.6 million) in compensation to the First Bank on behalf of the shareholders. This decision gave a boost to the momentum of the campaign and encouraged small shareholders to dare to challenge major corporations and *chaebols* in order to protect their rights.

The PSPD also took a series of actions against Samsung Electronics. In February 1997, the PSPD delivered to Samsung Electronics a formal request from minority shareholders for nullification of Samsung Electronics' issue of convertible bonds worth 60 billion won (US$43 million), of which 45 billion won were directed to the Samsung chairman's son and 15 billion won to Samsung Co.[11] The PSPD filed suit to nullify the issue of convertible bonds and filed a request for a temporary injunction against their conversion. In March 1998 the PSPD attended the annual stockholders' meeting of Samsung Electronics. During the record thirteen and a half hours of the meeting, the *chaebol's* intra-group loan to Samsung Motors was revealed. In response to revelations about that loan, the PSPD took a series of legal actions against illegal insider trading, capital injection and bank guarantees, and sales of holding securities at below-market prices.[12] The shareholders' derivative suit, following the Korea First Bank case, led to significant changes in the ways the responsibilities and authority of directors and auditors were specified and monitored. At the same time, it strengthened the rights of small shareholders.

The PSPD continued the campaign to demand management responsibility and transparency and prevent unilateral decision-making by majority shareholders, by attending the general shareholders' meetings of other *chaebols* including SK Telecom, Hyundai Heavy Industry, Dacom, Daewoo Corporation and LG Semiconductors. It also filed derivative suits to protect the rights of minority shareholders in those conglomerates and corporations. In response, several *chaebols* accepted their minority shareholders' requests to improve management transparency by amending their articles of incorporation, appointing independent outside executives and auditors, and establishing an audit committee. The PSPD also proposed a series of legislative reforms in corporate law that resulted in the promulgation of the Commercial Code and Securities Exchange Act. In 1999, the PSPD attempted to institutionalise the cumulative voting system that would enable small shareholders, in alliance, to appoint their own executive board members. However, it failed to gain approval from most *chaebols* to revise their articles of incorporation to allow for the cumulative voting system in the election of directors.

As is the case with many of the actions the PSPD has initiated, the Small Shareholders' Rights Campaign was essentially an attempt to introduce new ideas about 'the public good' into Korean society. The organisation's goal was to bring attention to, and expand, the rights of small shareholders that had been overshadowed by the arbitrary power of the directors, managers and major shareholders of *chaebols*. Prior to the PSPD's endeavour, the small shareholders had not challenged the omnipotence of the business elites that dominated the *chaebols*, nor had they the expertise and the organisational capacity to do so. The PSPD mobilised the small shareholders to form a 'public' that could articulate its demands and participate in the management of corporations in which it was a shareholder. Even though crucial shareholders' rights did not become fully institutionalised, it is indisputable that the PSPD campaign made minor shareholders much more active participants in corporate affairs. Indeed, the Small Shareholders' Rights Campaign has been described as 'the most influential citizen movement that has affected all sectors in Korea' (Sung 1999).

The CCEJ[13] is also a citizens' voluntary organisation. Founded in July 1989, by the end of 1999 the CCEJ had nearly fifty full-time staff and some 35,000 members. It was formed with the aim of eliminating economic injustice (CCEJ 1997). In deference to its largely middle-class membership, it eschews radical political philosophies. Instead it seeks to uncover the causes of economic problems and to propose alternative policies and reforms to realise economic justice at all levels of society. It concentrates on issues of income disparity, unbalanced distribution of wealth, speculation in real estate, environmental degradation and consumer rights. At various times, it has proposed equalisation of the tax structure, strengthening the antitrust and fair trade laws, dispersal of *chaebol* ownership and reform of the political system. In pursuit of that last objective, for example, the CCEJ worked through its local branches to increase citizen participation by launching a Fair Election Campaign. The campaign was designed to eradicate corrupt politics and restore the sovereignty of citizens' participation in the political arena. The CCEJ also actively focuses public attention on housing for the poor and environmental degradation (CCEJ 1997).

The CCEJ was one of a number of major civic groups, including the PSPD, the Korean Federation of Environmental Movements and the Green Korea United, that launched a new political reform movement on 27 December 1999. On 12 January 2000, over 400 organisations and groups proclaimed a coalition, CAGE, devoted to political reform.

CAGE declared that its goals were to establish democratic and transparent political procedures and guarantee citizens' rights to participate in the nomination and election of candidates (Kim 2001a). Hence CAGE's vision of 'the public good' was clearly couched in terms of people's participation in a representative democracy. Declaring the movement for political reform as the most significant movement in civil society in the year 2000, CAGE first sought to prevent unqualified and corrupt politicians and officials from running in the general elections to be held the following April, and to help voters make informed choices in the election. Second, in order to obtain legitimacy for the movement, CAGE proposed revising the election law that prevented citizens from campaigning actively for or against any party or candidates and restricted the sorts of campaign event that could be staged. Finally, CAGE sought to eradicate disaffection, apathy and distrust of politics – sentiments that were widespread in Korean society – by promoting political reform as an important social issue.

CAGE ran a negative campaign against politicians who were judged by civic organisations to be unfit to be elected. The first list of 167 'unfit' politicians was released in January by the CCEJ. The CCEJ's judgement was based on criteria such as an individual politician's participation in corruption, their violation of election laws, resistance to reform and fanning of regional antagonisms and, more generally, their lack of education or poor quality. Immediately after the revelations of the CCEJ, CAGE announced a list of sixty-six unqualified candidates: of those, twenty-nine contenders were from the opposition Grand National Party (GNP) and sixteen each were from the ruling Millennium Democratic Party (MDP) and its coalition partner the United Liberal Democrats (ULD). CAGE also unveiled an additional list of forty-seven incompetent, corrupt and lazy politicians who were proclaimed 'unfit' to run for office in the April polls. The CCEJ and CAGE lists touched off successive announcements of similar lists by other civic groups. For example, Political Watch, a civic movement for political reform, published its own list of eighty-nine 'unfit' politicians.

These lists caused major repercussions in the political arena because they included not only one of the most prominent political figures, Kim Jong-pil, who was the honorary president and founder of the ULD, but also dozens of key politicians in both ruling and opposition parties. As expected, the affected politicians and political parties unanimously denounced the publication of these lists and questioned the objectivity of the criteria and the fairness of the selection process. In response to appeals from those who had been declared 'unfit', the CCEJ was forced to change its list twice. All major political parties sought legal action against what they saw as an apparent violation of the law as well as the defamation of individual politicians, and urged that CAGE be prosecuted.

In order to obtain legal foundation for their campaigns, both the CCEJ and CAGE asked for a revision of Article 87 of the Election Law, which banned organisations such as civic groups from electioneering for candidates. The media and citizenry reacted favourably to this call for a revision of the law. Hence some ruling party members, including President Kim and members of the National Elections Commission – the political establishment – agreed that Article 87 of the Election Law be altered. Moreover, CCEJ and CAGE were granted the status of consultants, to advise on that revision. The two groups proposed that the scope of permissible campaign activities by NGOs should be expanded and the definition of civic groups should be amended. The revised Election Law, however, failed to meet their demands. Although the new law allowed civil groups to state their support for, or objections against, specific politicians and lawmakers, they were still banned from holding outdoor rallies and pre-election campaigns, including petition drives and certain other activities.

In response to the government's failure to approve their activities, the groups involved in the political reform movement filed a complaint with the Constitutional Court over the revised Election Law and petitioned President Kim to exercise his power of veto. This gained widespread media attention, and the number of NGOs participating in the campaign rose to 1,055.

CAGE launched a civil disobedience campaign to collect one million signatures from citizens in preparation for taking legal action to further amend the revised Election Law. It also drew participation from tens of thousands of people by designating 30 January as a 'Day of Declaration for Voters' Rights'.

As election campaigning gathered steam, CAGE activated civil monitoring task forces that questioned candidates, monitored any attempts to raise regional animosities, and held regular press conferences on the negative effects of regionalism and the dangers associated with voting for unqualified candidates. In a climate of growing public interest in the nominations, on 19 February the political parties disclosed their nominated candidates for most electoral districts. The nominations were denounced by CAGE because they were conducted in an undemocratic manner and violated Article 31 of the Political Party Law, which states that a candidate must be selected through due democratic process and with the support of district party members. Moreover, the candidates included forty politicians pronounced 'unfit' by the broad coalition of NGOs.

Claiming that the nominations failed to respond to the demands for political reform from the public, the CCEJ and CAGE used two-stage strategies to discourage the political parties from continuing to nominate 'unfit' candidates and to urge citizens not to vote for those who had been blacklisted. On 1 March, in spite of their illegality, the NGOs staged rallies to restore 'voter independence' and called on the political parties to reselect candidates. The movement escalated with the participation of a coalition of university students and various other civic groups. The CCEJ and CAGE also used their nationwide networks of affiliated organisations to demand an end to factionalism, regionalism and corrupt politics, and to mobilise a civil education and monitoring task force. Members of the Korean Teachers and Educational Workers Union began to lecture their students on the meaning of citizenship in a democratic country, and on desirable traits in politicians and voters. Finally, CAGE held a 'rejection campaign', staging massive outdoor rallies to restore 'voter independence' and appealing directly to the people for support in their quest to root out corrupt politicians and regionalism in politics. CAGE released a final list of eighty-six 'unfit' nominees, vowing to campaign for their defeat. The 'rejection campaign' centred primarily on twenty-two 'most problematic' candidates (seven from the MDP, nine from the GNP, four from the ULD and two from the Democratic People's Party or DPP), twenty 'focused blacklisted' candidates and seven 'most focused blacklisted' candidates in the metropolitan areas.

The success of the NGOs' strategy was demonstrated in the final outcome of the election. Nineteen out of twenty of the 'focused blacklisted' candidates (95 per cent) and all seven of the 'most focused blacklisted' candidates in metropolitan areas were defeated (Kim 2001a).[14] The election results for other blacklisted candidates were also negative. Fifty-nine of the eighty-six 'unfit' politicians failed to be win seats in the election (68.6 per cent), and fifteen of the twenty-two 'most problematic' candidates were not elected (68.2 per cent). In addition to its success in affecting the election results, the coalition of NGOs also succeeded in recalling the lawmakers to review the Election Law and readjust the electoral constituencies to prevent gerrymandering by political parties. The political reform movement created a landmark for Korean democracy by facilitating meaningful citizen participation in the political arena. Indeed, CAGE was described in the press as 'the only real winner' in the general election (*Korea Times* 2000).

On the other hand, the NGO coalition was not able to overcome chronic regionalism, as shown in the fact that eighteen 'focused blacklisted' GNP candidates in the Kyongsang provinces won seats. Moreover, because the 'rejection campaign' launched by CAGE was a negative campaign to undermine support for 'blacklisted' candidates, it fell short of offering alternatives to voters.

Conclusion

The conventional paradigm in Korean politics changed with the emergence and development of NGOs in the late 1980s and 1990s. To the extent that it had been realised at all after the demise of the authoritarian military regime, popular sovereignty was exercised only through the one-time voting rights of individuals in elections. Politics and the content of public policy were exclusively determined in interaction between the leaders of political parties and major corporations. Against this restricted form of democracy, NGOs began to demand an expansion of citizens' participatory rights. They raised new issues and values in the public sphere, and thus contributed to the creation of a new consensus on democratic principles and practice. They spoke a language of citizens' empowerment. They lobbied for the creation of institutions that could grant people the right and the capacity to monitor government and business activities. Even though the legality and objectivity of their activities were often challenged, NGOs and the civic coalitions they formed demonstrated that through voluntarily organising themselves and taking responsibility for economic management and the political process, citizens at the grassroots could enhance their rights and participate in their own governance.

Now, the task of governance is increasingly viewed as a partnership in which citizens, NGOs, businesses and the government face each other as equals in defining 'the public good' and providing public and collective goods (Etzioni 1973). In this new partnership, all sectors engage in constructive criticism, rivalry and cooperation with each other so as to create loci of public interest, organisation and collective action. Furthermore, it is deemed to be crucially important that citizens overcome their sense of dependence on bureaucracy, and take responsibility on themselves for developing and articulating their common interests and pursuing public purposes within society. Citizens become active agents not only in the selection and regulation of their governments, but also in the management of business, the organisation of civil society and the governance of themselves.

New roles and relationships are being created by the practice of delegating responsibility to NGOs. Accordingly, the arguments of those who once occupied extremes of the political spectrum – NGOs and governments occupy separate positions, perform different functions and act as antagonists – need to be discounted. Now, as this case study of Korea has demonstrated, NGOs are actively projecting their visions of what is in 'the public good', and lobbying for provision of the sorts of public and collective goods that might help to realise those visions. They have become a conduit, transferring functions previously performed by parts of the state not just to the NGO sector, but also to groups of individuals who have been well schooled in their powers and responsibilities as shareholders and voters. NGOs provide indispensable information to governments about new demands for public and collective goods, are often the most fruitful source of innovative suggestions about how best to organise citizens to provide their own public and collective goods, and offer an organisational mechanism for delivery of some of those goods. NGOs work in tandem with, or in order to reform, local and national governments, judicial organs, conglomerates and the media (Powell and Clemens 1998; Salamon 1995).

One of the implications of this process is that there has been a fundamental transformation in Korea's mode of governance. Korea moved from an authoritarian mode, in which the state monitored, and sometimes repressed, the activities of its citizens, to a participatory democratic mode in which citizens oversee the activities of government. In the past, the provision of public and collective goods was the domain of government and those in the private sector could be no more than beneficiaries of those goods. The organisation of political structures and processes and the design of legislation were solely the province of party leaders. But, as shown here, throughout the 1990s Korean NGOs helped to create institutions, languages and attitudes that allowed – indeed, encouraged – civilians to organise and provide public and collective goods for themselves. The Small Shareholders' Rights Campaign by the PSPD mobilised small shareholders to form a 'public' comprised of responsible individuals who should rightfully benefit from the 'good': the right of all shareholders to monitor and participate in management. The CCEJ's Fair Election Campaign and CAGE actively pursued the realisation of citizens' sovereign power in the political arena. Organised three months before the April 2000 election, these groups succeeded not only in educating voters to oust many unqualified politicians, but also in lobbying the government to revise the Election Law and readjust the electoral constituencies. The concerted efforts of the CCEJ and CAGE made citizens feel responsible for the exercise of their voters' rights and the conduct of the electoral process. Thus the three NGOs examined here played a significant role in consolidating democracy and decentralising governance functions – both in politics and business – to civil organisations and individual citizens. They helped to establish a 'responsibilising' pattern of governance in Korea.

Korean NGOs have emerged as important public institutions, and as alternative providers of public goods and services in the process of democratic transition. Their future tasks are to resist regionalism and popularise ever-more inclusive concepts of the political public, and expand the rights of responsible citizens both in politics and business. For this, there must be a recognition of the diversity of interests held by various 'publics', and a willingness on the part of citizens and NGOs to continue to engage in collective action to promote those interests. It can also be argued that although democracy was not necessary for the emergence of an independent NGO sector, the existence of such a sector has been essential in the consolidation and practise of democracy in Korea.

Notes

1 This research was supported in part by the Yonsei University Research Fund of 2000.
2 Beginning in the early 1980s, there was a dramatic expansion in the size of the NGO sector and in its involvement in the provision of public goods. The most telling indictor of NGOs' growing prominence is their increasing level of participation in world summits and conferences, including the Rio environmental 'Earth Summit' of 1992; the Vienna World Conference on Human Rights of 1993; the International Conference on Population and Development of 1994; the World Summit for Social Development in Copenhagen of 1995; the Fourth World Conference on Women in Beijing in 1995; the Istanbul UN Conference on Human Settlements in 1996; and the Kyoto Climate Change Conference of 1997. The increasing public interest is also exemplified by the expansion of such international NGOs as UNDP, UNICEF, Greenpeace, Friends of the Earth, Save the Children, Oxfam, the International Federation of Red Cross, Amnesty International and the Ralph Nader Consumer Group.
3 The concept of public goods is contested not because of an aggregation of individual interests, but because of divergence in social and cultural constructions of the public sphere (Calhoun 1998: 32), and because the concepts of both 'public' and 'good' are defined in various ways (Mansbridge 1998). Generally, in defining the term 'public goods' the properties of joint supply, non-rivalry, non-excludability, and externality are identified (see Chapter 1). The first of these states that the good is produced by people working together. The second, that consumption of the good by one individual does not reduce the quantity available to others, so that its benefits can be made available to all. The third refers to the assumption that the goods cannot be easily be appropriated for exclusive access, use and consumption. Finally, the costs and benefits of providing a good are externalised.
4 Negative externalities imply social costs that are not taken into account by individual decision-makers. On the other hand, positive externalities discourage private investment by spreading the benefits among the members of society.

5 With the constitutional amendments stipulating the state's duty to secure social welfare, the Elderly Welfare Act was enacted and amended respectively in 1981 and 1984. Also, the enactment and amendment of other related Acts was achieved in the 1980s (Moon 1999).

6 Kim (1997) based this analysis on the Directory of Korean NGOs. He selected 730 NGOs of the total 3,899 organisations listed in the Directory. For his analysis, he excluded international organisations including NGOs set up by overseas Koreans, trade organisations, labour unions, academic societies, media and publications, research institutions and religious groups.

7 In recent years the Korean media have begun to draw public attention to the importance of civil society and the operation of NGOs. Since the beginning of 1999 in particular, all major newspapers have devoted regular columns to detailing NGO events and activities, and they have published articles on civil movements. For example, the daily newspaper *Dong-A* reported on 'Civil movements: the fifth power'; there was *Jung-Ang* daily's 'Civil forum: NGOs', *Kyung-Hyang* daily's 'NGO forum', and *Hankyurae* daily's 'Newly rising civil power in the 21st century'.

8 The number of professionals in the PSPD is about 100, and it reaches 300 when non-active participants are included. This information was based on the PSPD website at *http://www.peoplepower21.org*.

9 There are nine action bodies in the PSPD: the Committee for a Transparent Society, the Justice Watch Centre, the National Assembly Watch Centre, the Centre for Restoring Citizens' Rights, the Participatory Economy Committee, the Social Welfare Committee, the Transparent Society Campaign, the Apartment Residents Community, and the Council for Democracy in Science and Technology. Among these acting bodies, the Participatory Economy Committee is responsible for the Small Shareholders' Rights Movement.

10 The PSPD, for instance, has formed the Citizen Lobbyist Group to reclaim the sovereignty of citizens. The group seeks to influence public opinion, exercise pressure on representatives, suggest alternatives, and train new citizen lobbyists. As its first enterprise, the Citizen Lobbyist Group is working for the establishment of the Corruption Prevention Law.

11 This information is to be found in the PSPD website archives at *http://www.pspd. org/structure.html*.

12 *Ibid.*

13 The CCEJ has more than 400 expert members including lawyers and professional activists in various fields.

14 This information has been compiled from various Korean daily newspapers. See Kim (2001a) for details of the election results.

5

CUSTOMARY REGIMES AND COLLECTIVE GOODS IN INDONESIA'S CHANGING POLITICAL CONSTELLATION

Carol Warren and John McCarthy[1]

Imagined communities: *adat* and the nation as commonweal

The most dramatic change in the focus of identity and the struggle over collective goods in post-Suharto Indonesia has undoubtedly been the radical shift in orientation from the nation to a complex constellation of constituent parts. In consequence, any discussion of collective goods and collective action in contemporary Indonesia has to recognise that the once powerful nationalist construction of common identity and interest faces increasing regional and local contestation.[2]

Historically, local 'customary' regimes governed access and use of land and other natural resources through local institutions grounded in kinship or community relations. *Adat* became the generic term in the Dutch colonial period for describing the plethora of religious beliefs, customary institutions and social practices throughout the Indonesian archipelago that tradition-ally defined collectivities and established rights and obligations within and between them.

Adat varies not only from one region or ethnic community to the next, but also from one local hamlet or social grouping to another within these. Notwithstanding the substantive critique of the instrumental and constructed nature of '*adat* law' in Dutch colonial policy and scholarship (Holleman 1981; Burns 1989; Warren 1993), numerous indigenous concepts and axioms[3] express the principle of respect for local variation in cultural codes and practices that characterised the quintessential notion of customary law in colonial scholarship. They attest at the same time to the significant degrees of autonomy claimed by the local domain in pre-colonial Indonesia.

While in no sense representing a homogeneous set of principles, or even universally accepted as an appropriate descriptor,[4] the concept of *adat* nevertheless conjures the disparate meanings associated with 'the local' across Indonesia. Stretching from the very specific ethnic, community or kinship group referents – *adat* Minangkabau, *adat* Desa Tenganan, etc. – to the broadly generic notion of pan-Indonesian beliefs and practices which predated and fused with the orthodox religious traditions of Hinduism and Islam, the notion of *adat* and roughly equivalent concepts in local languages is fundamentally concerned with the rights and reciprocal responsibilities of individuals to their communities or descent groups, and to the founding ancestors who continue to ensure collective wellbeing.

With respect to land and resources, *adat* is tied to varying notions of territoriality or community rights of avail, summed up in the legal term *hak ulayat*.[5] The encompassing religious, social and economic dimensions of *adat* make resource access much more complex than do concepts of individual property rights in Western law.

> Individual rights are defined by their relationship to the complementary rights of the community to which the individual belongs and from which individualised rights are derived. ... [But] the distinction between individual and communal rights cannot be drawn very sharply. *Hak ulayat* is a delicate balance of rights and restrictions, a give and take between the community and its members based on mutual agreement, that can only be really fully understood by the members of the community concerned.
>
> (Evers 1995: 2–3)

While individual possession of agricultural land is not uncommon in *adat* communities, it is normally qualified by conditions on alienation and through various access and redistributive requirements imposed by communities under *adat* rules.[6] Therefore the distinction between private and common property in *adat* constructs is a moot one.

The centrepiece of colonial scholarship and the cornerstone of indirect rule, *adat* was pragmatically asserted by the founding fathers of independent Indonesia as a core principle underpinning 'Unity in Diversity', the motto of the new nation-state. This homage to the place of *adat* as a common heritage of all Indonesian peoples was always characterised by ambivalence, however.[7] In practice, official recognition of *adat* rights was typically observed in benign neglect or breach, depending on the distance of these communities from the purview of interests at the centre and the extent to which their resources attracted outside attention.

From the founding of the Indonesian republic, celebration of cultural diversity and legal recognition of indigenous rights sat uncomfortably with the centralist and nationalist principles of the revolutionary movement. The rejection of a federal structure at the inception of Indonesian nationhood left this concept of governance virtually taboo (Kahin 1994; *Far Eastern Economic Review* 1999). Since the proclamation of Indonesian independence in 1945, the politically centralist tendencies of the 'Old Order' Sukarno period were compounded by the economic power concentrated at the centre under Suharto's 'New Order'. The cumulative impact of Jakarta-driven economic development policy in the late New Order period in particular has been the marginalisation or outright transgression of the *adat* institutions, claims and management regimes that traditionally operated in the local domain.

This chapter will focus on competing claims to natural, cultural and institutional resources that represent the most significant collective assets of local communities across Indonesia. It addresses the practical and rhetorical associations tied to the notion of *adat* and national 'communities' as sites of shared welfare – 'commonweal' – to which identities, institutional relationships and property or resource rights are connected. The contests over the amorphous but powerful links between the resource, identity and authority domains represented by *adat* and national regimes are an important feature of the changing political constellation of post-New Order Indonesia. While the term 'collective goods' is restricted to specific institutional resources, for the purposes of this chapter the metaphoric glossing of 'commonweal' captures the wider range of senses in which access to resources is implicitly associated with membership in local *adat* or national 'communities'.

It is precisely the metaphoric and rhetorical slippage in collective identities/citizenships and concomitant claims/rights that allowed the construction of the Indonesian nation-state as an 'imagined community' (Anderson 1991), and precipitated the contest of power and allegiance between this wider corporatist entity and its local constituents. The project of conflating local and national constructions of the commonweal was paralleled by a similar political and legal slippage authorising the capture of public goods by private interests. The rhetorical dimensions of governance (claims to represent 'the people', 'the common interest', etc.) and the discursive struggles situating collective identities are an important dimension of ongoing contests over the material resources that sustain communities, the legal mechanisms that govern them, and the leaderships that claim to represent them. The 'political rationalities' that catalyse new positionings and struggles in post-New Order Indonesia are forged from these diffuse and rapidly realigning configurations of local, national and global interests and imaginings.

Centring the commonweal: appropriating collective goods in the 'national interest'

At the heart of the disenfranchisement of local communities and *adat* regimes in Indonesia were several key laws that defined property rights, natural resource management and political authority relations between the state, local communities and individuals. The Basic Agrarian Law (UUPA 5/1960), the Forestry Law (UU 5/1967), the Basic Mining Law (UU 11/1967), and the Village Government Law (UU 5/1979) were the legal vehicles for the appropriation of land and resources from *adat* communities and for the marginalisation of autonomous customary institutions. These basic laws, following provisions in the 1945 Constitution, nominally recognise *adat*, but they do so only as long as these local customary practices and institutions do not conflict with national law and national interest.[8]

Both the 1945 Constitution and the Basic Agrarian Law of 1960 absorb the rights of *adat* communities into those of the Indonesian nation-state. In establishing a hierarchy of the commonweal, collective goods regimes were transformed, ensuring that local claims to land and natural resources were systematically overridden by the state in the name of a national definition of 'the people' and the 'common welfare'. The official explanatory notes to Article 3 of the Basic Agrarian Law do not mince words concerning the hindrance *adat* was regarded as representing to development and the wider good:

> nor can it be allowed for a community based on its *hak ulayat* [*adat* territorial rights] for example to refuse the large-scale opening of forests or the planning of large projects for the purpose of increasing food production and moving populations.

Such claims would 'stand in the way of great efforts to achieve the welfare of all the people'.[9]

The subordination of local customary rights to the national interest was rationalised by the same evolutionary developmentalist ethos that underpinned colonial policy and law. Taken into the legal-political regime of the new Indonesian nation-state, it legitimated the expropriation of millions of hectares of land belonging to *adat* communities. Indeed, the legal framework for land and natural resource management effectively appropriates the *adat* concept of territorial rights of avail (*hak ulayat*) writ large to the national scale: '[The] land, water and atmosphere, including natural resources within them at its highest level are controlled by the state, as the organisational authority of all the people' (UUPA 5/1960, §2.1). Mining and forestry laws, in adopting the Dutch legal principle of *domein verklaring*, by which land not legally recognised as private property is deemed owned by the state, go further still beyond the Basic Agrarian Law, which at least acknowledged residual local rights based on *adat* (Fitzpatrick 1997: 187).

The conflation of local with national interest was paralleled by the marginalisation of autonomous local forms of governance, as control of political authority structures was increasingly centralised (Warren 1993; McCarthy 2000). The Village Government Law (UU 5/1979) compounded the effects of basic laws on land and resources by instituting an undemocratic, top-down and culturally inappropriate model of local government throughout Indonesia, marginalising and disempowering indigenous *adat* institutions. The centrally driven framework it imposed facilitated collusion between carefully selected local officials[10] and developers with political connections, ultimately disenfranchising 'the people' in the interest of political–military–business elites.

The contest over collective goods: land law

Throughout the history of the Indonesian republic, land policy and law have been extremely sensitive issues, embodying long-standing tensions between private and public rights, local and central governance regimes, and between Indonesian national and transnational capital with respect to control over this fundamental resource (Hariadi and Masruchah 1995). With the final victory of the Indonesian revolution and foundation of the republic, land reform became a paramount priority for nationalist leaders. Public attention was focused on the need to overcome the inequities of colonial patterns of land use, as well as to recognise the primary rights of those working the land (Tjondronegoro 1991).

The Basic Agrarian Law (UUPA 5/1960), which established the legal framework for land tenure and use in Indonesia, was enacted in 1960 in the context of the development orientation of the newly independent republic. Formulated in the decade following the long revolutionary struggle, it represents a fusion of populist, socialist and nationalist ideas powerfully articulated by the nation's charismatic leader and first president, Sukarno. Reflecting nationalist sentiment, as well as the cultural significance and social security functions of land, foreign nationals were not permitted to obtain freehold title, and concentration of land ownership was restricted under the Basic Agrarian Law and its implementing regulations. In this sense national law, like *adat* law, regarded land as a social good,[11] inalienable from the national commonweal.

In the period of intense political struggle in the early 1960s, the Basic Agrarian Law and subsequent land reform legislation became associated with 'unilateral actions', conflicts between landlords and the Peasants' Front supported by the Communist Party (PKI). The killings of 1965–6 that accompanied the downfall of Sukarno saw the destruction of the PKI and the Peasants' Front, and with it the land reform agenda so central to the Indonesian revolution and national policy under the 'Old Order' of Sukarno. From that point the revolutionary promise of agrarian reform was left to wither (Tjondronegoro 1991).

In recent years even sacrosanct restrictions on foreign ownership have been relaxed as part of the New Order government's deregulation policies that aimed to facilitate access to land for investors (Suhendar and Kasim

1996). Major public and private development projects including hydro-electric dams, commercial forest plantations, urban infrastructure, residential estates and resort complexes for international tourism and the burgeoning middle class, brought tensions between public and private, national and local claims over land rights to a head (Lucas 1992; 1997; Benda-Beckmann and van der Velde 1992; Suyanto 1996; Hirsch and Warren 1998). Commercial pressures compounded the serious ambiguities that have plagued land tenure in Indonesia since the colonial period, and conflicts over land became increasingly acute as the Indonesian economy industrialised (CSIS 1991; World Bank 1995a).

The Basic Agrarian Law reflects the ambivalence over cultural pluralism and the integrity of *adat* regimes that has plagued Indonesian policy and practice since independence. As Fitzpatrick (1997) argues, despite its intent to establish a syncretic amalgam of *adat* and Western law appropriate to the unique circumstances of post-revolutionary Indonesia, it has neither given adequate recognition to the diverse social and cultural relationships to land and resources that *adat* traditionally secured, nor achieved the legal certainty that is supposed to be the hallmark of the Western legal system.

The most fundamental problem with the Basic Agrarian Law has been the contradiction between the thoroughly Western individualised system of statutory land holding categories it establishes and its principal assertion that the land law of the nation is to be 'based upon *adat*' and must have a 'social function' that emphasises the needs of the community over those of the individual (UUPA 5/1960: §6; Fitzpatrick 1997: 172–3; Evers 1995: 4ff).

Partly because of the lack of fit between state law and local understandings, and partly because of the great expense of registration, most land remained untitled into the 1990s (Evers 1995: 21). World Bank reports, produced in the context of a controversial twenty-five-year Land Administration Project (LAP) to provide private property land titles, estimate that only 20 per cent of land parcels in Indonesia are registered. However, this excludes the majority of land outside Java which is classified as forest land and which became subject to a separate legal regime administered by the Ministry of Forestry under the 1967 Forestry Law (World Bank 1993: 19; LAP 1994: 2ff).[12]

As a consequence of the inappropriate and ineffectual titling process, thoroughgoing registration of land rarely occurred outside urban areas. The practical regulation of land distribution and resource access remained a local affair except where significant external interests became involved. In these cases, the land and forest resources of local communities were left vulnerable to direct appropriation by the state or by private companies operating with state backing.

Paradoxically, the very 'social function' which was supposed to ensure that land and resources served the basic needs of ordinary Indonesians (a principle instantiated in land reform laws promulgated pursuant to UUPA in the early 1960s) was increasingly used to justify expropriation from local communities in the name of 'development'. Under the New Order regime especially, the 'national interest' became a euphemism rationalising development projects that primarily served to enrich a small group of powerful and well-connected conglomerates.

The role of the military in securing the interests of the Suharto family and allied business concerns in the process of 'freeing up' land for investment is well documented.[13] In the latter phase of the New Order regime, a rising tide of popular disaffection over land issues paralleled mounting numbers of cases of dispossession in which there was official complicity. By the 1990s, land disputes comprised the largest number of cases dealt with by the newly established National Human Rights Commission and administrative courts (see Lucas and Warren 2000: 223–6). In the latter phase of the Suharto regime, land reform lost even its place in the rhetorical agenda. The land reform courts were abolished, and underlying principles of legal limitation on landholding were grossly violated whenever commercial interests were at stake. Conflicts between the Indonesian state and local communities proliferated in tandem with the skyrocketing growth rates of the 1990s.

In 1991 the political furore created by the satirical 'Land for the People' (*Tanah untuk Rakyat*) calendar (see Lucas 1992) drew attention to the major development policy shifts that had taken place under the New Order. Thereafter the land clearance question became one of the key issues taken up by student activists and NGOs in Indonesia. In Java, most of the large-scale land clearances involved urban and industrial expansion at the expense of squatter settlements or resumption of lands (often former colonial plantations previously redistributed to local farmers in the land reform era) for golf courses, infrastructure or industrial development. At issue in these cases were the aborted land reform programmes that left most farmers without legal title, the consequent weakness of their position in the negotiation process, and the inadequacy of compensation. Although spiritual and social ties to the land were sometimes also involved, it was generally held that, as agricultural property rights had over the centuries become individualised in Java, *adat* no longer defined the nature of land and resource claims there to the extent it did in the outer islands of Indonesia.[14]

For the '*adat* communities'[15] throughout the rest of the country, the displacements wrought by late New Order development involved not only the loss of material resources enjoyed under customary law, but a threat to the cultural identities which were tied to them. Indeed, state policy was aimed on several fronts at dismantling those ties. Local administration, cultural and educational policies, and internal colonisation programmes had the twin objectives of developing the resources of 'outer' Indonesia while homogenising their populations. The appropriation of forested land to state control simultaneously served a nationalist political agenda and the private interests of Indonesia's political-economic elite. With sometimes tragic consequences, the displaced farmers and labourers of inner Indonesia became implicated in the disenfranchisement of local communities elsewhere through the transmigration programme. Pivotal to New Order centralist-developmentalist policies was a national legal arrangement that turned the vast forest areas of outer Indonesia into state property outside the land tenure regime regulated by the Basic Agrarian Law.

Resource policy in the outer islands – colonial and post-colonial displacements

The *adat* communities of what are often referred to as Indonesia's outer islands (primarily referring to Indonesia's periphery outside Java, the demographic and political 'centre') traditionally practised shifting cultivation and maintained notions of territoriality (*hak ulayat* or 'right of avail') over neighbouring land and resources. *Hak ulayat* constituted a type of *lebensraum* where, under specified conditions, members of a community had the right to open new plots of land under shifting cultivation and to harvest forest products (Parlindungan 1997: 218).

The self-governing authority systems of these *adat* communities enforced compliance with various types of community management systems. Lands cleared for swiddens were often held in common by residential or kin-based groups, and 'cultivators were given temporary use rights extending through a rotation cycle or cycles' (Poffenberger 1990: 9). Property regimes differed from those which emerged in the intensively cultivated wet rice regions of Java, where major investments of labour were required to build and maintain permanent terraces and irrigation systems, and where 'the concept of individual ownership and land sales became more common' (Poffenberger 1990: 9). In these areas, local kingdoms arose, and rulers concentrated on controlling the most valuable resources: people and the products of agriculture and surrounding forest. Pre-colonial states and their colonial successors were less successful in controlling land use in the vast forested regions far removed from the seat of government, however (Peluso 1990: 29).

The shift in the structure of property relations in the outer islands came with the emergence of a state forestry regime in the colonial period. In 1808, in the face of widespread forest destruction on Java, the Dutch Governor-General declared all forests to be the domain of the state and set up a government forest service. The first law punishing all uses of the forest not authorised by the state was introduced, in effect criminalising the exercise of customary use rights in the forest (Peluso 1990: 32).

The Agrarian Acts of 1870 were another legal turning point in the process of legal appropriation of property rights to the state. In order to facilitate further private investments in plantation agriculture, the Governor-General declared that all lands without certified ownership belonged to the state (*domein verklaring*). Swidden land lying fallow and forest used for hunting and gathering by *adat* communities were appropriated by the stroke of a pen (Kano 1996). Thereafter, commercial interests could obtain seventy-five year leases from the state for plantations on these lands (Suhendar 1994: 7).

In claiming control over the forested areas, the Dutch colonial system had at least on paper overridden the tenurial systems of *adat* communities in forestlands that were not under constant cultivation. Given the enormous size of the area concerned, however, the Forestry Service had limited ability to control access to forests. In most of the extensive forest areas outside Java, the traditional management systems were able to continue as *de facto* property regimes, albeit without recognised legal status (Goor 1982; Poffenberger 1990). As in other parts of the world, the colonial regime set up a regulatory order that co-existed with and overlaid a pre-existing customary regime with its own concepts of property rights. The scene was set for conflict in the post-colonial period between elites using national law to justify access to local resources and local people seeking to preserve their own tenure systems.

Following their colonial predecessors, as we have seen, the Indonesian Constitution and the Basic Agrarian Law declared all natural resources to be under the control of the state (UUPA 5/1960: §2.1). Initially, under the post-revolutionary government of Sukarno, the 'social function' clauses of the Basic Agrarian Law and land reform legislation were used to redistribute concentrated land holdings, in particular plantations expropriated from foreign commercial interests. But an important shift took place after 1965 under the New Order regime of Suharto, with respect to whose claims would be identified with the common good and national interest when it came to the disposal of land and forest assets.

In the early years of the New Order (1967–70) the country faced a severe economic crisis. As the state treasury could gain large economic rents from logging, forestry policy focused on bringing in urgently needed revenue (Tjondronegoro 1991). The Basic Forestry Law (UU 5/1967) was promulgated soon after the Suharto government wrested power from Sukarno. It gave effect to the *de jure* sovereignty the state had long asserted over the 'forest area' under the Indonesian Constitution. Despite the claims of isolated *adat* communities over traditional territory, in the name of revenue generation for the nation, the state allocated twenty-year timber harvesting rights across large areas of state forests to urban elites with strong political connections.

Suharto handed out logging concessions 'to benefit loyal military officers, appease potential opponents and bolster the military budget' (Dauvergne 1997c: 7). Partnerships between political and bureaucratic power holders within the central, provincial and local bureaucracies, the military apparatus and private business interests created power networks supporting logging activities at odds with declared state forest policy and the national common good it was supposed to represent. When Suharto was forced to resign in 1998, the Ministry of Forestry and Estate Crops (MFEC) revealed that 422 concessionaires (HPH) controlled some 51.5 million hectares of production forest. With cross-ownership, hidden deals and silent partnerships, ownership of forest concessions was anything but transparent.[16] The Ministry of Forestry report showed that just twelve companies controlled 'virtually all' of Indonesia's forest concessions, with three groups holding more than 2 million hectares each (*Republika* 1998; *Timber and Wood Products* 1998).

The tragedy of competing regimes

The Basic Forestry Law of 1967, which established state control over all forests in Indonesia, divided the 'forest area' into distinct land-use categories, setting separate areas aside for timber production, conversion to agriculture and conservation.[17] From 1980 to 1983 the government embarked on a series of forest mapping exercises that extended the boundaries of 'forest area', placing 75 per cent of Indonesia's landmass under the jurisdiction of the Minister of Forestry (Peluso 1990).[18] In classifying 143 million hectares of the nation's land surface as 'forest land', state ownership was extended over vast areas inhabited or utilised by some 65 million people.[19]

In spite of legal sanctions, local communities continued to cut wood, collect forest products and open land for agriculture, in some cases according to local customary rights and in other cases outside *adat* regulatory regimes. Accordingly, the state has held the activities of shifting cultivators and 'forest squatters' responsible for a large amount of deforestation (Angelsen 1995; Colfer and Dudley 1993; Dove 1983; 1993a; 1993b; Guha 1994; Hayes 1997; Myers 1980). Government rhetoric persistently attempted to divert responsibility for the destruction of Indonesia's timber resource from the networks of patronage and collusion between political elites and timber conglomerates, whose practices contradicted the aims of state forest policy and contributed to the underlying legitimacy problem it faced.

As proved the case in the colonial period, *de jure* status is one thing, *de facto* control another. Given the amount of land under forestry department jurisdiction, the forest authorities were unable to defend the extensive 'state forest', and in many cases areas set aside for their extensive biodiversity and conservation values or ecological functions were only protected on paper.[20] At the same time, the allocation of property rights over vast areas of production forests to external interests lacked local legitimacy and led to acute ecological problems. The widespread misuse of the nation's forests means that, despite the stated policy aims to maintain a large area of 'permanent forest', deforestation rates increased over the 1990s to some 1,000,000 hectares per year.[21]

At the local level, concessions allocated to commercial interests overlaid pre-existing property regimes. The state-declared 'forest areas' under the *de jure* administration of the Forestry Department were based on a mapping exercise that failed to take into account the concepts of territoriality and land tenure in use among the local *adat* communities in or surrounding the forest. As in the colonial period, where the Ministry of Forestry allocated land considered by local communities to be subject to *hak ulayat*, 'right of avail', there has often been conflict. Despite the formal exploitation rights allocated by the state in the form of forest concessions (HPH), agricultural and timber plantation leases (HTI), timber use permits (IPK), or as land grants to transmigrants, in practice, settlers, commercial interests and agents of the state frequently found it necessary to come to terms with these *de facto* property systems of local *adat* communities. Often tentative *ad hoc* accommodations emerged which left neither management regime intact.

The consequence of mutually disabling *adat* and state regulatory regimes and the competing constructions of the commonweal they served has turned competition for Indonesia's forest resources into a variation of Hardin's 'tragedy'. The destruction of the forest resource base of both national and local commonweal had begun well before the economic crisis and tumultous political events of 1997–8 brought about the collapse of national authority and intensified the contest over these resources.

A 1992 study carried out by a team of Indonesian researchers from Gadjah Mada University (Mubyarto 1992) illustrates the impact of overlapping *de facto* regimes on forest management. Traditional community based tenure systems operating in Jambi (Sumatra) involve a complex bundle of group and individual property rights under the control of a customary (*adat*) authority system. Forest, land and dispersed resources such as minor forest products are ultimately the property of an interdependent community of users. However, individual use rights over resources that are more concentrated may be obtained in various ways. Villagers who want to work an unused swidden area previously worked by another forest farmer may do so with the consent of those who previously worked the area or through the arbitration of the *adat* authorities.[22]

As in many other areas of the world, for all practical purposes, control of trees confers control of the land on which they stand. Consequently farmers gain control and long-term tenurial rights over land by planting trees (Bruce and Fortmann 1991: 473). To mark their continuing rights over a piece of land, before abandoning a swidden, forest farmers often plant fruit trees. After harvesting a swidden, farmers also may plant the area with rubber trees, thereby turning the shifting cultivated fields (*ladang*) into a permanent forest garden (*kebun*). While property rights over rubber *kebun* are abiding, property rights in *ladang* areas are not enduring. As Dove (1996) has shown, under certain conditions the combination of market-oriented rubber production with extensive, subsistence-oriented agriculture offers a successful and sustainable strategy to indigenous farmers. Among other advantages, rubber and other perennial tree crops with high market value, such as nutmeg and cloves, generate cash for essential needs while enabling forest farmers to avoid the occasional failures of swidden. At the same time, swidden cultivation helps farmers avoid over-dependence on the substantial price fluctuations of cash crops (Dove 1996).

The Gaja Mada researchers (Mubyarto 1992) found variability in traditional land tenure systems that incorporated rules geared in different ways to guarantee the resource security of local communities in Jambi. In Sarko district, for example, there is a category of village land known as *pungko* land, an area set aside for food crops and made available to needy villagers each year with the consent of *adat* leaders according to customary law. In this district, villages also set aside *hutan rimbo sejati*, areas of primary forest protected according to *adat* connected with traditional belief systems. In other areas, villages simply divide their lands into two areas: permanent areas for rubber cultivation and areas reserved for swidden agriculture cycles. Geared toward maintaining sufficient forest reserve for opening swiddens, food security is assured through *adat* systems of tenure and access rights. The local management system depends on the social cohesiveness that results from the reality that many tasks, such as opening a *ladang*, depend on collective labour. It also relies on religious beliefs and ritual relations defining the collective, and on customary rules enforced with sanctions, including fines.

In the 1970s, logging companies and agricultural plantations began to flood the Jambi area. By 1990 there were thirty HPH concessions operating in Jambi, controlling 2,662,000 hectares of forest (Mubyarto 1992: 39) The Gaja Mada researchers found that Forestry Department policy to control logging failed in Jambi, as has been amply evidenced across Indonesia, due to technical, managerial and political difficulties. As a 1998 newspaper article (*Suara Pembaruan* 1998a) notes, widespread collusion between concessionaires and Forest Department personnel, who in any case lacked the numbers and resources to monitor state policy, ensured that criminal sanctions for infringement of state regulations were not applied. For instance, although Jambi forest police (*jagawana*) confiscated almost 2,000,000 cubic metres of illegal wood connected with HPH operations over 1996–7, not one case was brought to court.

As reported in other studies (Fox 1993; Peluso 1992), the Gajah Mada researchers also discovered a link between the allocation of extraction rights to concessionaires and the decline of indigenous land management practices. Concessionaires and plantations secured legal leases (HPH, HTI, etc.) from relevant government agencies. However, within the local regime, land was inalienable from the community, whose members obtained rights by investing labour and time. Within this local system, trees marked tenurial rights, and local farmers had no need for additional evidence of their property rights. When concessions enclosed land previously available for opening new swiddens, land shortages emerged, a problem exacerbated by population growth and in-migration (Colfer and Dudley 1993; Potter 1996).[23] In areas close to logging concessions, forest farmers lost access to traditional reserve areas and had to re-work fields after as little as three- or even one-year fallow periods, rather than the stipulated seven to eight years. This led to increased erosion, falling fertility, smaller harvests and poverty.

As local people lost customary rights over traditional *hak ulayat* territories, taking wood now became 'theft', and those opening land in forest under *de jure* state control were now classified as 'forest squatters' (*perambah hutan*). In this context, according to official figures, cases of illegal clearing, uncontrolled logging and obtaining wood without valid documents increased by a third over the 1987–9 period (Mubyarto 1992: 40–1). While logging concessionaires attempted to control access to their areas, officially classified protection forests under primary forest cover were poorly protected by forestry officials. Local people continued to open land in these areas, despite the state's statutory claims over land and trees. Accordingly, in the 1982–90 period, the actual area of protected forest in Jambi fell from 1,147,500 hectares to 181,000 hectares (Mubyarto 1992: 89).

Other research from Sumatra and Kalimantan has indicated that, besides the forest clearing carried out for plantation, logging or transmigration projects, government-sponsored claims on behalf of external users intensified forest clearing by local people (Angelsen 1995). Expectations of future land shortages stimulated a race to clear new areas of forest among local farmers. In failing to recognise the various forms of traditional territorial rights (*hak ulayat*), state land and forest policies have created a 'tragedy of competing regimes', in which short-term intensive exploitation becomes the most rational response.

Burning down the house

In 1997–8 this tragedy of competing regimes culminated in forest fires that ravaged Sumatra and Kalimantan. The fires were directly linked to government policies that transferred large timber concessions and plantation leases to national politico-business interests. While government officials and the timber industry blamed the exceptionally dry El Niño year and shifting cultivators' farming practices, evidence from satellite photographs proved most of the fires were burning in concession areas. Fire was the cheapest means of clearing remnant vegetation for conversion to oil palm plantations. Despite claims that those responsible for the fires would be fined heavily and have their permits cancelled, none of the major timber conglomerates were prosecuted (*Bisnis Indonesia* 1997; *Kompas* 1998; Reuters 1998).

Indigenous forest farmers traditionally use fire to open up small areas of land for growing food crops in accordance with forest management principles regulated by *adat*. Farmers burn off at the end of the dry season in the weeks before the first rains, carefully establishing fire breaks to ensure that the fire does not spread. But in some areas social change has radically altered local farming practices (KLH/UNDP 1998). In many places forest pioneers, including unemployed migrants from other areas of Indonesia, sponsored and spontaneous transmigrants, have taken up farming. These migrants were either unfamiliar with traditional management practices or not subject to *adat* authority structures. This meant that some farmers burned without taking precautions, contributing to the spread of uncontrolled fires (KLH/UNDP 1998: 72–5; Schindler 1998). Meanwhile, social change, in-migration and loss of property rights decreased social cohesiveness among indigenous forest communities, with similar consequences for the forest.

Throughout Indonesia, intervention to increase central government control had contributed to the decline of *adat* systems of authority controlling resource use (Nababan 1996). Following implementation of the Village Government Law (UU 5/1979), the institutional linkage between *adat* and village government was cut. The displacement of *adat* leaders and councils contributed to the decline of the traditional regulatory regime.[24] Several reports reveal that property disputes were associated with widespread arson in the Sumatra and Kalimantan forest fires of 1997–8. While these disputes had a wide variety of causes, they were ultimately connected to unresolved conflicts between interests based on officially unrecognised customary tenure regimes and those claiming property rights under national law. Reports from Kalimantan mention that some community members who had never accepted the loss of customary tenure to outside interests retaliated by setting fire to plantations (Gonner 1998; KLH/UNDP 1998: 72).

The fate of the 'million hectare' project in Central Kalimantan, one of the great environmental and social disasters of the late New Order, epitomises the compound effects of centralist developmentalism and the state's failure to protect the resources on which community livelihoods ultimately depend. Faced with the embarrassing loss of rice self-sufficiency, due mainly to the diversion of some 20 per cent of Indonesia's agricultural land to non-agricultural uses in the previous decade (*Kompas* 1999b), and coaxed by logging interests anxious to gain access to more timber, President Suharto announced a mega-project to convert the peat swamp forests of Central Kalimantan to wet rice agriculture. Ultimately intended to cover 5.8 million hectares and to involve the transmigration of 1.6 million people (mainly from Java), the first million-hectare stage of the project started up in 1996 without an effective environmental impact assessment and without local consultation.[25]

Indigenous Dayak communities lost their traditional lands to the project, along with the fish, wild boar, and rattan agro-forest resources that had provided a good and sustainable standard of living[26] within the forest ecosystem. When the denuded peat swamps dried out and the project went up in smoke in the forest fires of 1997–8, transmigrants found themselves stranded in an area wholly unsuitable for intensive agriculture (WALHI 1997; *Tempo* 1999b). They abandoned their new farmland, demanding to be returned home or relocated. Dayaks sued the government and called for the reafforestation of the damaged ecosystem. Subsequent central and regional administrations are still trying to sort out who has responsibility for the disaster and how to mitigate its worst effects (*Tempo* 1999a; *Jakarta Post* 2000; *Indonesian Observer* 2000b; *Kompas* 2000c).

An effective property regime entails the existence of an effective authority structure: an institutional arrangement able to establish and regulate access rights to a resource. Although property rights are ultimately enforced by legal sanctions, they also require a degree of moral legitimacy. Both the Jambi and Central Kalimantan examples illustrate the failure of the state to institute a legitimate and effective alternative to the local regulatory regimes that it had pushed aside. In the case of the 'million hectare' project in Kalimantan, responsibility for the fires which ravaged the delicate peat swamp ecosystem has been attributed variously to the departments of Public Works and Planning for draining the peat swamp to create irrigation channels, regional and central government for collusion with vested interests, concessionaires and transmigrants seeking to clear the land cheaply, and traditional owners taking revenge for the loss of their land and resources. In the post-Suharto era, forests beyond the areas destroyed in the fires continue to be felled by concessionaires as well as local people who have lost other means of subsistence, in contravention of both national and *adat* law.

Collective goods and collective actions: constructing the reform agenda

There is often an inherent conflict between the state's role as developer and as protector and steward of the nation's collective goods. In Indonesia by the 1990s it became increasingly evident that the first role had eclipsed the second. During the New Order, private interests had been able to capture resources theoretically reserved for the benefit of the nation.[27] By co-opting or marginalising state managers and local communities, these private interests ensured that Indonesia's resources slipped beyond public control.

In the name of 'development' and the 'national interest', politico-business elites diverted collective assets in the local domain to secure their own interests. Accordingly, the economic and environmental crisis of late 1998 was also a legitimation crisis for state institutions.[28] As these began to crumble under the weight of discredited policies, repressed local claims and institutions began to reassert themselves. The political momentum of the '*reformasi*' era offered the first opportunity to unravel networks of patronage and collusion that had worked against the collective interests of the nation, and to redress the misappropriation of local resources and the marginalisation of local communities. Following Suharto's political demise, advocates of reform have pressed for the dismantling of the previous land and natural resource regime, and for return of management responsibility and the flow of benefits to the local domain.

Among the most spectacular signals of the dramatic nature of political change during the last months of the Suharto regime and the transitional interregnum, was the direct action taken by aggrieved local groups. Sometimes with the support of legal aid and environmental NGOs, villagers began purging officials accused of corruption and collusion, reasserting prior resource claims, and even reoccupying lands lost to the mega-projects of the late New Order. In Java, victims of the notorious Kedung Ombo dam revived protests against their forced removal from ancestral lands (*Suara Merdeka* 1998). In East Kalimantan farmers demanded fair compensation for lands taken for retired military transmigrants twenty years earlier (*Banjarmasin Post* 1999).[29] In South Aceh the local group, Rimueng Lamkaluet, announced that if the government did not revoke the long contested forest exploitation licenses, they would 'run *amuk*', attack timber camps and 'burn to the ground all forest concessions operating in South Aceh' (*Serambi* 1998; *Waspada* 1998).

Under the New Order, ambiguities in the law, the closed nature of administration, corruption in the bureaucracy, lack of independence in the judiciary, and military backing had allowed state agencies to act arbitrarily in land expropriation and the allocation of forest and mining concessions. In the reform atmosphere that swept Indonesia in 1998, local communities, student groups and NGO activists attempted to reverse the excesses of the previous regime. During the power vacuum that followed the resignation of Suharto, NGOs were eager to make the most of the fragile political base of the transitional Habibie government, demanding radical changes on the legal front. They called for new laws that would revive land reform, fully recognise *adat* institutions and customary land tenure, and facilitate community-based forest management (FKKM 1998; Latin 1998; Simon 1998; KPA Munas 1998).

Caught between vested interests which it was clearly established to preserve, and its illegitimacy in the eyes of the public, the shaky transitional government sought to assuage criticism by making concessions on resource access and introducing legal reforms. In the face of the economic crisis, food riots and land occupations, the government granted permission for farmers to work 'sleeping' land not being utilised by its legal owners. The Forestry Agency allowed farmers to plant subsistence crops on land under its jurisdiction with the understanding that this did not give them ownership rights (*Suara Pembaruan* 1998b).

Under intense pressure and at breakneck speed, the transitional government drafted new laws on land, forests and the decentralisation of political authority and financial distributions that purported to scrap or alter the workings of some of the most important pieces of national legislation affecting the regions. A Presidential Decree (KepPres 48/1999) established a study team to review the policy and legal framework of land reform, an issue which had been buried with the bloody events that brought Suharto to power in 1965.

A Ministerial Regulation (Per MenAg 5/1999) also put *adat* peoples' territorial rights (*hak ulayat*) on the public agenda. For the first time, *adat* lands could be registered in the name of the village, as opposed to individual titling. Debate continues over whether titling of *adat* lands under national law would increase the legal standing of *adat* communities or simply facilitate the delivery of local resources to the international market. NGO and academic opinion was firmly against titling, and for the time being the controversial World-Bank-funded Land Administration Project, originally intended to issue titles covering all non-forest land across Indonesia, has been shelved, due largely to the pressure these loans would place on Indonesia's foreign debt. Into 2002 debate continued over the extent of revision of the Basic Agrarian Law, in particular concerning the definitions of 'national interest' and 'state control' of natural resources.

Legislative initiatives from the Minister of Forestry moved a step towards recognising the overlap between state claims over forest areas and local notions of territoriality. A new regulation on forest utilisation (PP 6/1999) granted communities the right to take forest products for their daily needs within concession areas. Under another ministerial decision (KepMen 677/Kpts-II/1998) communities could gain officially recognised rights to manage areas of forest.[30] The Ministry would permit community groups to form cooperatives which could apply for thirty-five-year 'community forestry leases' over production and protection forests as well as in specific conservation zones. The decree allows for community rights to harvest timber and to utilise traditional forest management systems as long as they do not conflict with 'forest sustainability' (*Suara Pembaruan* 1998c; 1998d).

By early 1999, in areas that have been sites of long-standing community-based conservation programmes, groups in South Aceh and West Kalimantan had processed authorisations to manage areas of forest in accordance with *adat* principles (Dephutbun 1988; *Suara Pembaruan* 1998e). But while the new initiatives represent a step forward and will facilitate co-management strategies advocated by NGOs, it is unlikely that forest communities will gain these rights on a wide scale. Moreover, the new approach does not break with the legislative regime for forest management developed under the New Order. Haverfield (1998: 63) warns that by entering into such agreements, the community is 'unwittingly acknowledging the land's status as state land and admitting that they only have specified rights of use, rather than traditional tenure'.

A new law (UU 41/1999) replacing the despised Basic Forestry Law (UU 5/1967) similarly indicated that lawmakers were reluctant to break from the underlying assumptions of the prevailing state property regime. While the new forestry law recognises the existence of *adat* forest (*hutan adat*), it maintains the concept of all 'forest areas' (*kawasan hutan*) falling under the dominion of the state. Under this law, the Minister retains managerial responsibility for some 70 per cent of the nation's land surface.

In the week before the June 1999 election, the umbrella environmental organisation WALHI, representing over 300 NGOs across Indonesia, issued a statement that rejected the 1999 forestry law (still at that stage in draft form) and other natural resource legislation then in preparation by the transitional Habibie government, claiming they showed no substantive reforms (*forestry-ind@mbe.ece.wisc.edu*, 3 June 1999). Many doubt whether cooperatives, legislated to become the vehicles for a `people's economy' in the new regime, could be extricated from the existing systems of privilege and patronage or would actually reallocate resource rights to local communities.[31] NGOs representing *adat* groups have been particularly critical of the lack of consultation with indigenous communities in the legal revision process, and of the failure to develop participative mechanisms as a systematic part of any reformed administrative regime.[32]

The fact that much of this 'reform' legislation was already being formulated in the last years of the Suharto regime indicates the intensity of the pressures that were building against government policies well before cracks in the façade of the New Order appeared to threaten its foundations. But while there is no question that the pressure of popular opinion is having some impact on policy, the origins of the revised legislation suggest the limited extent to which it is likely to bring about the real transformation that the public expects.

With respect to pressures for land reform, the government planning body BAPPENAS was resisting calls to revive the programme on grounds that it is not economically viable or politically acceptable, presumably because it would not be well received in investment circles. Land reform would not necessarily serve the elite interests which continue to be well represented across the political spectrum.

Political party policies put forward during the 1999 parliamentary election campaign were noticeably lacking detail on these fundamental reform issues. Party platforms included the usual appeals to 'the people's welfare', but none of the major parties made specific commitments regarding land reform or traditional resource rights beyond these rhetorical gestures (*Kompas* 1999b). Nevertheless, the effect of direct action through land occupations, acts of sabotage and local resource appropriation, as well as the changing vicissitudes of electoral politics, were apparently forcing the Wahid government to put out reformist messages on populist issues.[33] Most prominent and contentious among the reform measures have been legislative steps toward the decentralisation of finance and authority to regional government.

Decentralisation: local and global contentions

Since Suharto was forced to step down during nationwide demonstrations and riots at the height of the economic crisis of 1998, the political constellation has altered dramatically. These events had been preceded by the growing strength of NGOs and a resurgence of *adat* institutions, often the only organised groupings at local level which could claim credibility in the void left by bankrupt government institutions. Backed by activist students and *ad hoc* community groups, they began to take on the mantle of a long-repressed civil society.[34] Government departments and international agencies now found themselves in round-table discussions with NGOs they formerly treated with suspicion, exchanging ideas and proffering collaboration (KPA Munas 1998; Soesangobeng 1998). Networks of *adat*-based local organisations sprung up across the country, in 1999 combining to form the Alliance of *Adat* Communities of the Archipelago (AMAN), with considerable international support from both NGO and foreign government aid agencies.

One issue upon which all parties agreed was the need for greater decentralisation. International agencies and NGOs had been advocating different versions of decentralisation policies for some time. The Regional Government and Revenue Allocation Acts (UU 22/1999 and UU 25/1999), probably the most sweeping of the Habibie legal changes, were intended to give greater powers to regional government and assuage some of the resentment which has made local autonomy one of the driving issues of the *reformasi* era. The new laws offer 'federalism without the "f" word', an inner-circle informant reportedly quipped (*Far Eastern Economic Review* 1999: 10). The expectation was that more direct control over development planning and investment, and a larger proportion of tax revenue will benefit the regions, decentring the commonweal in political and economic terms.[35]

The ultimate consequences of decentralisation are difficult to read from the new legislation. While some powers are devolved to the district level, these do not include full rights over the exploitation of natural resources. In any case, without effective accountability mechanisms, rather than benefit ordinary people, decentralised management may simply serve to enrich and consolidate the position of local elites, who now take over the privilege of dispensing resource access. On the other hand, it is possible that a central government with an effective system of checks and balances and less to gain by way of rent-seeking opportunities could develop an impartial umpire role. There is little indication of capacity to move in this direction, however.[36] The turnover in political leadership which brought Megawati Sukarnoputri to power in 2001 may signal a reversal for regional interests aspiring to a thoroughgoing redistribution of power and resources. To date there are no signs of policies which would contribute toward further reform of the role of the state in the provision of collective goods.

There is no reason to assume that decentralisation to regional (*kabupaten*) level will by definition bring greater public participation or a fairer distribution of resources. Notably, it was the regional government of Central Kalimantan itself that originally proposed the disastrous 'million hectare' project, and is still actively engaged in promoting special arrangements to attract business to the area through tax concessions and relaxation of permits (*Kompas* 1999a; *Suara Pembaruan* 1999b; *Bisnis Indonesia* 1999; *Banjarmasin Post* 2000).[37]

In broader structural terms, if significant financial powers are taken over by resource-rich regions as part of the decentralisation process, what will be left at the centre for provision of collective goods to less well endowed provinces? The resource distribution issue poses real difficulties to any government serious about devolving power over its most valuable natural resources to the regions. On average the timber industry generates 20 per cent of total foreign exchange earnings; and in 1998/9 the industry was expected to contribute US$8.5 billion to national revenue (Kartodihardjo 1999: 2; *Tempo* 2000).

Indications of conflict between global and local policy objectives are also emerging. International creditors, including multilateral donor agencies such as the IMF, are anxious that the central government meet its debt repayments. To this end they are said to be applying pressure behind the scenes to limit decentralisation and revenue sharing initiatives so that the central government retains the majority of revenue generated from natural resources (*Jakarta Post* 1999; *Down to Earth* 1999).

Tensions between popular demands for redress of past grievances and the sensitivity of Indonesia's economy to global capital markets were already appearing in the first months of the Wahid government that replaced Habibie after the 1999 national election. Negative overseas investor reaction met the new government's expressions of intent to renegotiate its contract with PT Freeport in West Papua (formerly Irian Jaya).[38] Similarly, its efforts to seek compensation through the courts for Riau villagers whose lands were illegally appropriated by the powerful Salim conglomerate, closely connected to the former President, attracted adverse international reaction (*Kapital* 1999; *Newsweek International* 1999; *Business Times* 2000).

Although the Wahid government initially raised the hopes of the reform movement, during 2000–1 protracted power struggles between the president and the legislature constrained the reform process. For many reformist elements the possibility of further reform was diminished when, with the support of the army and Suharto's party Golkar, Megawati became president in August 2001. Megawati has strong nationalist and centralist inclinations, and she is less sympathetic to the decentralisation process. Her election has boosted revisionist efforts 'to reduce regency administrations' control over natural and financial resources' (*Jakarta Post* 2001).[39]

During 1998–9 it had seemed possible that a sea-change would take place in the distribution of power in Indonesia, on the basis of new alliances surrounding a different constellation of political interests and new imaginings of the relationship between nation and community as 'commonweal'.

But even if, perhaps especially if, the 'rule of law' were to take hold, local people might well remain as marginalised as they have ever been. A more radical political and legislative programme and new political rationalities, not suggested by policy indications of the current government, would be required to substantially overcome a situation where elites rely on national law to substantiate their claims over resources while ordinary people seek to preserve their claims to land and resources through *ad hoc* procedures. Consequently, it appears likely that the disjunction between *de jure* and *de facto* property relations associated with earlier conflicts over collective goods will continue.

Reformists operate on the expectation that legal instruments can be used to shape Indonesia's future. In the past, implementation of law was erratic and applied only where it served or at least did not conflict with elite interests. In the reform era, the lost credibility of Indonesia's governing institutions, compounded by power struggles at the centre and on the periphery, are impeding the capacity for implementation of new legislation. To date, much of the 'reform' at local level has involved reappropriation of property or the ousting of accused officials from office by local groups, entirely outside legal structures. But the balances of power between central and local government, and between popular and elite interests, are not the only ones reformers have to contend with. If reform is to have a significant effect on collective goods regimes, other serious issues will have to be confronted.

While the 'national interest' and 'social function' platforms of the Constitution and Basic Agrarian Law provided the foundation for redistribution under subsequent legislation on land reform, those same principles also became the rationale for expropriation of the lands and resources of minority peoples in the sparsely populated and resource-rich 'outer islands', sparking horizontal struggles over resources. Over three decades, the New Order (and on a less grand scale its predecessors) used transmigration policy as a tool for colonising Indonesia's periphery. Millions of people have been moved from the heavily populated islands of Java, Bali and Madura to Sumatra, Sulawesi, Kalimantan, Timor and Irian Jaya. The reassertion of local interests in the reform era has been expressed also in explosions of intercommunal conflicts both instigated and suppressed by centralist policies of earlier regimes. In many parts of the country, the appeal to a national concept of commonweal has lost its hold, and national law its claim as a ground for determining the distribution of rights.

In addition to the question of fair distribution of land and resources among Indonesia's constituent communal groups, the question of long-term sustainability versus satisfaction of short-term needs will not be resolved simply by reversion to traditional management regimes. As *adat* institutions were marginalised by the nation-state or integrated into wider clientelist structures, their cultural grounding, local authority systems and management practices came under challenge. In many cases they too have been unable to maintain customary rules covering resource distribution and management. Local *adat* regimes will be least likely to offer a coherent and workable set of institutional arrangements where large-scale in-migration and commercialisation have taken place. To date the implications of new political developments for collective goods regimes governing the protection and distribution of land and other resources remain uncertain. There are cases of *adat* regimes reasserting authority over local resources.[40] On the other hand, the press is also full of reports of national parks and forest reserves devastated in the absence of effective governance at any level.[41]

A fundamental goal of the reform movement in Indonesia is the development of collective goods regimes that provide for the fair distribution and sustainable management of land and national resources. Re-sorting central and local government priorities with respect to Indonesia's natural resources, the relationship between customary (*adat*) and national law in their management, and the ground rules for resolving the competing claims among different segments of 'the people' disenfranchised by previous regimes will take extraordinary vision, new and more complex foundations for building common identities, and careful institutional balancing of power and checking of interests at national, regional and local levels.

Competing claims over collective goods in the changing political constellation of Indonesia have also to be considered in the context of pressures operating at the international level, where redistributive, sustainability and economic growth objectives find themselves similarly at odds with each other. World Bank and IMF prescriptions, while pressing for transparency, decentralisation and democratic reform of governance in Indonesia, are at the same time insisting on liberalisation of the market in land and accelerated exploitation of natural resources,[42] often at the expense of local people and long-term ecological sustainability. Issues surrounding the place of *adat* regimes and collective goods conjure the full panoply of political tensions and cultural imaginings implicit in debates about the impacts of globalisation on struggles between the 'national' and the 'local', growth and distribution, short- and long-term sustainability, individual and group rights. They are unlikely to be resolved in the interests of ordinary Indonesians independently of broader transformations on a global scale.

Notes

1 Research for this paper was partly funded under an Australia Research Council Grant (1998–2000) held by Dr Anton Lucas (Flinders University) and Dr Carol Warren (Murdoch University) on land tenure policy and law in Indonesia. Support was also provided by the Australia Research Council funded Asia Research Centre of Murdoch University, which supported John McCarthy's fieldwork. The authors wish to thank Anton Lucas and Tim Babcock for comments on earlier drafts of this manuscript. Translations of Indonesian language documents quoted in the text are by the authors.

2 These devolutionary pressures coincide with an opposite movement toward constituting global frameworks of common interest and collective goods centred on free trade, human rights and environmental protection. International markets, agencies and non-government organisations are playing an increasingly significant role in the shifting patterns of power in Indonesia and other parts of the Asian region.

3 *Desa mawa cara* (the village is bearer of custom); *desa kala patra* (according to village, time, circumstance); *adat sapangjang jalan, cupak sapanjang batuang* (mutual respect for the *adat* of each community), etc.

4 As an Acehnese *adat* leader put it at a national congress on land reform

> We have to discuss the range of functions of *adat* land. It is different in each case. Otherwise it will get messy. Java doesn't have *adat* land [*tanah adat*]; It is different from one end of Sumatra to another; In Madura people wouldn't call it *tanah adat*, but they would pull a kris if you denied it was *tanah Madura*.
>
> (the farmer 'Aba', speaking at Konsortium Pembaruan Agraria Congress, 4 December 1998).

5 The term *hak ulayat* was adopted from Minangkabau by Dutch scholar-administrators and translated as *beschikkingsrecht* (right of avail) in their many treatises on *adat* law. According to the *adat* law scholar, van Vollenhoven, 'right of avail applies when an indigenous jural community, whether territorial … or genealogical … claims to have within a certain area the exclusive right to avail itself of the land' (Sonius 1981).

6 Psota (1998: 131) argues that distributive requirements arising from the intimate connection between kinship, community and agricultural production in the Sumatran communities he studied dissolves the apparent contradictions between individual and common property in this context. Warren (1993: 38–43) makes a similar case for Bali, even in those communities where individuals hold legal title to land. The Benda-Beckmanns (1999) insist that prevalent categories of private, communal, state property and open access resources do not adequately represent the variety of property rights or the overlaying effects of the social and cultural functions to which property relations are tied. Even the most individual forms of private property are nevertheless part of a 'bundle of rights' and obligations which are collectively defined. *Adat* concepts of property in Indonesia can not be extricated from culturally specific social security and social continuity functions (1999: 15–16).

7 This ambivalence has to be understood in the context of the awkward colonial grounding that underpinned the construction of the Indonesian nation, as well as Western notions of modernity which the founders of the newly independent Indonesia sought to build upon. See Article 33 of the 1945 Constitution on transitional provisions pending the 'development of laws better suited to a modern independent nation'. See also Fitzpatrick (1997: 175).

8 Article 3 of the Basic Agrarian Law states:

> The application of *hak ulayat* [territorial right of avail] and similar rights of communities based on adat law, so long as these evidently continue to exist, must be in accordance with the interests of the nation and the state, based on national unity, and may not conflict with higher laws or regulations.

9 A rider in the explanatory notes to the legislation adds, 'But ... this does not mean that the needs of these [*adat*] law communities will be disregarded completely' (UUPA 5/1960: §3 *Penjelasan Umum*).

10 Screening processes ensured that potentially non-compliant nominees were culled before local elections. Localities which found themselves unwilling hosts to particularly sensitive development projects were sometimes arbitrarily reclassified as *kelurahan*. Under the Village Government Law, government in areas so classified was handled by civil servants, appointed rather than elected, and often from outside the local area. Retired military officers were favoured for these positions.

11 Literally the law states: 'All rights in land have a social function' (UUPA 5/60: §6).

12 This regime will be discussed separately below.

13 The Indonesian Legal Aid Foundation notes direct military involvement in twenty-two of the land conflict cases that it handled in 1998 (YLBHI 1998: 6–7). See accounts of some of the more notorious land conflicts at Kedung Ombo (Stanley 1994; Aditjondro 1998), Tanah Lot (Warren 1998a) and Tubanan (Lucas 1997). See also publications of the Consortium for Agrarian Reform (Bachriadi 1997; Ruwiastuti *et al.* 1997; Hardiyanto 1998; KPA 1998), a non-government umbrella organisation which brings together the large number of local organisations struggling for land reform and *adat* rights, and publications of the social research group AKATIGA (Suhendar and Winarni 1998).

14 This point requires qualification. It is true that privatisation of land was more thoroughgoing in Java because of the length and intensity of its colonial occupation as opposed to the so-called 'outer islands', and that the Islamisation of Java altered the ancestral grounding of *adat* institutions. The distinction clearly has rhetorical significance in the centre/periphery debate, and was a prominent policy consideration in the introduction of the World Bank land-titling programme. That project was restricted to Java for its first five-year phase because of the assumption that titling where land was already largely individualised would be least problematic. Nevertheless, local institutions on Java retain many of the features of *adat* communities, including cultural ties to land and corporate mechanisms for resource management.

15 The term *masyarakat adat* (literally '*adat* communities'), often glossed in English as 'indigenous peoples' (Ruwiastuti n.d.; YLBHI 1998), has become preferred usage by NGOs referring to non-Javanese ethnic minorities, in lieu of the denigrating connotations of government manufacture such as *suku terasing* (isolated – implicitly backward – ethnic groups). The concept of 'indigenous peoples' has always been rejected by Indonesian governments, both Old and New Order, which gave overriding importance to national unity and downplayed ethnicity (Evers 1995: 7). For the reverse reason, the notion of '*adat* communities' as 'indigenous peoples' has been systematically deployed by activists to discursively extricate minority cultural populations in Indonesia from Javanese hegemony. The 'indigenous peoples' label became popular, despite the arguable legitimacy of the way the concept is applied, when the UN Draft Convention on the Rights of Indigenous Peoples offered possibilities of legitimating local claims on international human rights grounds.

16 By buying up smaller concessions, a company might control a much more extensive area than it is formally registered as controlling (Mubyarto 1992: 80). Following the resignation of Suharto, public pressure mounted to make a clean slate of the intricate networks of patronage that flourished under the former president. In December 1998, the Minister of Forestry and Crop Production, Muslimin Nasution, announced that the Ministry had discovered that Suharto's family had shares in concessions operating over 4.22 million hectares of state forests (*Republika* 1998).

17 Under the forest classification system, 30.8 million hectares was set aside as 'protection forests' and 18.8 million hectares as nature reserves/conservation areas. Another 64.3 million hectares area was mapped as 'production forest' or 'limited production forest', over which the forest authorities granted long-term leases to log the forest (HPH) to concessionaires, theoretically under Forestry Department supervision (KLH/UNDP 1998: 364). In areas mapped as 'conversion forest' (26.6 million hectares), land is set aside for 'planned deforestation'; here the Forestry Department issues leases for conversion of forest to plantation agriculture, granting use rights (HGU) over what remains state land.

18 Previously, large areas of the 'outer islands' of Indonesia were not classified under any land-use category. However, as part of the TGHK forest mapping process, much of this land was classified as 'forest land' and put under the jurisdiction of the forestry agency. According to Ascher (1993), this involved a fourfold increase in the 'forest area' compared with 1967 categories. However, large areas of this land were actually unforested.

19 See McCarthy (2000) for the widely ranging estimates of forest dwellers and those dependent upon forest products for subsistence.

20 Very few resources are available for forest protection. There are 8,500 forest guards (*jagawana*) responsible for policing over 100 million hectares of the 'forest area' (KLH/UNDP 1998: 378).

21 Figures for the rate of deforestation vary depending on the sources and methods of analysis, the most accepted estimates ranging from between less than 600,000 hectares to 1.3 million hectares per year (KLH/UNDP 1998: 364).

22 It is worth noting that the customary *adat* system described here is by no means a static one. Historically farmers in Jambi also cultivated wet rice fields (*sawah*). The authors note that villagers only began to cultivate rubber around 1910. As rubber produced greater profits compared to sawah, forest farmers began to turn areas previously used for sawah as well as newly opened dry cultivation (*ladang*) areas into rubber plots (Mubyarto 1992: 40–1).

23 Population growth caused by in-migration is clearly a serious threat to forests: Colfer found that in-migration was the principal source of East Kalimantan's population increase, which in turn was one of the principle threats to its forests (Colfer and Dudley 1993: 79) For a discussion of the effect of migration on forest management in Kalimantan, see also Potter (1996).

24 See McCarthy (2000) for a full discussion of the debates surrounding the relative responsibility of in-migrant 'forest pioneers' as opposed to 'traditional' farmers for unsustainable forest use, particularly where the latter's practices are affected by modernisation and economic pressures.

25 Local involvement consisted in becoming the objects of 'information sessions' (*penyuluhan*) and 'letters of appreciation' (*surat penghargaan*) to those whose land was taken for the project (*Notulen Rapat Kabupaten Kapuas*, 24 April 1996), as well as the 'socialisation' (promoting acceptance) of project goals (*Kompas* 1999a).

26 Dayak incomes were reported to have declined from 150,000 rupiah per day from collecting rattan to 200,000 (heavily devalued) rupiah per month in the two years since the project began (*Tempo* 1999b).

27 A comparison of royalties from forest concessions with royalties gained from the oil sector illustrate the extent to which claims of common benefit were disingenuous. In 1991 a series of reports disclosed that the Indonesian government only collected about 30 per cent of the 'surplus or rent accruing from logging'. The World Bank and the economic ministries considered this to be too small compared with the 85 per cent of rent the government collects from the petroleum sector. However, while the economic ministries were keen to collect

more revenue from the forestry sector, they were reluctant to take on the powerful concessionaires who collect most of the surplus flowing from the timber industry (Ross 1996; Ramli and Ahmad 1994).

28 Well before the fall of the Suharto regime, under pressure from international agencies, the media and non-government organisations, public sector directors within the National Land Board (BPN), the Ministry of State for Environment (KLH), the National Development Planning Board (BAPPENAS) and the Ministry of Finance became troubled by the growing incidence of land conflicts, the declining condition of Indonesia's forests, the low rents extracted by the state from the timber industry, and the social insecurities resulting from the current land and resource regime (CSIS 1991; Barber 1998; Johnson and Keehn 1994: 70–3).

29 Compensation issues were among the most often protested grievances precipitated by New Order developmentalism. Farmers who were victims of the land speculation explosion of the later years of the New Order in particular, had been paid a pittance (sometimes as little as 30–250 rupiah per square metre) for land that now had a market price as much as 1,000 times the compensation they received, if they had received any compensation at all (see *Far Eastern Economic Review* 1998a; *Suara Pembaruan* 1999b).

30 This seems to be a realisation of earlier statements of reformist state sector managers. As early as 1993, the Biodiversity Action Plan, a policy document prepared under the auspices of the National Planning Board (BAPPENAS), recognised that an estimated 40 million people live in or are dependent upon resources in the 'public forest estate' and that these people were the '*de facto* forest managers' (BAPPENAS 1993).

31 See 'Pemerintah gegabah beri IPK kepada Orang Rimba' (*Republika*, 2000) which reports a case under this new policy in which the Department of Forestry issued a forest exploitation permit (IPK) to a cooperative consisting of one individual at the expense of the wider indigenous community claiming traditional rights.

32 See Statement by the Alliance of Indigenous Peoples of the Archipelego (AMAN) Jakarta, on the draft forestry law (*forestry-ind@mbe.ece.wisc.edu*, 26 May 1999). See also *Down to Earth* (1999).

33 See *Kompas* 2000a, 'UUPA dan UU landreform cenderung direvisi', which suggests that restrictions on concentrated land holdings will be reintroduced through revision of the Agrarian and Land Reform Laws.

34 See 'Activists thrust agendas into post-Suharto void'. *New York Times* 1999.

35 East Kalimantan, for example, was demanding ten times its current disbursement on the basis of a greater share of its huge natural resource base (*Far Eastern Economic Review*, 1999).

36 Real reform depends upon a radical realignment of institutions at every level: the practical capacity of legislatures to exercise control over the executive, of the civilian authority to assert itself over the military, of judicial and administrative systems to monitor and sanction misuse of power, of civil society to insist on an active role in defining the terms of governance.

37 Provincial and regional government officials were responsible for setting compensation rates for traditional landholders of 500 rupiah per square metre (approximately US$0.50 at that time) at a meeting at which no local representatives were present (*Notulen Rapat Kabupaten Kapuas*, 24 April 1996; WALHI 1997: appendix). Recent reports allege local legislators have attempted to halt prosecutions associated with the case (*Indonesian Observer* 2000a).

38 At the same time the Indonesian parliament announced plans to reassess Freeport's contract, on the grounds of imputed corruption involving its dealings with the Suharto regime. Wahid appointed Henry Kissinger, former US

Secretary of State and a member of the Board of Directors of the Freeport-McMoran company, as political adviser. After the meeting with Indonesia's president, Kissinger commented: 'It is in the interests of Indonesia that the contract is respected since you want investment from all over the world' (AFX Asia, 28 February 2000). This provoked a stinging attack from the Indonesian Environment group WALHI, which argued that the contracts had been made in a business atmosphere that did not respect the people's aspirations and did not involve local people in the decision-making process (*Indonesian Observer*, 2000a).

39 At the time of writing, while legal experts within government were engaged in re-writing the two laws to reassert the powers of central and provincial governments, it was unclear whether legislators would create a new law altogether or merely amend the 1999 laws. Key changes being discussed included reasserting the vertical hierarchical relationship between provinces and districts, and spelling out in concrete terms the specific authorities held by districts in both cases restoring some of the control central government formerly exercised over the regions (McCarthy, Interview with officials, Ministry of Internal Affairs and Regional Autonomy, August 2001).

40 Warren (1998b) describes such a case just before the fall of the Suharto regime at Padanggalak in Bali; *Suara Pembaruan*, 2000a, reports nine holders of forest concessions in Kutai, East Kalimantan subjected to 'sanctions according to *adat*' imposed by Dayak *adat* leaders; The *Riau Post* (2000), 'Karet masyarakat di hutan lindung dicabut', reports the revived enforcement of *adat* regulations on a traditional forest reserve by local *adat* leaders who ordered the destruction of rubber trees illegally planted by some villagers.

41 See *Suara Pembaruan*, 2000b, 'Taman Nasional Kutai kini jadi kebun pisang' [Kutai National Park becomes a banana garden]. *Kompas* 2000b reports forest destruction in Gunung Palung National Park (Kalimantan) carried out by gangs of timber cutters including security forces. *The Guardian* 2000, 'Indonesia's chainsaw massacre', describes the state of the nation with 'the world's second richest biodiversity ... raped and pillaged by illegal loggers, poachers and greedy farmers'. Even timber companies were finding it difficult to operate in the face of local hostility: 'Conflicts between locals and timber companies to grow', *Jakarta Post* 2000c; 'Indon timber firms halt work due to conflicts with locals', *Jakarta Post* 2000cb

42 A World Bank-sponsored report on Indonesian Forestry noted that Indonesia was 'consuming its natural capital at a worrying rate', and pointed to the contradictory IMF policies to reduce forest conversion while promoting liberalisation of the oil palm industry which is increasing pressure for the conversion of forests to plantations (World Bank press release, 26 January 2000; Isalazar@world. bank.org).

6

FROM VILLAGE COMMONS TO SHAREHOLDING CORPORATION

Collective property reforms in a Chinese village[1]

Jian Zhang

This chapter examines collective action problems in the management of collectively owned enterprises in Chinese village communities during the post-Mao reform era, and the property rights institutions that have been created in response to those problems. The rapid development of community-owned enterprises at the township and village level is a unique feature of China's transition to a market economy. While the rural reforms inaugurated in the early 1980s dismantled the Maoist People's Commune system and allowed a greater role to be played by individuals and markets in the rural economy, collective property did not simply disappear. Townships and villages, which replaced the commune and brigade as the rural administrative units, assumed the ownership and management of land, most collective enterprises, infrastructure and services. This collective property comprised the village 'commons'. Townships and villages capitalised on opportunities brought about by market reform to expand their commons. Now, in many parts of China, it is the commons that is the major source of employment, income, and such collective goods as social welfare and infrastructure funding (Oi 1990; 1998).

The continuities and changes in property rights institutions in the rural collective economy raise important questions concerning management of a common property regime. In the absence of clearly defined individual rights over collective property, how do villagers deal with these collective action dilemmas in the management of their commons? And how is the industrialisation and urbanisation of the countryside affecting the provision of the collective goods that have been funded by the commons?

One prevailing view on the management of conflict in the rural collective economy in China is that village communities have the capacity to undertake effective collective action because of their unique cultural attributes. In an influential article, Weitzman and Xu (1994) argue that a Chinese village community traditionally has a 'cooperative culture' that enables villagers to solve potential conflicts over collective property in the absence of explicitly defined individual rights. In a similar vein, Pei (1998) explicitly defines the collective economy at the village level as a common property regime, and reasons that the low information cost, kinship ties, trust and cooperative spirit embodied in Chinese village communities minimise the possibility of free riding, shirking and opportunistic behaviour by their members. Moreover, according to Pei, because of the increasing independence of village leaders from the state, village communities can now enjoy the net collective benefits of community-based development that were formerly captured by the state. Hence collective management of the village economy is a preferred alternative to privatisation in Chinese villages.

However, recent developments in the rural economy in the 1990s made such assertions highly questionable. In that decade, the transformation of collectively owned property gained momentum. The lack of the clarity of the property rights relations in rural collective organisations was viewed as a major obstacle to the further development of the rural economy (Smyth 1998). Institutional arrangements aiming to grant individual villagers clearer rights over collective property were created. A number of recent empirical studies have identified a gradual but steady shift from collective ownership towards privatisation in many parts of rural China (Oi and Walder 1999).

The objective of this chapter is to provide a corrective to the earlier mentioned prevailing view on the capacity of Chinese villages to avoid collective action problems in management of the commons. It disputes the view that the Chinese village collective is not susceptible to a 'tragedy of commons'. Instead, the chapter argues that as a common property regime, rural collective property in China is indeed subject to the opportunistic behaviour of members of the village community. Moreover, collective action problems in rural China have been complicated by the attempts of village governments to maintain their monopoly of power in the management of collective properties in the context of market-oriented reform. In fact, local property rights institutions have been shaped by the political interests of village governments.

The argument is supported by a case study of Yujia village, on the outskirts of Hangzhou, the capital of Zhejiang province. Conflicts between individual villagers and village officials, rooted in the ownership and management of collective property and intensified by the rapid marketisation and urbanisation of Yujia, prompted changes in property institutions and the management of collective assets. In the early 1990s, a shareholding cooperative system was introduced in Yujia to restructure the ownership and management of collective property. The consequences of those changes demonstrate that village cadres acted to protect their economic and political power in the rapidly growing local economy. Villagers' rights to benefit from collective property were enhanced by the restructuring. However, the distribution of shares, dividend payments and disbursement of economic welfare were all manipulated by the village government in such a way as to generate political support and to ensure villagers' compliance with government regulations. The newly established village shareholding cooperative (*cunji gufen jingji hezuoshe*, hereafter VSC) still operated as a collective organisation under the control of village cadres. The resultant institutional arrangement is likely to generate further conflict.

The argument is presented in three sections. The first explains the common property characteristics of collective ownership in Chinese villages, and describes the collective action problems that have arisen in the management and allocation of the commons in the context of rapid industrialisation and urbanisation. The second section focuses on conflicts over the commons that occurred in Yujia village. These conflicts led to changes in the ownership and management of collective property and the creation of the Yujia VSC. This property rights transformation not only affected the provision of collective goods in Yujia, but also enhanced the control of local governments over the village community. These consequences are discussed in the final section of the chapter.

Collective property as a commons

In Chinese villages, collective property (*jiti zichan*) refers to the economic assets – land, enterprises, services and funds – that are owned collectively by all members of a village community. The village committee as a collective organisation represents all its members in exerting ownership rights.

The post-Mao rural reforms in the early 1980s abolished the People's Commune system. However, they did not dismantle collective ownership. In agriculture, the adoption of household responsibility system (HRS) resulted in a household-based land tenure system within a collective ownership framework. Under the HRS, farmlands were divided and contracted to farming households for a specified period which, in 1984, was initially set by the central government for fifteen years. In 1993, the contract period was extended to thirty years. Farming households gained substantive autonomy in making decisions in agricultural production and, more importantly, fully enjoyed the surplus incomes generated from their contracted land after fulfilling the state grain quotas. Yet the formal ownership of land still remained with the village collectives, represented by the village committee (Cheng and Tsang 1995–6; Kojima 1988; Zhu and Jiang 1993; Li 1995).

In the non-agricultural sector, collective ownership was even more significant. In many places former brigade-run enterprises and collective funds remained undivided and were taken over by the village authorities in the name of the village collectives. Based on these resources, many communities managed to expand the non-agricultural collective economy by establishing new collective enterprises (Byrd and Lin 1990). These collective enterprises were directly managed by village leaders and Party secretaries or their appointees. Villagers were employed in collective firms, and benefited from the services, welfare and infrastructure that was funded from collective enterprise profits (Oi 1990).

In this system, collective property shared two important attributes of a common property regime: non-excludability and rivalry in consumption. First, while every villager that was a registered resident of the community had a nominal share in ownership rights to collectively owned property, those rights were not clarified and represented in any specific individual form such as stocks. Neither the collective as a whole, nor any village members, had the right to exclude any rural-registered resident of the village from ownership of the collective property. Hence, every one and no-one in the community was the owner of the collectively owned property (Weitzman and Xu 1994). This 'open to all' feature of collective property created an excludability problem. Second, collective property was finite and rival in consumption (Jefferson 1998: 431). Consumption of collective property by one villager left less to be consumed by the others.

In situations where there were perceptions of scarcity, untrustworthiness and inequity, individuals had an incentive to grab as much as they could from the commons. Moreover, there were few constraints on them extracting more value than they had contributed towards the provision of collective property. Consequently, collective property was susceptible to over-consumption and free riding.

One of the most common manifestations of these collective action problems was asset stripping by village authorities. While some scholars argue that these collective action problems were avoided or minimised in Chinese village communities due to the cooperative spirit and cohesive structure of rural Chinese society (Weitzman and Xu 1994; Pei 1998; Lin 1995), evidence from empirical studies renders such claims problematic. For example, it is well documented that corrupt village leaders took advantage of their control over collective assets to amass individual wealth during the reform era (Oi 1986; Nee and Lian 1994; Nee 1989). A government investigation of the financial management in 2,196 villages in China found embezzlement of collective funds in 1,493, or 68 per cent of the villages surveyed (Pei 1995: 74).

The malfeasance of village leaders not only reduced the amount of collective assets and the benefits available to all villagers from common property, but it also inspired suspicion, resistance and self-interested opportunistic behaviour on the part of individual villagers (Li and O'Brien 1996; Pei 1995). Consequently, many villagers took a 'free rider' attitude to the development of the collective economy and the benefits provided by the village collectives. They generally had low incentives and were reluctant to do their jobs in the collective enterprises. Official reports complained that

JIAN ZHANG

villages were only concerned with the amount of the bonuses and welfare provided by the village collectives (Guowuyuan Yanjiushi 1993; Wang and Wu 1993). Creating incentives for villagers to work harder was often a great concern of village officials. Thus, in managing its collective property, the Chinese village community faced the same collective action dilemma as did the participants in other common property regimes.

However, the nature of political authority and collective ownership in Chinese villages meant that these collective action problems also exhibited unique features. Consider, first, the consequences of the fact that although collective property was nominally owned by all members of village, the leaders of the village committees represented the villagers in executing their ownership rights. In many instances, they acted as the owners of collective assets, rather than on behalf of all the owners. To a certain extent, then, nominal collective ownership in rural China became *de facto* ownership by village authorities. This 'local government ownership' (Oi 1995) of collective property not only provided village leaders with an incentive to maintain the collective ownership of village assets, but it also gave them the economic means to exert control over members of the community. Collective action problems were thus complicated by conflicts between local authorities and villagers. Individual villagers wanted to participate in decision-making regarding collective property, while village leaders tried to monopolise control over collective property. At the same time, villagers whose behaviour was not in accord with government regulations were at odds with leaders able and willing to use their control over collective property to enforce those regulations.

Moreover, while all major property, including farmland and non-agricultural enterprises, is owned by the village collective, individual villagers have different bundles of rights to particular types of collective asset. Their property rights to farmland are stronger and more clearly specified than are their rights to non-agricultural enterprises. Rural industrialisation and urbanisation, which turns a village's collectively owned farmland into industrial and commercial property, reallocates property rights among villagers and between individual villagers and the village collective. This impact can be seen in the process of converting farmland to non-agricultural use. When upper-level government requisitions farmland to expand municipal boundaries or develop industrial enterprises, village committees, representing their communities, are compensated for the transfer of ownership rights to the land. Land compensation funds have become an important source of capital for the development of non-agricultural collective enterprises in these villages. Villagers whose farmlands have been requisitioned receive two sorts of compensation. First, they receive compensation for their crops and any facilities they built on the requisitioned land.[2] Second, some members of households that have had land requisitioned are given jobs and registered as urban residents.

106

In the process, villagers lose out. Agricultural assets, over which villagers have relatively strong property rights, are transformed into non-agricultural assets over which they have little control. Villagers whose land is requisitioned and who become urban residents also become ineligible to receive benefits from the village's collective property, as they are no longer classed as village residents. It is not surprising, then, that land requisition has become a contentious issue in places where the collective economy is well developed. Village leaders face a dilemma in deciding which households' land should be requisitioned. Villagers frequently have refused to give up their land. And demands for clearer property rights to collective property have increased significantly, particularly in suburban villages where the majority of the farmland already has been requisitioned and the collective economy is highly industrialised. In some areas, villagers have requested the outright privatisation of collective property since the early 1990s (Huang 1992).

In sum, collective property in Chinese villages is very much akin to a commons. As in other common property regimes, the opportunistic behaviour of members of village communities leads to problems in ensuring the sustainability, not to mention the potential for growth, of collective assets. Those collective action problems have been exacerbated by the rapid industrialisation and urbanisation of villages that has occurred in China's coastal provinces. With conflicts between villagers and village leaders becoming increasingly intense, pressures for restructuring the collective ownership system mounted, leading to important property rights reforms. In the following section, I will take Yujia village as a case study to show how collective action problems in the village economy led to the emergence of a shareholding cooperative system, and how the political interests of village officials influenced the design of this new institution.

Corporatising the village commons

Yujia village: the local setting[3]

Yujia village consists of twelve natural villages organised into nine sub-village groups (*cunmin xiaozu*). At the end of 1993, the village had 438 households with a population of 1,756. The land area of the village has shrunk considerably due to the expansion of Hangzhou city during the last two decades. In 1983, the village had about 200 hectares of farmland. In 1996, the village only had about 10 hectares of farmland, 16.7 hectares of fish pond and a small area of other categories of land (Yujia cun dang-zongzhi 1995).

Industrial growth and urbanisation have profoundly changed the economic structure in Yujia over the past two decades. In 1996, apart from a few households that contracted fish ponds from the village and grew flowers, all residents were employed in the non-agricultural sector. Collective industrial enterprises were highly developed and contributed greatly to local prosperity. Villagers' per capita income in 1995 was 6,501 yuan. This was four times higher than the national average amount earned by rural residents and thirty times greater than the average income in Yujia in 1978 (Yujia cun dangzongzhi 1995; *Zhongguo Tongji Nianjian* 1996: 281).

Village leaders in Yujia attributed the village's economic success largely to their commitment to the development of the collective economy. As soon as local agricultural production was de-collectivised in 1984, Yujia's leaders decided to develop collectively owned industry. Village enterprises quickly formed cooperative links with state enterprises in Hangzhou city, which gave them access to much-needed technology and market information. Moreover, in the following decade the village received some 80 million yuan in compensation fees for land that was requisitioned to accommodate the growth of Hangzhou municipality. Village authorities invested these funds in collective enterprises. In the early 1990s, the village leaders adopted an ambitious plan to improve their enterprises' long-term prospects in the marketplace. Several new, high-tech firms, including an air-conditioner factory with a total investment of 85 million yuan, were established jointly with overseas and domestic corporations (Yujia VSC 1996). By the end of 1994, the village had eighteen village collective enterprises with a gross value of output of 136 million yuan, which contributed 5.6 million yuan per annum to the village authority's budget.

However, along with the rapid development of the collective economy in Yujia, management of the village's collective assets became increasingly difficult. First, villagers showed little enthusiasm for the development of collective enterprises. Although individual villagers regularly demanded increased economic benefits from the village collective, they put little effort into programmes or activities that expanded the enterprises or improved their profitability. Indeed, according to collective enterprise managers the work ethic of village employees was particularly poor. Yet because of the non-excludability features of collective property, village leaders could not enact punitive measures by firing slack workers or barring them from enjoying access to the collective goods funded by enterprise profits.

Second, conflicts erupted between villagers and village leaders over the lack of transparency and democratic participation in the management of collective property. Villagers in Yujia had a deep distrust of the leaders that managed collective enterprises and funds, whom they generally saw as unaccountable, dishonest and self-serving. Their suspicions may have been well founded. As early as 1987, the then village party secretary of Yujia was found to have expropriated public funds and was sentenced to seven years imprisonment. In 1996, when I was conducting fieldwork in Yujia, the villagers were lodging a collective complaint over poorly constructed housing that had been subsidised by the village collective. The villagers suspected that village cadres had received kickbacks from the builders for having awarded them the construction contract.

A third problem was the increase in disputes between villagers and village leaders caused by the exclusion of growing numbers of villagers from collective ownership and from the distribution of land compensation funds. Between 1984 and 1994, as a result of land requisition, the residential status of 1,032 out of the 1,756 residents of Yujia was changed from rural to urban. Consequently, these people lost their rights to the rapidly growing collective property of the village. Infuriated, they demanded a share of the collective assets and asked for a reversal of their residential status. Moreover, remaining members of the village refused to relinquish their land and change their residential status. In the early 1990s, many villagers started to call for the privatisation of the collective economy.

In response to these problems, in early 1993 the Yujia village committee decided to reform the property rights system of the village collective economy by introducing a shareholding cooperative system. The chief of the village committee led a team of village cadres to the thriving metropolis of Guangzhou to study the organisation of VSCs there.[4] In May 1993 the village government set up a working committee, which included the village party secretary, the chief of the village committee, the village accountant and all village cadres, to plan the transformation of collective property rights. At the end of that year, a VSC was established to assume responsibility for the economic functions of the village committee. The VSC would represent the owners of collective property and take over the management of all the collectively owned properties including land, enterprises and funds.

While documents of the Yujia village government claimed that the establishment of the VSC was aimed primarily at clarifying the property rights of collective assets, establishing a system of democratic management of collective assets and raising capital, interviews with village cadres indicate that they had other, more complex, agendas in adopting this model. According to the chief of the village committee, village leaders intended to use the organisation of the VSC to transform villagers from being simply the beneficiaries of collective economic development into being risk-takers who felt responsible for collective economic development. The village chief complained that because of the ambiguity of collective ownership and government management, villagers were free riders who were solely interested in demanding more and more benefits from the village leaders. With the establishment of the VSC and their transformation into shareholders, villagers would not only have an incentive to contribute towards the growth of enterprises, but they also would have to bear the economic risks together with the collective. The chief also acknowledged that village authorities had no intention of giving up their control over collective property. Instead, they intended to use the property rights reform to facilitate their future administration of the village. In short, the interests of the village leaders influenced the creation of the VSC. This is illustrated in the following examination of the share structure and the power distribution of Yujia VSC.

Shares in Yujia VSC

The share structure of Yujia VSC was largely determined by the village leaders and reflected their political and economic concerns. Three types of share were created: collective shares (*jiti gu*), household distributed shares (*nonghu fenpei gu*) and household investment shares (*nonghu touzi gu*). These were intended by the village government to assign limited property rights to villagers to ease their increasing demands on collective property, and to maintain a collective framework for the village economy that was under their control.

Collective shares are shares owned collectively by the VSC, which is supposed to represent all villagers. These shares comprise assets that were collectively owned by the village prior to the establishment of the VSC. According to the regulation of Yujia VSC, in Yujia the collectively owned assets included:

(a) the collectively owned land, water resources and other natural resources according to law;
(b) all the buildings, traffic tools, machinery, equipment, the infrastructure of the agricultural irrigation system and public infrastructure for educational, cultural, public health and sports purposes which were invested by the collectives (village or sub-village branches);
(c) all the village-owned collective enterprises and all the village's shares in the partnership enterprises (*lianying qiye*), shareholding cooperative enterprises and Sino-foreign joint-ventures;
(d) all the assets from the donation, support and help of the state government, units, and individuals received by the village collective;
(e) all the securities, including stocks and bonds purchased by the village collective;
(f) all the monetary assets generated from the incomes of using the collective assets. These include contracting payments, rents, share interests, share dividends, land contracting payments, compensation payments for the land, rents for the land and village's levies;
(g) the intellectual property rights owned by the village collective, such as patents rights and brand rights;
(h) all other collective assets owned by the village collective.

(Yujia VSC 1993: 5)

According to the assessment of the village government, in April 1993 the village had a total of 1.2 billion yuan collective assets, including land and non-productive assets. Although the village's farmland and non-productive

110

assets such as public facilities were owned by the VSC, they were excluded from the issue of collective shares. Moreover, if farmland is requisitioned by the city government in the future, the entire land compensation fee and farmers' employment arrangement fee will go to the VSC. All the remaining collective assets, which included such productive fixed assets as workshops, machinery, investments and the monetary assets held by the village collective, were valued at 21.60 million yuan. It was these assets that were converted into collective and household shares in the VSC. The majority of these became collective shares.

A smaller part of the collective shares became household distributed shares, allocated among village households by the village committee. Household distributed shares lack most of the attributes of shares in a Western market economy. Formal ownership of these shares is still in the hands of the collective, that is, the VSC. Shareholders only have rights to the share dividends. They have no right to sell or to transfer the shares to others.

Household investment shares consist of the investment made by the individual villager households in the VSC. While these shares are fully owned by villagers and inheritable, subscriptions to these shares are compulsory. It is a village committee regulation that to be eligible to receive their household distributed shares, each household must invest 10,000 yuan, but only 10,000 yuan, in the VSC. The village chief of Yujia acknowledged that this regulation was meant to forge a close link between the personal interests of individual villagers and the collective interests of the VSC. According to him, 'by asking them to invest in the VSC, they have to be concerned with the development of the collective economy, rather than just want to get more and more benefits from the collective'. However, to avoid differentiation within the village, the individual household investment was limited to only 10,000 yuan.

Not surprisingly, many villagers were unsatisfied with the ways in which the village government designed and allocated shares in the VSC. The village chief of Yujia frankly admitted that when the above share structure was first proposed by the village government, many villagers in Yujia were not happy with the compulsory subscription of household investment shares. They complained that the village already had many collective assets and these should be distributed to all villagers for free, rather than that villagers be required to invest even more in collective accumulation in order to protect their ownership share of existing assets. Many villagers suspected that the aim of establishing the VSC was not to provide them with greater rights over collective property, as claimed by the village government. Instead they believed that it was intended by the village government to raise money from villagers. Hence villagers were reluctant to invest in the VSC, and again demanded the complete privatisation of collective property.

In response, the Yujia village leaders insisted that it was not only impossible to privatise the village's collective assets, but for several reasons, it was also undesirable. For one thing, they argued that a strong collective economy was the only way to guarantee that all villagers would become wealthy. Privatisation might disadvantage many villagers who were incompetent in the marketplace. Further, they argued that the majority of the collective assets had to be kept in the hands of the collective so as to take care of the senior and disabled villagers and provide welfare and infrastructure for the community. Third, they pointed out that the collective economy was an inter-generational public good. The collective assets had been accumulated largely through investment of the compensation payments for requisitioned farmland, which not only belonged to the current residents but also to their descendants. If the collective assets were divided, villagers would spend the money quickly and future generations would not have economic resources on which to depend. Therefore, maintenance and development of the collective economy was necessary not only to benefit current villagers, but also to ensure the wellbeing of future generations of villagers.

While the village government in Yujia insisted on maintaining a collective framework for the VSC, they also took measures to obtain cooperation from the villagers. For example, to reduce villagers' resistance to the mandatory subscription to household investment shares, payment for household investment shares could be made over two years. The village leaders also guaranteed that the household investment shares would receive an interest payment that would be higher than the interest paid on the same bank deposit over five years, in addition to their dividends.

Distributing power in the Yujia VSC

The founding charter of the Yujia VSC stipulates that the VSC is an independent collective economic organisation that owns and manages all the collectively owned assets in the village. The economic functions of the village committee were transferred to the VSC. In return the VSC would issue the contract for farming land to village households, provide services to households engaged in agricultural production, determine the management system of the village collective enterprises, develop new enterprises and accumulate collective assets. Village cadres claimed that the establishment of the VSC would realise a separation of the village government from the management of the village economy and establish a democratic management system of collective property. Shareholder villagers could effectively protect their interests by participating in the decision-making process of the VSC and monitoring the management of collective property (Yujia VSC 1993: 1–2).

In Yujia, the organisational structure of the VSC was superficially not much different from that of a Western shareholding limited company. The highest organ of power was the Shareholders' Representative Assembly, members of which were elected by all shareholder-villagers. For every ten households, there was one representative in the Shareholders' Representative Assembly. So from the 438 households in Yujia, forty-three members were elected. The major power and responsibilities of the Shareholders' Representatives Assembly listed in the founding charter of Yujia VSC included: setting and amending the VSC founding charter; electing and dismissing members of the Board of Directors of the VSC; hearing and assessing the report of the Board; making decisions on the development plan for the village collective economy; setting wages of the Board members and performance appraisal criteria and supervising the financial affairs of the VSC.

Under the Shareholders' Representative Assembly, a board of directors, which included thirteen elected members, was established. The board held the responsibility for drawing up the development strategy of the VSC and for making decisions on investment, production and income distribution in the VSC. The chairman of the board was the legal representative of the VSC and represented the VSC externally. The board was accountable to the Shareholders' Representative Assembly. Its management and performance were to be monitored and assessed by the Shareholders' Representative Assembly. Each board member was appointed for three years, and board members could serve an unlimited number of terms if they continued to be elected by the shareholders.

However, the creation of this organisational structure in the VSC resulted in little change to the way that the village leaders controlled collective property. Board members were selected by the village leaders, rather than by the Shareholders' Representative Assembly, and village leaders monopolised all the positions on the VSC board. The thirteen members of the board included the village party secretary, the chief of the village committee, the deputy-chief of the village committee, the village accountant and managerial cadres of the nine sub-village groups (cunmin xiaozu zuzhang). The village party secretary became the chairman of the board of directors. No ordinary villagers sat on the board.

The complete congruence between the membership of the board and leadership of the village indicates that the establishment of the VSC did not offer villagers greater power in the management of collective property. The Shareholders' Representative Assembly had little influence in protecting the interests or assets of the shareholder-villagers. For example, as a result of the rapid expansion of the village economy, between 1993 and 1995 the total value of shares in Yujia VSC increased from 25.98 million yuan to 96.88 million yuan. However, the value of the household distributed and individual shares remained unchanged. The increased value, worth more than 70 million yuan, was all accredited by the VSC board to the collective shares that it controlled. In fact, by establishing a corporate form of governance, village cadres even further legitimised their power and strengthened their control over the commons.[5]

The above account of the establishment of the VSC in Yujia demonstrates that although property rights to the collective assets were disaggregated and some of these rights were granted to the village households, village leaders directed the whole process in such a way as to consolidate their overall control of collective property. To this end, the designation and distribution of shares all reflected the interests and aims of the village leaders rather than those of the villagers. While in principle the VSC board should be responsive to the interests of the villager-shareholders, in practice it still exerts its will over the villagers. Collective ownership remains at the core of the local economy, property rights in collective assets remain ill defined, and the village government still acts as the *de facto* owner of the commons.

Collective goods provision by VSCs: organising support and ensuring compliance

Although the interests of village leaders have dictated the design and formation of the VSCs, it would be a mistake to suppose that those leaders acted without any consideration for the interests of villagers. As mentioned in an earlier section, the need to maintain the provision of collective goods to villagers was one of the main reasons village authorities chose to maintain a collective framework for the VSCs. In wealthy villages, a very comprehensive range of collective goods and services is provided to villagers by the VSCs. Yet the ways in which village leaders deliver these goods, particularly economic welfare, also reflect their political objectives. As shown in this section, village cadres have disposed of the revenues generated from VSCs under their management in such a way as to win political support and ensure compliance from villagers.

Creating a constituency: dividend payments and local social welfare

While village leaders retained their control over collective property by establishing VSCs, they understood that in order to consolidate that control over time, they still had to enlist the support, or at least the compliance, of the local populace. In Yujia, village cadres went to considerable lengths to convince villagers that the creation of the VSC was for 'the public good'. One strategy used to achieve this was to manipulate the distribution of profits in the VSC to pay abnormally high share dividends and supply generous collective goods and services to villagers.

According to the founding charter of the Yujia VSC, dividend payments to shares are determined by both the profit margins of shareholding companies and the long-term development strategy of the enterprises. In this way, the necessity to invest in the long-term development of the VSC is balanced against the immediate wants and needs of individual villager-shareholders.

114

Therefore it was ruled that after deducting the relevant taxes and fees, the net profits of the VSC would be divided as follows: 50 per cent would be held by the VSC as public accumulation funds (*gong ji jin*), which would mainly be used for reinvestment; 10 per cent would be used by the VSC as public welfare funds (*gong yi jin*), which would be used for the provision of public welfare for villagers; and 40 per cent would be distributed to shareholders as dividends (Yujia VSC 1993: 7–8).

However, the VSC board has not always followed the rules spelled out in the founding charter when distributing profits. The decisions made by the village leaders on dividend payments often reflect their political goals. In Yujia, since the VSC was set up, the board has paid considerably more than 40 per cent of net profits as dividends. In 1994 and 1995, each household in Yujia received 7,560 yuan and 7,058 yuan in dividends from its total 20,000 yuan of shares (Yujia VSC 1996: 1). Given that each household in Yujia invested only 10,000 yuan, the return on investment was extremely high. Moreover, villagers also received a guaranteed interest for their household investment shares. Such a yield, which greatly exceeded the real profitability of the Yujia VSC, helped the village leaders to mollify villagers who were dissatisfied with the partial nature of the property rights reform, and to legitimise their continuing control over collective property. A document of the Yujia village committee explained that the high rate of return received by the villagers from the VSC justified its refusal to relinquish control over the village economy. As a village cadre commented:

> If we had divided collective assets between villagers, things would have been different. The villagers could not handle this money properly and could not get such good returns elsewhere. What they would have done is to spend the money quickly without caring about the future.

The dividends enjoyed by the villagers constitute only part of the benefits produced by the VSC. One of the major functions of the VSC is to provide a funding basis for the provision of social security. In Yujia, the village leaders have spent a considerable amount of the revenue from the VSCs to set up and sustain a comprehensive local welfare system. The welfare available to the villagers is superior to that provided by the central state for its tenured employees. Villagers receive old-age and disability pensions, subsidised education and healthcare, family planning rewards and subsidised cremations. Senior villagers are given free holiday travel every three years.

In Yujia, large amounts have also been spent on physical infrastructure. In 1995, the village leaders initiated a rehousing project for the entire 438 households of the village. Under this project, all households moved into an entirely new residential complex of free standing three-storey villas. The village leaders offered a 20,000 yuan subsidy towards the construction of each dwelling. In addition, they financed the construction of new roads, the connection of water and electricity, the external decoration of the dwellings and the installation of cable TV and telephone. To be sure, villagers have benefited from this generous provision of collective goods and services.

However, we should not be beguiled into accepting that this is solely evidence of the village leaders' commitment to realising 'the public good'. The provision of these collective goods and services is also tailored to generate political support for local officials. An illustration of this is to be found in the particular emphasis placed by village leaders on the provision of welfare for senior villagers. In 1995, more than one million yuan was spent on welfare just for the 258 elderly residents. In addition to payment for old-age pensions, the VSC spent more than 500,000 yuan on building a senior citizens' entertainment centre and supplying various entertainment facilities and programmes. Another 400,000 yuan was spent on providing seniors with a free holiday in Beijing. A free health examination was offered to each senior villager. On the one hand, these benefits were provided because senior citizens generally are among those most in need of assistance. But on the other hand, looking after older people is a highly respectable philanthropic activity in Chinese society, and so this was an effective way for village leaders to establish their reputation as 'filial', 'public-spirited' leaders. Moreover, since the elderly have great informal authority and influence on local affairs within their communities and families, their backing for the village leaders became quite significant.

The political considerations of the Yujia village leaders also have prompted them to provide collective goods in such a way as to strengthen the villagers' sense of collective identity. The new rehousing project in Yujia exemplifies this utilitarian approach to identity construction. Building subsidies were offered to villagers on condition that all houses would be built on a location determined by the leaders to an identical architectural plan selected by the leaders, and that construction of the houses would be organised by the village committee. The resulting visual uniformity expresses community unity and demonstrates the success of the collective management of the village economy.

In Yujia, the village leaders' generous disposal of the collective revenues in the VSC to provide benefits to villagers has effectively won them considerable support from villagers and led to the expansion of their patronage in the local community. The prosperity of the village and the comprehensive welfare enjoyed by villagers have often been perceived, by village cadres, many villagers and higher-level government, as the results of the development of the collective economy and the successful management and benevolent personalities of the village leaders. The popularity of village leaders is reflected in their high rate of retention in office. The village party secretary and village chief in Yujia began their third three-year term of office in 1996.

Ensuring compliance: providing collective goods selectively

Besides manipulating the profit distribution in the VSC to enlist political support, village cadres in Yujia also use their control of the VSC to ensure compliance with national and local policies and regulations. They accomplish this by setting restrictive rules for villagers to gain access to membership of the VSC and to the collective goods and services it finances. The social and political behaviour of villagers and the loyalties of villagers to the collective economy are all criteria by which village leaders determine the eligibility of villagers for benefits from the VSC. In this way, village governments effectively generate the cooperation of villagers with national authorities and themselves, and fragment any potential opposition to their power.

From the very start, the VSC was designed by village cadres in Yujia to function as an arm of village government, rather than purely as an economic organisation. To be eligible as shareholders, villagers are required not only to invest in the VSC, but also to obey various regulations ranging from central government legislation to village codes. The failure of villagers to observe these regulations adversely affects their rights to receive shares, share dividends and welfare. For example, if villagers refuse to fulfil their military service obligation during army recruitment, their families lose their entitlements to receive dividends or other economic benefits supplied by the VSC for three years. Families of villagers who commit a legal offence receive only a proportion of the dividends they would otherwise receive from the VSC (Yujia cun 1994: 10–11). Villagers who breach the central government's family planning polices permanently lose their entitlements to the economic benefits that are financed by the VSC. In Gujia village, which is adjacent to Yujia, it is stipulated that if villagers seriously violate village committee regulations, not only do they lose the right to receive dividends and economic welfare from the village, but they also lose their right to work in any of its collective enterprises (Gujia cun 1994: 6, 11). Similar rules can also be found in many other places in rural China. In Henggang town in Baoan county, Guangdong province, villagers who breach the government's one-child policy are, together with their children, excluded from the shareholders' lists for a certain period (Zhou and Wu 1992).

Furthermore, in many of the suburban villages that surround Hangzhou the distribution of collective goods and services is designed to discourage private economic activity and encourage dependence on the collective economy. Indeed, in some villages, local business people and the self-employed are denied all entitlements to collective goods and services, or are only eligible for a small proportion of the goods and services that are supplied to other villagers. Leaders in Yujia made no pretence about the fact that they used their control over the distribution of profits from the VSC to discriminate against villagers who set up their own businesses. As the chief of the village committee explained, 'they compete with the collective firms and undermine villagers' commitments to the collective economy'. In 1995 in Gujia village, profit distribution of the VSC consisted of two parts: dividends on shares held by all village households, and year-end bonuses for all villagers working in the collectives. A case study on the collective economy in four villages in Shangdong province also found that households engaging in private business were virtually denied all the economic benefits provided by the collective enterprises (Chen 1998).

By using the profits from the VSC to reward compliance, punish opposition and encourage membership of the village collective, village leaders have maintained effective control over the behaviour of villagers in the context of rapid marketisation and rural democratisation. Yujia village has been selected as one of twenty model villages in Zhejiang province, due to its highly developed collective economy. Yujia has also been acclaimed as a model village by Hangzhou's city government, because of its enforcement of central government policies, maintenance of law and order and remarkable prosperity. And the village possesses a stable, popularly elected leadership.

However, while village leaders in Yujia have retained command over the VSC and, *ipso facto*, are able to elicit political support from villagers and manipulate their behaviour, their controls are contingent. In the past, their power, legitimacy and popularity have been underpinned by the growth that has taken place in the collective economy. In the future, it will continue to depend on the capacity of that economy to fund the collective goods and services that are necessary both to pave the way for further growth and to satisfy villagers' growing expectations. If the profits of the VSC fall, its purchase of costly technology and infrastructure and provision of an extremely generous welfare system will have to be scaled down. In that event, it is unlikely that village leaders would continue to receive high levels of political support.

Moreover, despite the introduction of the shareholding system, property rights in the village commons are still fuzzy. The VSC suffers from overconsumption by village leaders and villagers. Villagers are still shirking their obligations to invest more and work harder in collective enterprises. Conflicts still occur between villagers and village cadres over the management of collective property, the payment of land compensation fees and the distribution of dividends from the VSC. Therefore, the VSC, which has been shaped by the economic and political interests of village cadres, has not effectively resolved collective action problems in the village commons. How collective ownership in Yujia will evolve is still uncertain, but it is clear that the various interests involved, in particular those of village cadres, will continue to shape these and other property rights institutions governing the commons in rural China.

Conclusion

This case study of the transformation of collective ownership in Yujia village disputes the view that the cooperative culture embodied in the Chinese village community can save rural collectives from the classic problems of common property regimes. Intense conflicts erupted between individual villagers and village leaders over the management of collective property. The absence of clearly defined individual property rights led to excessive consumption, shirking and opportunist behaviour by all kinds of members of the village community. Resistance from villagers to the monopoly of control by village cadres over collective property resulted in the modification of the management institutions of collective property.

At a more general level, this chapter has shown that institutions governing collective property in rural China have been engineered to facilitate achievement of the objectives of national policy elites and local government leaders. Yujia village officials were under great pressure from villagers to clarify property rights over collective assets. Nevertheless, they refused to privatise the collective economy. By manipulating the allocation of shares, nominations to the VSC board and the distribution of dividends and provision of collective goods and services from the VSC, village leaders managed to maintain their economic and political controls and even expand clientelist ties.

The resulting institutions are not likely to be an effective solution to the collective action problems in village communities, however. In part, this is because in villages such as Yujia, the VSC primarily has been designed to fulfil the interests of those who created the institutions, rather than those who collectively own, and benefit from, the property. Property rights in the commons have remained unclear in order to maintain and bolster the power of village leaders. Conflicts between villagers and village officials are likely to arise whenever profits from the commons decline, or when there are perceptions of mismanagement, corruption, scarcity and over-exploitation. As Warren and McCarthy conclude in their study of *adat* in Indonesia in Chapter 5 of this volume, despite the growth of markets and decentralisation of decision-making, competing claims over the commons in rural China will not be resolved in a manner that protects the rights and interests of villagers unless there are fundamental changes in national structures and practices of political authority.

Notes

1 The author wishes to thank Sally Sargeson, Garry Rodan, Tim Wright and participants in the conference on 'Shaping Common Futures: Case Studies of Collective Goods, Collective Actions in East and Southeast Asia', Perth, Australia, 7–9 October 1999, for their constructive comments on an earlier draft of this paper. I am solely responsible for all remaining faults.

2 For a discussion of land ownership and the distribution of the compensation fund for requisitioned land, see Zhang *et al.* (1993).

3 Data in the following sections on Yujia village are drawn from my fieldwork in Hangzhou during April and July 1994, and May and June 1996. To ensure confidentiality, the names of Yujia and other villages have been modified.

4 The VSCs originated in suburban Guangzhou in the early 1990s and later developed quickly in other areas. According to a national survey of seventy-five counties, up to July 1992, there were 6,820 VSCs in these counties (Ministry of Agriculture 1992). For discussions of the development of VSCs in China, see Kong (1995); Guo and Zhou (1997).
5 In some other places, local governments explicitly regulated that the VSCs were subject to the supervision of the village governments. For example, a regulation of Tianhe district of Guangzhou city concerning the VSCs stated that the VSCs should ask the approval of the 'two committees' – the village party branch committee and the villager committee – on all key issues, such as important projects, economic development plans, large loans and personnel arrangements in important departments, budgets and income distributions (Guangzhou shi Tianhe qu nongwei 1992: 23).

7

THE PRIVATISATION OF PUBLIC INFRASTRUCTURE IN TRANSITIONAL SOUTHEAST ASIAN ECONOMIES

The case of build-own-operate-transfer projects in Vietnam and Laos

Andrew B. Wyatt

The transition from centrally planned to market economies that began in the mid-1980s in the Lao People's Democratic Republic (Lao PDR) and Vietnam undoubtedly resulted in rapid economic growth and an improvement in the average standard of living in both countries. It was, therefore, viewed as being in 'the national interest'. Nevertheless, rates of growth were not uniform. Certain regions, economic sectors and social groups benefited disproportionately from market reforms, while others were seriously disadvantaged (EAAU 1997).

As a result of divergence between winners and losers in the reform process, the pace, scope and process of reform have been divisive issues for the governments of Laos and Vietnam. In Laos, leadership changes at the Sixth Party Congress of the Lao People's Revolutionary Party in March 1996 signalled concern that economic growth was resulting in an inequitable distribution of benefits between urban and regional areas (KPL 1996). In Vietnam, though concerns arose over increasing regional inequity, debates centred on the position of the nation-state and the Party. Conservative politicians argued that certain reforms could threaten Vietnamese sovereignty, damage society and undermine the government's leading role in the economy and the Party's political power (Kolko 1997).

Another divisive issue concerned the privatisation of state owned enterprises (SOEs). In Vietnam, the preferred approach to privatisation – equitisation, in which managers and workers are offered an equity stake in the enterprise – was considered to be progressing satisfactorily until the early 1990s. After that time, progress slowed and was of a piecemeal nature

(Probert and Young 1995). In contrast, in the Lao PDR after an initial slow start the privatisation of SOEs accelerated in 1991 and 1992, and most major SOEs were in private hands by 1994 (Livingston 1997).

However, in both countries, privatisation mainly took place in SOEs in the sectors of manufacturing, food processing and agriculture, rather than in economic infrastructure (Tuan 1994). Economic infrastructure is defined as instrumental infrastructure goods that are required to facilitate economic growth and development. It includes public utilities such as power, telecommunications, piped water supply, sanitation and sewerage, and transport facilities such as roads, bridges, railways, ports and waterways and airports. Since it is deemed to be crucial for economic growth, is of strategic importance, and provides essential services and social welfare functions that benefit entire populations regardless of geographical location, ethnic origin, or class, the governments of Vietnam and Laos concur that development of economic infrastructure is in 'the national interest'. For these reasons, it has been off-limits to enterprise-level privatisation and, until recently, often has been heavily subsidised by the state.

In Vietnam, the extremely poor state of economic infrastructure as a result of the war years, lack of capital and rapidly growing demand has placed considerable pressure on SOEs to attract new investments. By contrast in Laos, were economic infrastructure is in a similar state to that of Vietnam, domestic demand has been somewhat lower and, until the economic crisis of 1997, came predominantly from neighbouring countries such as Thailand or developing regions within Laos.

While both countries ruled out the privatisation of SOEs already operating in the sector, in the 1990s they began to implement a lesser known form of privatisation in the provision of new economic infrastructure. Sometimes called a policy 'soft option', build-own-operate-transfer, or BOOT, projects are recognised by their proponents as useful mechanisms by which new private sector investment can be mobilised into sectors that remain in public hands for political reasons (World Bank 1994c). They are implemented as discrete projects and therefore do not threaten the overall ownership structure of the SOEs.

International financial institutions (IFIs) have been central to the introduction and implementation of BOOT projects in developing countries, including Laos and Vietnam. Since the early 1990s, agencies such as the World Bank, the International Finance Corporation (IFC) and the Asian Development Bank (ADB) have enthusiastically espoused the benefits of the BOOT approach (World Bank 1994c; Smith 1996; IFC 1996; Ferreira and Khatami 1996; ADB 1997a; 1997b). Indeed, the IFC through its Foreign Investment Advisory Service, has been sponsoring round-table meetings on privately funded infrastructure between developing country governments and the private sector since 1993 (IFC 1996). The IFIs maintain that BOOT projects represent the best means by which the main material constraint on infrastructure improvement in developing countries, lack of public funds, can be overcome through the mobilisation of private sector funds. According to the World Bank (1994c), market forces and competition can improve the production and delivery of infrastructure, lower the costs of provision and introduce new technologies. The allocation of private property rights in infrastructure encourages owners and stakeholders to make wise investments and use resources in a sustainable fashion. In short, it is argued that the privatisation of economic infrastructure can serve 'the national interest'.

However, the IFIs tend to ignore significant problems associated with BOOT projects. First, these projects are difficult to regulate and involve major public costs and risks. Second, little is known about how the high risk investment environments of transitional economies might foster sets of private interests that, in seeking to benefit from the provision of economic infrastructure, act in a manner that is antithetical to both 'the national interest' and the interests of certain regions, sectors and social groups. Third, insufficient attention has been given to the consequences of implementing BOOT projects in the absence of well constructed regulatory regimes, and of altering long-standing property relations so as to allow BOOT projects to exploit common pool resources.

This chapter examines these problems in the context of efforts by governments in Vietnam and Laos to upgrade national economic infrastructure. It first provides a brief overview of the BOOT concept and its popularisation by IFIs in developing countries. It then addresses the three sets of problems identified above by comparing the implementation of BOOT infrastructure projects in Vietnam and Laos. A concluding discussion analyses the consequences of these projects for the BOOT industry, the region, the two nation-states, and the governments and peoples of Vietnam and Laos.

Build-own-operate-transfer: benefits, costs and risks

BOOT involves the private sector financing, building and operating a public infrastructure facility for a concessionary period. That period may last up to ninety-nine years (Levy 1996), but more usually is between ten and thirty years, depending on micro-economic factors. During the concession period, the project company is allowed to charge users a fee or sell its products and services at a rate high enough to repay debt within maturity periods of ten to fifteen years, and to generate a profit at internal rates of return (IRR) of 15 per cent or more. At the end of the concession period, the facility is transferred to government ownership at no cost to the government. Many other variants such as build-transfer-operate (BTO) and rehabilitate-operate-transfer (ROT) exist, and are essentially similar in nature to the BOOT approach that is discussed here. Certain countries, such as Vietnam, and IFIs such as the World Bank have preferred the term build-operate-transfer

(BOT) as a politically more palatable alternative to the term BOOT, which explicitly indicates a property rights relation. However, in a legal sense there is no difference, since BOT schemes as they are implemented in Vietnam confer the right of asset transfer to the private developer and investor. In this chapter I use the term BOOT to refer to both the Lao and Vietnamese cases. I use the term BOT when referring to the Vietnamese case specifically.

The main proponents of the BOOT concept have been the IFIs such as the World Bank and ADB, many developed country governments including Australia, Japan and the United Kingdom, and the BOOT industry itself. The industry comprises international financiers and banks, large engineering corporations and companies with specialist expertise on the complexities of BOOT, including international legal firms. Proponents argue that the approach brings private sector efficiency to public infrastructure provision. Synergy is gained when one consortium finances, builds and operates the same facility. Under competitive tendering conditions, which is not always the case, creative solutions to financing and technology result. It also allows the public sector to transfer risks to the party best able to manage that risk. For example, in BOOT projects the risk of construction cost and time over-runs are assumed by the constructor. Hence, BOOT allows governments to overcome material impediments to the provision of infrastructure while avoiding public borrowing.

Yet borrowing and risk allocation remain crucial issues in BOOT projects. Infrastructure projects often involve large sunk costs. This means that investors are restricted in their ability to move equity out of the investment once committed. The result is that most BOOT projects are highly geared, with debt to equity ratios of 70 per cent or more. Investors attempt to reduce their risk exposure by forming large international consortiums that also serve to bring in complementary expertise. Risk allocation makes or breaks a project. One reason why risk allocation is of central importance is that projects usually utilise limited or non-recourse financing techniques. Financiers fund the developer's project company solely on the basis of the commercial viability of the project, that is, full revenue and risk projections. Should the project fail, the financiers have no recourse, or limited recourse, to the assets of the developer companies. Given that financiers provide the bulk of investment, it is they who have the ultimate say in whether a project goes ahead or not. Unwise investment decisions are supposedly avoided through the exercise of 'due diligence'.

Although there are incentives for both investors and project companies to exercise 'due diligence', there often are misplaced incentives that prevent BOOT projects from delivering the outcomes desired by governments. It is not often stated that 'due diligence' exercised by financiers does not go beyond the period of debt and interest recovery, a period that may be as short as a third of the life of the project. Other misplaced incentives occur when developers who are equipment or service suppliers stand to benefit even if the project fails commercially. There may be incentives that encourage investors to make unwise decisions, as is evident from early experiences with BOOT projects in Australia. In the case of the Sydney Eastern Distributor motorway and the Melbourne Citylink, where equity was raised from local share markets, public interest groups took the project companies to court for publishing misleading revenue estimates based on overly optimistic traffic projections that were designed to attract investment (Morris 1997).

There are also numerous situations where the risks of a project have been misunderstood. In the case of the Sydney Harbour Tunnel, the NSW government provided a minimum revenue guarantee, a guarantee that covered a commercial risk (NSW Auditor General's Office 1994). Risks incurred by BOOT projects can be magnified by dramatic changes in foreign exchange rates. The Asian financial crisis left the governments of Indonesia and the Philippines bearing the risks of power purchase agreements denominated in US dollars. The devaluation of their currencies during the crisis raised government purchasing costs and increased retail prices (Gray and Shuster 1998). Another important category of risk is sovereign or political risk. These non-commercial risks include the possibility of governments expropriating assets without compensation, contractual undertakings not being enforced, projects being affected by acts of war or civil disturbance, and governments making regulatory changes that reduce project revenues (IFC 1996). In practice, however, it is often difficult to separate some forms of commercial risk from political risks (Handley 1997).

Partial risk guarantees (PRGs) provide the private sector developer and financier with partial protection against these risks. In theory, these guarantees are restricted to political or sovereign risks. In the early 1990s the World Bank played a key role in catalysing private sector investment in the construction of economic infrastructure, through its provision of PRGs to member countries of the International Bank for Reconstruction and Development (IBRD), one of the World Bank's two constituent organisations (Benoit 1996).

However, in May 1997, the World Bank Board also approved the provision of PRGs in International Development Association (IDA) countries, to which the World Bank lends at concessional rates. IDA countries are considered by international credit rating agencies and financiers to be politically unstable, and to have poorly developed regulatory and legal systems and less than transparent decision-making processes. They have high levels of risk and low credit worthiness. Consequently, in the absence of protective guarantees from an IFI such as the World Bank, foreign private capital is reluctant to finance projects in IDA countries. Vietnam and Laos are IDA countries in which World Bank PRGs were offered specifically to support BOOT approaches to the development of economic infrastructure. The US$1.5 billion Nam Theun 2 hydro-power project in the Lao PDR was one of the first projects where the investor called for a PRG. In Vietnam, the World Bank offered a PRG to encourage investment in the proposed US$400 million Phu My 2.2 gas-fired power station.

PRGs are meant to reduce the cost of financing projects where risk premiums would make such projects uneconomic. But their provision in IDA countries appears to be inconsistent with the arguments regarding the efficiencies that can be achieved from market competition that are advanced by proponents of the BOOT concept, including the World Bank. First, PRGs function like a public subsidy of a project's viability under conditions in which, without the guarantee, the project would be judged non-viable by the market. Second, the availability of the PRG allows governments to avoid creating the legal and regulatory systems that would foster investor confidence under normal circumstances. And finally, the provision of PRGs promotes large-scale, complex and extremely expensive projects in countries that may lack the institutions, skills, administrative agencies and financial resources necessary to ensure their success. Laos' Nam Theun 2 project is a case in point. The projected US$1.5 billion cost of this single project is three quarters the size of the Lao PDR's GDP.

In contrast to the claim by IFIs that BOOT projects allow the public sector to shed risk, Handley (1997) argues that governments, particularly in developing countries where risks are much higher, have in fact taken on the bulk of the risks. Governments have provided guarantees on fuel supply, power and water off-take, and protection against foreign exchange risk (Handley 1997). Governments that have given the private sector such guarantees have taken on contingent liabilities that, in most cases, have not been costed and accounted for. Nevertheless, they are real liabilities that potentially have significant negative implications, not only for government budgets, but also for intergenerational equity (Mody and Patro 1996). Infrastructure projects typically require financing by present generations, since debt maturities are usually in the order of ten to fifteen years. However, a developer's potential call on a government guarantee is good for the operational life of the project under a BOOT concession. This can be anything up to fifty-five years. The call on guarantees can potentially create major budgetary shortfalls and follow-on consequences for future generations. In one attempt to account for the contingent liabilities of three private infrastructure projects in Colombia, the World Bank estimated that expected government losses from government guarantees could amount to as much as US$93.2 million (Lewis and Mody 1998).

The following case studies of BOT and BOOT projects in Vietnam and Laos respectively illustrate how and why, despite the similar historical trajectories of the two countries, the IFIs, their client governments, the BOOT industry and certain NGOs are constructing two very different regimes for providing collective goods. They also explain why, in the absence of effective regulation, misplaced incentives and risks have radically divergent consequences for people at different levels of geo-political scale and at different periods of time.

BOT in the Socialist Republic of Vietnam: contested regulations and the agents of international capital

After Vietnam began its transition to a market economy under the reforms of *Doi Moi*, foreign debt ballooned, reaching more than 20 per cent of GDP by 1995 (Figure 7.1).

The end of Soviet aid in 1991, which had accounted for up to 40 per cent of the government budget (Probert and Young 1995), and the lack of access to loans from the IFIs as a result of the US embargo, impacted heavily on the fiscal position of the government (Thayer 1994; Kolko 1997). When Vietnam implemented its five-year Public Investment Program for the period 1996–2000, targeted versus actual figures showed shortfalls in all three sources of capital for infrastructure development: that is, the state budget, credit including overseas development aid, and general revenues from SOEs. The total estimated realised capital for the five-year plan would, at best, provide only US$19.5 billion or 90 per cent of the required US$21.7 billion (Vietnam 1996). Of this, the Ministry of Planning and Investment (MPI) estimated that approximately $7.5 billion was needed for transportation infrastructure, $1.5 billion for telecommunications, $2 billion for water supply, $3 billion for urban development, and $4–$5 billion for power. Annual expenditure on economic infrastructure would amount to approximately 15 per cent of Vietnam's GDP (Foster and Knight 1997).

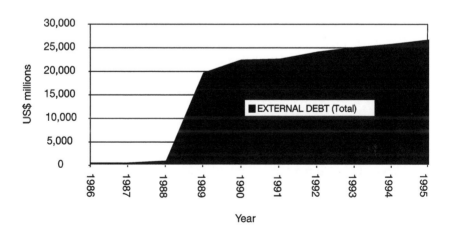

Figure 7.1   Vietnam's external debt 1986–95, not including Council for Mutual Economic Cooperation/Central and Eastern European countries

Source: World Bank 1997b

Demand in some infrastructure sectors was acute. For example, electricity consumption was growing on average by 12.6 per cent annually between 1990 and 1995, much faster than the average GDP growth rate of 7.8 per cent. World Bank projections to the year 2010 estimate that electricity supply would need to increase 70 per cent faster than GDP in order to meet demand under planned economic growth targets of 4–5 per cent (World Bank 1999).

Faced with chronic budget deficits, ballooning foreign debt and increasing demand for economic infrastructure, the government had two options for financing infrastructural development. It could draw on more concessional credits from the IFIs, or seek private sector investment in infrastructure projects to supplement IFI credits. The former option had unpalatable political implications. It could crowd out desperately needed social infrastructure. Moreover, after fighting for its independence against foreign invaders and colonialists,[1] the realisation that Vietnam's economy was becoming more indebted to foreigners made Vietnam's political masters reluctant to draw on concessional credits.[2] The ministries that hold Vietnam's purse strings, the Ministry of Finance and Ministry of Planning and Investment, concurred with advice coming from the IFC and the World Bank that concessional credit should be reserved for social infrastructure such as health and education. Private sector investment would be utilised for economic infrastructure.

In December 1992 an Amendment to Article 2 of the Foreign Investment Law invited foreign investors to finance Vietnam's economic infrastructure through build-operate-transfer (BOT), build-transfer-operate (BTO) and build-transfer projects.[3] On 23 November 1993, Government Decree 87-CP was released to spell out the regulations under which private investment would be able to operate in infrastructure development.

From the time they were released, the Amendment and Decree were judged to be deficient and unworkable by the foreign investment community and their facilitators, the IFIs (Foreign Investment Advisory Service 1995). The following issues were of particular concern:

- While Decree 87-CP states that, subject to the approval of the state body authorised to enter into a BOT contract, the BOT company has the explicit right to create 'mortgages' over its assets, Vietnam does not have laws relating to mortgages and other forms of security that are required to secure the of foreign investors and lenders over project components such as immovable physical assets, land use rights, contractual rights that have an economic value, bank accounts etc.
- Decree 87-CP allows disputes over ancillary contracts between the BOT company and its subcontractors to be referred to a court in an arbitration body in Vietnam, an *ad hoc* arbitrator established by both parties, an arbitration body in a third country, or an international arbitration

tribunal. However, BOT contracts, defined as those between a Vietnamese state agency and a foreign investor, cannot be referred to international arbitration bodies or those in a third country.

- Article 8 of Decree 87-CP only authorises guarantees of 'financial obligations' of Vietnamese business enterprises (e.g. Electricity of Vietnam, hereafter EVN) that have contracts with the BOT company. Certain BOT projects, such as power generation plants, have required guarantees of performance beyond simple 'financial obligations', such as fuel delivery obligations.
- The regulation does not specifically entitle BOT project companies to receive payment for off-take deliveries in a foreign currency. Payments in Vietnamese dong are tied to the US dollar exchange rate so that the BOT company receives sufficient amounts of Vietnamese dong to meet foreign currency obligations to foreign lenders. Lenders also need to receive guarantees regarding the convertibility of dong into dollars, the availability of dollars, and the transferability of dollars out of Vietnam. While the government is entitled to appoint a financial institution or a bank of Vietnam to act as guarantor of the financial obligations assumed under a contract by a Vietnamese business enterprise, the value of this guarantee is questionable because such guarantees need to be at the level of a sovereign guarantee, and a state bank guarantee is not as reliable as one issued by the Ministry of Finance. However, no provision is made for sovereign guarantees (Foster and Knight 1997).

In 1998 Vietnam released a reworked version of Decree 87-CP, Decree 62/1998/ND-CP. That, too, was immediately criticised by the foreign legal fraternity because Vietnam remained unwilling to subject disputes between investors and its agencies to a foreign arbitration court (Skinner 1998). Investors were reluctant to risk their investments in local courts that were widely recognised to uphold Vietnamese interests. For the Vietnamese, the issue was politically sensitive since international arbitration was viewed as an infringement of sovereignty.[4] As of 2000, the issue of legally enforceable sovereign guarantees was still unresolved (Skinner 1998), as were the other points of contention over Decree 87-CP.

By early 1999, a little over five years after Decree 87-CP was issued, of ten currently active foreign-invested BOT projects, only one project, the Thu Duc water treatment plant, had reached financial closure. Three others had received the necessary approval from the Prime Minister of Vietnam and had been granted investment licences (see Table 7.1).

Indeed, the only power project to have received an investment licence, the diesel-fired power plant for Ba Ria-Vung Tau Province proposed by the Finnish diesel engine manufacturer Wartsila, became a focus for contestation between the BOT industry and the government of Vietnam. Although Vietnam accepted the conditions stipulated in the Wartsila concession

Table 7.1 Foreign BOT projects under development or negotiation in Vietnam as of January 2001

Project	Location	Investor/s	Cost, US$, millions	Status
Power projects				
Wartsila 120MW diesel	Ba Ria-Vung Tau	Wartsila NSD Corporation (Finland)	110	Investment licence granted in 1997. Financial closure stalled due to lack of security for financiers and poorly allocated risks. Re-negotiations are stalled over the tariff price of electricity.
Quang Ninh 300MW coal	Quang Ninh Province	Oxbow corporation (USA)	360	Under negotiation. Coal supply and tariff price of electricity under dispute. Govt received US Trade and Development Agency funding (US$250,000) to help advise with negotiations. Oxbow ready to pull out.
Phu My 2.2 720MW	Ba Ria-Vung Tau	10 consortiums tendered for project in Feb. 1998, led by Mitsubishi, Tomen and Nissho Iwai of Japan; Unocal, GE Capital, Enron and AES Transpower of US; and British Petroleum, EdF and Asea Brown Boveri (Swiss-Swedish group). EdF-led consortium including Sumitomo Corp. and Tokyo Electric Power Co. won bid in Jan. 1999.	Cost not announced as yet, due to incomplete tender. Original estimate was US$400–$500 million.	World Bank facilitating first competitive BOT tender. Awarded K&M Engineering (US consultants) contract to draft bid documents. Gas supply from Soc Son Gas field delayed due to construction delays. Consortium asking for a cost renegotiation since bid price was valid for one year.
Phu My 3 720 MW	Ba Ria-Vung Tau	BHP (sold share to BP Amoco/Statoil in Nov. 1998), Tomen Co. (Japan), Mitsui Co. (Japan), Agrium (Canada).	600–700	Negotiations stalled over plans for the Nam Con Son Gas pipeline that will deliver fuel and the tariff price of electricity. Project began in 1992; first feasibility finished in 1997.

Project	Location	Company	Value	Status
Soc Trang 475 MW	Soc Trang Province	Enron	270–310	
Ormat 50MW geothermal	Quang Ngai Province	Ormat (USA)	Under negotiation	Negotiations proceeding
Water treatment plants				
Binh An water treatment plant	HCMC–Dong Nai River		30	
Thu Duc water treatment plant	HCMC–Cai Canal	Suez Lyonnaise de Eaux, Pilecon Engineering Berhad (Malaysia). BOT company: Lyonnaise Vietnam Water Company	120 (investment capital). 36 in equity	Investment licence granted 26 Dec. for 25-year concession
Transport				
HCM City–Bien Hoa–Vung Tau Expressway	HCMC, Ba Ria-Vung Tau	Daewoo (Korea)	590	Stalled due to ceiling on toll level set by government being too low for investor.
Sao Mai Ben Dinh deep water sea port	Vung Tau	Tredia (Singapore), Low Yat Group (Malaysia), Yamaichi (Japan)	637	Investment licence withdrawn Dec. 1998. Failure to commence project due to the Asian financial crisis.

contract, the project failed to gain the approval of the final arbiters of all BOT-type projects, the international financiers. They were concerned that unacceptable amounts of risk lay in their hands (Irvine 1997). In particular, the legislatively unsupported letters of comfort that assured the Vietnamese government's agreement to foreign currency rates and availability, the repatriation of revenues and profits, security in fuel supply and pricing, and off-take commitments, were judged to be unenforceable by the foreign legal consulting fraternity, who were trying to hammer out deals on a number of much larger and therefore riskier projects (Irvine 1997). Legal consultants pointed out that Wartsila's acceptance of higher risks was due to self-interest. Whether or not the project became financially viable, Wartsila stood to profit from the sale of its diesel engines, while limited recourse would protect the company in case of financial collapse.

Faced with what they considered to be intractable problems, the IFIs hosted a number of forums to highlight 'weaknesses' in the regulations and emphasise the government's obligation to offer enforceable guarantees. At the September 1995 IFC-sponsored round-table,[5] the IFIs and members of the foreign financial and legal community explained details of international standards and the intricacies of risk-sharing through a range of enforceable sovereign guarantees to their increasingly beleaguered Vietnamese audience (see Foreign Investment Advisory Service 1995).[6]

By 1996, the World Bank had become concerned that some sections of the Vietnamese government were not in favour of BOT projects. It began to search for a suitable 'demonstration' project to assist the government 'in creating an appropriate legal and regulatory framework' (World Bank 1996b: 1). In 1997 it helped to fund a consulting company based in Washington DC, K&M Engineering, to draft a bid document for the Phu My 2.2 gas-fired power plant in Ba Ria-Vung Tau Province that would meet international financiers' requirements for risk allocation. Several considerations prompted the Bank's intervention. Until Phu My 2.2, all BOT projects in Vietnam had failed to follow the Bank's best practice models because they were negotiated projects undertaken without competitive bids. The Bank was keen to demonstrate to the Vietnamese government that competitive bidding could deliver financial, management and technological efficiencies. However, with an estimated cost of US$400–500 million, Phu My 2.2 would be one of the biggest and riskiest investments in the untested waters of Vietnamese BOTs.

To alleviate the risk and fulfil its role as facilitator of private sector investment, the Bank offered to provide a US$75 million PRG. Guaranteed such protection, thirty international companies and consortiums, including major power companies and equipment manufacturers such as Electricité de France (EdF), Asea Brown Boveri, Unacol, Enron, BP, Mitsubishi and Tomen (Vietbid 1998), stampeded to bid for the project, despite the fact that key fuel supply details from the incomplete Soc Son gas field development were still not available. An EdF-led consortium won the bid on technical and pricing criteria (Hung 1999). According to an elated Anil Malhotra,[7] the World Bank's Regional Energy Adviser, the price, while still not finalised because of the incomplete gas development, appeared to be 8 per cent less than negotiated proposals for an equivalent-sized gas powered plant.

The provision of a PRG by the World Bank at Phu My 2.2 still required approval from the Vietnamese government, since it had to provide a counter-guarantee.[8] However, key decision-makers in the government lacked the skills necessary to calculate the implications of a counter-guarantee and its costs, and carry out risk analysis of contingent liabilities.[9]

The Vietnamese government's cautiousness about the BOT concept and concerns about the offer of counter-guarantees led the World Bank's Country Assistance Program Policy Advisory Services to provide the government with capacity-building support in the area of 'private provision of infrastructure'. The consultant was Beca Worley International of New Zealand, an engineering and environmental consultant with a long involvement in Laos' private hydro-power projects. This support was designed to provide technocrats in ministries and line agencies at the central, provincial and city level with an understanding of international principles and requirements for successful BOT implementation.[10]

The capacity-building efforts of the World Bank may have assisted the Vietnamese government in dealing with the complexities of BOT projects, but the Bank itself seriously underestimated the politically sensitive nature of electricity pricing in Vietnam. In almost all cases except Phu My 2.2, where the bidding process resulted in a power price that was acceptable to the government, BOT power projects stalled over the price of electricity. The Government Pricing Committee, a standing committee within the National Assembly, controlled electricity prices in Vietnam, and those prices were subsidised by the state. However, under increasing pressure from the World Bank for structural and pricing reform in the energy sector, EVN was allowed to raise prices by an average of 9.1 per cent in 1996. While the rise met with a storm of objections from SOEs in heavy industrial sectors, the government stood firm. The price rise brought EVN's cost recovery to 70 per cent of its long-run marginal costs. That was not enough for the World Bank, which threatened to withhold further concessional funding if EVN did not move to full cost recovery through increases in tariffs by the year 2000 (Quan 1998). While the Bank stated that its threat was meant to ensure that EVN would be in a better position to pay back its debts in the future, the arm twisting also served to increase the price of electricity to a level that the BOT investors needed in order to make an attractive return on their investments of around 15 per cent. By late 1998, it appeared that the Government Pricing Committee had conceded. It announced that from July 1999, EVN would be allowed to increase electricity prices by 3.6 per cent from a long-run marginal cost of US$0.048/kWh to US$0.052/kWh. The price rise was delayed for four months because of protests from the SOEs.

One outcome of the dissatisfaction triggered by electricity price rises was that questions were raised publicly about whether BOT projects did indeed serve 'the national interest'. On the one hand, all foreign BOT power projects had stalled. In April 2000, Deputy Prime Minister Nguyen Tan Dung chaired a round-table meeting with MPI, concerned ministries and line agencies including EVN, over a range of stalemated projects. Included in the list of projects was Phu My 2.2. Dung ruled that the Phu My 2.2 project company, which was asking to negotiate a higher construction price because the one-year price validity of its bid had lapsed, was now subject to a deadline of May 2000 to conclude a deal. EVN was instructed to consider an alternative form of investment if negotiations failed.

Dung's rulings were broadcast in the state-run media, together with reports that EVN was seeking permission to terminate the Wartsila and Phu My 3 negotiations and look for other sources of financing. The media pointedly contrasted these reports with news about successful domestically funded power projects. EVN had surplus generating capacity, lower than projected industrial demand as a result of the economic downturn, and new capacity coming online. Also, EVN and Song Da Construction Corporation had concluded a BOT deal for the 72MW Can Don hydro-power project (see Table 7.2). Song Da is a leading domestic hydro-power firm that had been involved in constructing the two largest hydro-power projects in the country, the 1920MW Hoa Binh hydro-power plant and the 720MW Yali hydro-power plant. Song Da had negotiated a tariff of US$0.045 /kWh and secured financing from four domestic banks (Mai 1999). The investor in the other two proposed domestic BOT power projects, VINACOAL, was Vietnam's largest energy producer through its monopoly over coal production. VINACOAL's refusal to provide Oxbow with a price guarantee for the supply of coal had been a stumbling block in negotiations over the Quang Ninh power plant (see Table 7.1).

Sceptics in the foreign investment community characterised these events as an attempt by the government to force the hand of foreign BOT developers and investors to accept terms more favourable to Vietnam. In 2000, there still was much to unravel in negotiations over the future of BOT projects in Vietnam. However, the progress made by the Vietnamese Government at Can Don demonstrated that it was possible for Vietnam to mobilise domestic capital into its economic infrastructure on its own terms.

BOOT in the Lao PDR: political realities, conflicts of interest and the privatisation of resources

As in Vietnam, Laos was faced with serious material constraints in the provision of economic infrastructure. It, too, suffered from the loss of Soviet aid (Livingston 1997), chronic budget deficits and large growing foreign debt that, while only one tenth as large as Vietnam's, still represented 39.6 per cent of GDP in 1995 (see Figure 7.2). However, Laos faced an even greater constraint.

Table 7.2 Domestic BOT power projects under development or negotiation in Vietnam as of January 2001

Project	Location	Investor/s	Cost, US$, millions	Status
Can Don 72MW hydro-power	Binh Phuoc Province	Domestic investment: Song Da Construction Corporation	86	Power purchase agreement with EVN to sell power at US$0.045/kWh for 25 years. Financial closure reached with financing provided by domestic banks. Construction proceeding.
Na Duong 100 MW coal	Lang Son Province	Domestic investment: VINACOAL	124.6	Received government approval. Land clearance proceeding. Negotiating PPA with EVN.
Cao Ngan 100MW coal	Thai Nguyen	Domestic investment: VINACOAL	124	Prime Minister's approval given.

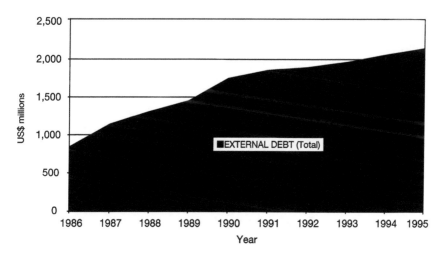

Figure 7.2 Laos' external debt 1986–95, not including Council for Mutual Economic Cooperation/Central and Eastern European countries

Source: World Bank 1997b

135

As a result of the 1975 exodus of approximately 90 per cent of its technically qualified civil servants and managers following the communist takeover of that year, the country lacked skilled human resources (Stuart-Fox 1993).

In its 1994–2000 Public Investment Programme, the Lao PDR allocated US$671 million to develop basic economic infrastructure (EAAU 1997). However, just one of its planned hydro-power dams, the Nam Theun 2 hydro-power project, was projected to cost US$1.5 billion.

Confronted with that material reality, senior government officials toured the region looking for ways to finance infrastructure. In the corridors of the ADB and World Bank in Thailand and the Philippines, they came across what appeared to be a free and painless model for infrastructure development: the BOOT concept.

The first BOOT project to be built in Laos – indeed, in the whole of Indochina – was the Tha Ngon bridge over the Nam Ngum River, 25km north of the capital Vientiane. In this venture, Laos had to deal with political fallout from the commercial principle of 'users pay'. Before the construction of the Tha Ngon bridge, for a minimal charge a government-operated ferry transported passengers and cars across the river at irregular times during the day. The idea for the bridge came from the then Australian Ambassador to Laos, Michael Mann. The Ambassador had family links to a village located on the northern side of the Nam Ngum river. Faced with the inconvenience of waiting for the ferry and wishing to meet the Australian government's directive to encourage investment in the region, the Ambassador proposed that Australia's leading BOOT developer, Transfield, could build a toll bridge at Tha Ngon. Transfield had been involved in the construction of the bilaterally funded Friendship Bridge, the first bridge connecting Thailand and Laos across the Mekong River. The Ministry of Communication, Transport, Post and Construction (MCTPC) and Vientiane Municipality accepted. The project became a 50/50 US$4.2 million joint venture between Transfield and the government of Laos. Australia's Export Finance and Insurance Corporation provided debt finance. Construction began in October 1993 and the bridge was opened in July 1994.

In order to capture traffic and secure tolls on the route, the project contract required that the existing ferry service be dismantled. Within weeks of the closure of the ferry service, bridge users, led by a group of retired and disabled revolutionary veterans living on the northern side of the river, protested against the toll, which was considerably higher than the old ferry charge.[11] A month later, the MCTPC succumbed to the protests. The government of Laos approached Transfield with a proposal to reduce the toll by 40 per cent. Transfield refused, since such a toll would not have provided sufficient revenue to service debt and to generate the projected IRR. A year later, with the threat of negative private sector sentiments being generated and spreading to the hydro sector, which was negotiating several BOOT projects, a settlement was achieved. In a contract buy-out, the government agreed to compensate Transfield for its equity in the project and the full projected IRR over the contracted ten-year concession period. The MCTPC reduced the toll to the same level as the old ferry charge. In 2000, it was still paying off its original debt, as well as the loan it arranged to buy out Transfield, at commercial rates of interest. The project burnt the MCTPC so badly that no other BOOT project has been considered in the transport sector.[12]

Bureaucrats in the power industry faced a different dilemma. The significant foreign exchange earned since 1971 from the country's first major hydro-power dam, the 150MW Nam Ngum Dam (Worley and Lahmeyer International 2000) and advice from the World Bank and ADB encouraged the Lao government to commit itself to large-scale hydro-power as the backbone of its drive for economic development. The ADB recommended that 'the exploitation of hydro-power resources represents the best immediate route for the Lao PDR to increase exports and raise growth of gross domestic product' (ADB 1996). Most of Laos' low domestic demand was provided by 38 per cent of Nam Ngum Dam's capacity (Somboune 1997). New capacity was specifically for export to Thailand. But how was Laos to find the required investment?

The first visible commitment to an increased investment in hydro-power since Nam Ngum Dam was the signing in late 1992 of a Memorandum of Understanding with Thailand to sell 1,500MW of electricity by the year 2000. The second was a speech by Khammone Phonekeo, the then Vice-minister of Industry and Handicrafts,[13] at a conference on the 'Emerging Private Power Sector in Asia' in Bangkok in March 1993. He identified a range of nineteen small (30MW) to large (950MW) hydro projects that Laos was prepared to develop through joint venture BOOT, with a view to later considering 100 per cent foreign-invested BOOT schemes (Khammone 1993).

After Khammone's speech, the country saw an influx of dam builders and consultants from countries such as Sweden, Norway, Australia, the USA, Canada and France, where environmental concerns had all but shut down the dam building industry (Usher 1997). The number of potential projects in Laos' hydro-power development plan had grown to about sixty by 1996. Many of these utilised a BOOT approach, and in 2000, sixteen BOOT hydro-power projects were listed as active (Somboune 1997; see Table 7.3). Several projects with investors from Asian countries, such as the Sepian-Senamnoy project, were inactive because of financial difficulties or the low price for electricity being offered by the Electricity Generating Authority of Thailand (EGAT), which made them non-viable.

In favouring BOOT over more traditional ways of financing dams through IFI loans, Khammone (1993) explained that the government saw 'risk shedding' as an attractive aspect of the approach. But unlike Vietnam, Laos did not promulgate special regulations relating to BOOT projects. While foreign investment in economic infrastructure was legislated under

Table 7.3 BOOT hydro-power projects completed or under development as of January 2001

Project	Location	Investor/s	Cost, US$, millions	Status
Theun Hinboun	Bolikhamsai	EdL 60%, Nordic Hydro-power 20%, MDX/GMS Power (Thailand) 20%.	260	Operational 4 April 1998. 30-year concession period.
Houay Ho	Attapeu	Daewoo (Sth Korea) 60%, Loxley (Thailand) 20%, EdL 20%.	192	Tariff agreement signed Nov 1995. Construction complete 1998. Electricity sales to Thailand begin September 1999.
Nam Theun 2	Khammou-ane	Transfield 10%, EdF (France) 30%, EdL 25%, Ital-Thai (Thailand) 15%, Jasmine (Thailand) 10%, Phatra Thanakit (Thailand) 10%.	1,200	MOU signed. FS and EIA completed. Negotiating PPA with Thailand.
Xekaman 1	Attapeu	Austral Lao Power (Australia) 5%, EdL 25%, Idris Hydraulic (Malaysia) 35%, unspecified Thai investors 35%.	500	MOU signed. FS submitted Feb 1995. EIA proceeding.
Nam Lik 1/2	Vientiane	M Group, EdL.	160	MOU signed. FS submitted March 1995.
Xekaman 1 +2	Attapeu	?	308	MOU signed. PFS submitted March 1995.
Nam Theun 3	Bolikhamsai	Heard Energy (USA), EdL.	170	MOU signed. FS submitted Oct 1995.
Sepian/ Senamnoy	Champasak	Dong Ah (Sth Korea) 45%, EdL 35%, unspecified Thai investors 20%.	1,000	MOU signed. FS submitted July 1995.

Nam Ou	Luang Prabang	Daelim Co. (Sth Korea), EdL.	735	MOU signed. PFS submitted Aug 1995.
Nam Ngum 2	Vientiane	Shlapak (USA), EdL.	510	MOU signed. FS submitted Aug 1995.
Nam Ngum 3	Vientiane	MDX/GMS Power (Thailand), EdL.	667	MOU signed. FS submitted Oct 1995.
Nam Theun 1	Bolikhamsai	Susco Group (Thailand), EdL.	334	MOU signed. FS submitted Oct 1995.
Nam Nhiep 2 + 3	Bolikhamsai	MDX/GMS Power (Thailand).	?	MOU signed. FS pending. FS pending.
Nam Suang 2	Luang Prabang	Hyundai Engineering.	296.4	MOU signed. FS pending.
Nam Tha 1	Bokeo	Campenon (France), EdF (France), EdL.	296	MOU signed. FS pending.
Nam Ngum 5	?	?	?	MOU signed. PFS submitted Jan 1997

Notes:
MOU: memorandum of understanding
FS: feasibility study
PFS: pre-feasibility study
EIA: environmental impact assessment
PPA: power purchase agreement

joint-venture arrangements in the 1998 Foreign Investment Law, the government intended to spell out the detailed regulations in individual sectoral laws. For example, the Ministry of Industry and Handicraft in charge of electricity generation planned to incorporate BOOT regulations in its Electricity Law. However, by 2000 BOOT developments were still subject to poorly enforced *ad hoc* administrative guidelines.[14]

In addition to the inadequate legal environment, BOOT hydro-power projects in Laos were plagued with problems that made it difficult for the government to achieve its aim of using hydro-power as a basis for broad social development. Some of these problems derived from the conflicts of interest and added risks that arose as a result of the government's own decision to take an equity stake in BOOT projects. The government believed that as an equity holder it stood to gain more revenue than it would otherwise do through royalties and resource rents. In that situation, however, it simultaneously acted as a regulator and an equity-holding developer. Despite its belief

139

that it could better regulate the industry by being on the boards of the private power companies, its power was limited by the number of votes it held: the government's stake was usually no higher than 30 per cent. It was also limited by its inadequate analytical capabilities.

Moreover, as an equity holder the government took on project risks that it originally had sought to shed. An illustration is provided by the Houay Ho hydro-power project, in which the government had a 20 per cent equity stake. The South Korean corporation, Daewoo, owned the remainder. Even before the project had made its first sale to Thailand, it was in financial trouble. First, the Power Purchase Agreement with EGAT, a key agreement that determines the project's financial viability by setting the purchase price and currency used, was concluded in 1995. The substantial devaluation of the Thai baht during the Asian financial crisis impacted on the projected earnings of the project. Second, the amount of power generated was below projected figures because the preliminary feasibility studies had underestimated the extent of sub-surface leakages from the reservoir (IRN 1999). By January 2001, Daewoo's financial troubles at home had forced it to look for new sources of financing and investors, with HSBC as the primary source of project finance.[15]

Serious problems also arose over the environmental consequences of BOOT hydro-power projects.[16] Environmental impact assessment (EIA) was seen by both the IFIs (see for example World Bank 1996a) and the Lao government as a way to deliver equitable benefits and compensate for the local costs of infrastructure development. However, the process of EIA in Laos' BOOT projects failed to meet these expectations for several reasons, not least of which was that conflicts of interest occurred when private developers were allowed to carry out their own EIA without independent review. For example, in the Theun Hinboun hydro-power project the developers utilised consultants with whom they had a commercial relationship. At Nam Theun 2, the company conducted its own EIA. In both cases, the developers directed the EIA to their advantage and externalised the costs of the project.

Second, profit considerations ensured that areas of potential impact were defined very narrowly for the purpose of EIA. In the Theun Hinboun project the assessed area was delimited so that it did not even include communities downstream of the dam. The Theun Hinboun Power Company (THPC), in which the Lao government holds a 60 per cent share, thereby minimised its contracted compensation package for affected areas. After the International Rivers Network (IRN) revealed numerous uncompensated impacts, and international NGOs[17] contested inadequate compensation plans, the company conceded that there was a need to assess downstream communities (IRN 1999). By the end of 2000, in response to external pressure from international NGOs, the THPC had released a ten-year mitigation and compensation programme costing US$2.7 million and a further US$1.9 million in conditional and contingent costs (THPC 2000).

A similar conflict of interest resulted in the Transfield-led Nam Theun 2 Electricity Consortium (NTEC), including its government partner Electricité du Lao which holds a 25 per cent equity stake, questioning whether the 4,500 villagers that resided at the dam site on the Nakay Plateau were in fact indigenous peoples. Because the project provided its financiers with a World Bank PRG, it had to comply with World Bank guidelines for EIA and the resettlement of indigenous peoples. International NGOs and the World Bank itself argued that the residents did fit the Bank's criteria[18] for an indigenous people, and therefore required culturally appropriate resettlement. A six-month stand-off ensued in the first half of 1996 between NTEC and the World Bank before a satisfactory agreement was reached. However, that was not the end of the matter. Another debate arose over the World Bank's suggestion that if NTEC could come up with a 'better off'[19] situation for the resettled, Nam Theun 2 would show the world that a BOOT hydro project could be both efficient and equitable (World Bank 1995b). Aware that making the resettled 'better off' might escalate costs, NTEC and its Lao government partner argued that the Bank's objective violated Lao equity concerns because it meant only the affected peoples were to be made better off (Wyatt 1996).

Intervention to secure the control of foreign hydro-power BOOT companies and the Lao government over watersheds has also eroded the traditional, collective rights of local communities to common pool resources. Some observers have labelled hydro-power development in Laos a 'rent a river' scheme (Usher 1997). Resource rights in the Lao PDR are ambiguous (Hirsch 1996). Much of the land and many resources within watersheds are classified as being owned by the nation and managed by the state. However, at the local level in remote watersheds, customary tenure and resource management systems have continued to exist and exert considerable informal authority (Kirk 1996). In 1995, much debate ensued about how customary tenure over forests could be formalised. One outcome of that debate was the production of a draft[20] regulation that detailed the conditions under which customary rights to forests could be exercised, and the conditions under which they could be extinguished. Article 7 of that draft regulation states that where the highest interests of the state, or 'the national interest' are at stake, customary rights could be extinguished. Further, it explicitly states that the development of hydro-power, communications and transportation are judged to be in 'the national interest'.

Nam Theun 2 provides an illustration of how the relatively short-term interests and newly bestowed property rights of BOOT investors, sanctioned by the draft national regulation, have taken precedence over the interests, pre-existing property relations and resource management systems of local communities. The 4,500 people who lived in the area inundated by the dam not only lost their tenure over productive agricultural land, under early proposals they would also have lost their customary rights to harvest non-timber products, fruits and food plants in the forests upstream. The watershed is also a National Biodiversity Conservation Area which is classified as being of international significance by the International Union for the Conservation of Nature (IUCN). During initial resettlement consultations in 1996, villagers were told that Nam Theun 2 was a matter of 'the national interest' and NTEC was therefore justified in denying local communities access to the watershed (Wyatt 1996). Later, the IUCN, acting as consultants to NTEC, brought a more integrated perspective to the watershed management plan. Local communities would be allowed to exercise limited use-rights to the forests in the watershed. However, NTEC-employed rangers would monitor and restrict their access. Technically, the state still owned the land but, in return for rents, it had transferred use-rights to the land to be inundated and the upstream watershed, including the National Biodiversity Conservation Area, to the BOOT developers for the concession period. Local institutions regulating common pool resources were to be eliminated in order to allow exploitation and development of the watershed by foreign investors.

Conclusion

In Vietnam and Laos, similar aims and similar material constraints led to the search for alternative ways to provide collective goods such as economic infrastructure. Partly as a result of the support given to the BOOT concept by the World Bank and ADB, both countries looked upon this as an attractive option for financing infrastructure development. But there are important differences in the regulatory regimes that each country established to oversee BOOT projects. In consequence, there are also important differences in the extent to which these projects are providing collective goods that are in 'the national interest', or that are in the interest of other countries, industries and groups in Southeast Asia.

The intention of the Vietnamese government was always to regulate the foreign BOT investor in a way that would, first and foremost, protect Vietnamese interests. The government promulgated a set of explicit regulations, Decree 87-CP and Decree 62/1998/ND-CP, to control BOT projects. Supported by the pro-BOT ministries such as MPI and on the advice of the IFIs, it also put in place policies and processes that were intended to satisfy investor needs. No doubt, BOT decrees sometimes conflicted with other national codes. However, the main points of contention between the government and foreign participants in BOT projects – sovereign guarantees, dispute arbitration and pricing of the inputs and products of BOT projects – clearly related to divergent notions of what actually constituted an 'equitable' sharing of benefits, costs and risks.

The impasse over guarantees to fix foreign exchange rates illustrates the contradictory interests at play in BOT. As Handley (1997) pointed out, and as happened in Indonesia (Gray and Shuster 1998), government guarantees of foreign exchange rates leave governments carrying risks that the private sector will not tolerate. The Vietnamese government was acutely aware of the risks it would incur from providing such a guarantee, including the possibility that it would restrict its ability to adjust Vietnam's fixed exchange rate in response to changing macro-economic conditions. Yet instead of applauding the prudent nature of the government's approach, the IFIs continued to push for legal changes that would support such guarantees. Responding to the continuing World Bank Policy Advisory Service on BOT, one prominent foreign legal practitioner lamented, 'the Vietnamese do not need further capacity building, they know very well how BOT works'.[21]

Indeed, as the World Bank's provision of PRGs demonstrates, the IFIs have supported the involvement of multinational corporations and international capital in the construction of economic infrastructure in countries such as Vietnam, even where that support appears to run counter to their own argument that market competition delivers efficiencies, and where it imposes unacceptable burdens of risk on national governments. Given the Bank's promotion of foreign, private finance and construction and its long-standing neglect of schemes involving domestic financing and provision, cynical observers might suspect that the Bank's major aim is to facilitate international business rather than national development. Moreover, the Bank's argument that foreign BOT investment speeds up technology transfer patently ignores the fact that domestic finance is equally capable of importing technology. In fact, the IFIs might provide better assistance by strengthening the development of domestic capital markets so as to support the role of Vietnamese investors in the construction of economic infrastructure.

Clearly, the World Bank advisers underestimated the potential political costs of BOT and the degree to which the concept might be resisted by powerful domestic industries. Rising electricity pricing drew attention, and opposition, to what many Vietnamese viewed as ideologically suspect policies. The state-owned media's reporting of the successes of the domestically invested power industry indicated that in pursuit of its vision of 'the national interest', the Vietnamese government was willing to contemplate other approaches to infrastructure financing. This played into the hands of EVN, which itself was ambivalent about BOT because foreign investment potentially diluted its role in Vietnam's power generation industry. Certain sections within the ministry controlling EVN always espoused the view that BOT should be the investment form of last resort. The impasse over guarantees and electricity prices in the late 1990s provided EVN with an opportunity to cancel negotiations over three of the most high-profile foreign BOT power projects. Similarly, VINACOAL's refusal to concede in price negotiations with Oxbow demonstrated that powerful local players had begun to jostle for position in the BOT market. While those industries exert considerable clout, however, it is by no means certain that they can raise enough capital domestically to invest in massive projects.

Laos chose not to implement formal regulations for BOOT. In part, that was because it lacked the technical capacity to do so. More importantly, however, the government of Laos chose to take an equity share in BOOT projects in the hope that it could regulate from within the boardrooms of the project companies. It negotiated and monitored BOOT projects on a flexible case-by-case basis, and administered them in an *ad hoc* way. By the end of the 1990s, there was a recognition by some members of the bureaucracy, particularly within the Ministry of Industry and Handicrafts, that some early deals had little commercial or technical merit. It was also becoming clear to some members of the government that the lack of enforceable regulations had led to conflicts of interests and compromised EIAs. The failure of the government of Laos to systematically regulate the BOOT industry meant that the government's vision of BOOT hydro-power projects serving 'the national interest' was being subverted by the pursuit of profit by both foreign investors and government stakeholders.

A second important difference between Vietnam and Laos is that while BOT in Vietnam was being used by the government specifically to facilitate the construction of economic infrastructure for domestic use, in Laos BOOT projects played a dual-purpose role. Certainly, the government hoped they would facilitate domestic development by providing localised physical infrastructure, rural electrification and jobs in some areas. But the government's primary aim was to earn foreign exchange that would be used to finance the national budget. As this chapter has demonstrated, that aim has not always been achieved.

The aims of the IFIs and other development agencies such as the Mekong River Commission were not the same as those of the Laos government. They viewed Laos' hydro-power primarily as an export industry that served regional and industry needs, especially in Thailand. The benefits for Thailand are obvious. It has had energy delivered to its industries with private sector efficiency at competitive prices. At the same time, it has avoided the investment risks of hydro-power and the social and environmental costs of building hydro-power in its own territory. The BOOT industry in Laos was able to repatriate its profits and international financiers accumulated capital. In short, BOOT-financed infrastructure in Laos largely served the interests of the region, Thailand in particular, and of a host of international investors and consultants.

Sadly, the financial risks and the social and environmental costs of those BOOT projects were internalised in Laos, one of the poorer countries of East and Southeast Asia. In cases such as Transfield's construction of the Tha Ngon bridge and the Houay Ho hydro-power project, BOOT agreements have transferred private risks and debts to the public sector and created hardship for the Laos government, consumers and communities. At Theun Hinboun, in the context of a weak regulatory regime, BOOT investors and sections of the government have siphoned away most of the benefits from infrastructure development, leaving local communities to bear the costs. Villagers' ability to create and utilise collective goods such as cheap ferry services have been effaced in order to ensure profits for international investors. Traditional community rights to common pool resources such as fisheries, agricultural land and forests are being extinguished in 'the national interest' and transferred to international corporations. Local authority structures and practices that regulated human extraction from rich ecosystems have been eroded, and the resources that offered immeasurable benefits not just to contemporary communities, but also to future generations, have been converted into a single resource, hydro-power, that is being exported.

This examination of BOOT projects in Vietnam and Laos demonstrates that definitions of 'the national interest' and assessments of the benefits of collective goods are sensitive to scale. The idea that a collective good is for the use of a particular group of users means that the good has both inclusive and exclusive properties. The boundaries that determine inclusion and exclusion are not immutable, and may be altered by the reform of regulatory systems or the design and implementation of new legislation. While BOOT-financed economic infrastructure is considered to be a collective good that has helped to achieve the intrinsic good of development at one end of the scale, in international and regional arenas, in the absence of effective regulation it sometimes has been a destroyer of livelihoods and customs at the other, local, end of the scale. Indeed, where the concept has been implemented according to the prescripts of the IFIs, it has created outcomes that are the antithesis of the nationalist developmental aims of governments in transitional Southeast Asian economies.

Notes

1 Independence and freedom from foreign domination is a powerful motivator in the national psyche. The populace is reminded of the importance of these two tenets of its national life through the national motto 'Independence-Freedom-Happiness'.

2 Interview: Nguyen Minh Tu, Director, Economic Management Policy Research, Central Institute For Economic Management, Ministry of Planning and Investment, Hanoi, 15 January 1999.

3 All three forms are subject to the same law and regulations. However, this paper focuses only on the BOT form, since it is the only form of interest to foreign investors to date.

4 Interview: Nguyen Minh Tu, Director, Economic Management Policy Research, Central Institute For Economic Management, Ministry of Planning and Investment, Hanoi, 15 January 1999.

5 This round-table included twenty-five government officials, seventeen private sector executives and five multilateral organisation representatives (IFC 1996).

6 Interview: Peter Block, Senior Associate, Phillips Fox, Hanoi, 22 April 1999.

7 Interview, 27 July 1998.

8 Phu My 2.2 is the first project in any sector in Vietnam that has been offered the use of the PRG.
9 Interview: Nguyen Minh Tu, Director, Economic Management Policy Research, Central Institute For Economic Management, Ministry of Planning and Investment, Hanoi, 15 January 1999.
10 Personal communication: Anil Malhotra, Regional Energy Adviser, World Bank, Hanoi, 8 June 2000.
11 200 kip higher than the ferry charge for a motorbike and 500 kip for a car (approximately 720 kip to US$1 at the time).
12 Interview: Math Sounmala, Acting Director General, Ministry of Communications, Transport, Post and Construction, Vientiane, 19 May 1999.
13 Hydro-power developments come under this ministry's jurisdiction through its electricity utility, Electricité du Lao (EdL) and the Hydropower Office.
14 Interview: Soukata Vichit, Director, Department of Environment, STEA, 21 February 1998.
15 Interview: In Jin Paik, Managing Director, Hoauy Ho Power Company, 16 February 2001.
16 In this paper, environmental impact assessment is taken to include social impact assessment.
17 There are no local NGOs in the Lao PDR since there is no legal basis for such organisations.
18 To be found in World Bank Operational Directive 4.20.
19 The World Bank criterion is actually 'no worse off'.
20 Order on Customary Rights and the Use of Forest Resources: Draft no. 5, 4 April 1995.
21 Personal communication: Peter Block, Senior Associate, Phillips Fox, Hanoi, 7 June 2000.

8

SOCIAL POLICIES AS COLLECTIVE GOODS

Lesson from Malaysia and Singapore

M. Ramesh

The intellectual and political outlook toward statutory social welfare – here broadly understood to include education, health, housing and income maintenance – has come almost full circle in the last hundred years. Until the end of the nineteenth century, these were seen as private goods that individuals consumed according to what they could afford. It was only in the twentieth century, especially in the post-World War II years, that liberals and conservatives alike began to accept that these services had collective goods characteristics which meant welfare would be consumed less than was desirable for the society as a whole, unless the state intervened to increase its supply.

The widespread acceptance of this principle forms the foundation for what is called the welfare state. The view suffered a setback in the 1980s, following the election of governments in some Western countries which attacked extensive state involvement in the provision of social welfare for leading to economic and moral ruin. Many intellectuals, led by neo-classical economists, expressed the same sentiments in more formal terms and argued for a roll-back of state involvement in social affairs. The critics found empirical evidence for their position following the demise of central planning in Eastern Europe. The Soviet experience was contrasted with that of the Asian newly industrialising economies (NIEs), which were said to have grown rapidly by maintaining slim social programme commitments except in the area of primary education (see for example World Bank 1993). The governments in the NIEs, for their part, renewed their commitment to avoiding the emergence of the welfare state in their country.

Characterising social policies in East and Southeast Asia in minimalist terms is, however, misleading. A closer examination shows that no such generalisation is possible, as public policies vary greatly across the region and across sectors, ranging from heavy intervention to leaving vital functions entirely to the private sector. This chapter compares the role of the state in four key social policy areas – education, health, housing and income maintenance – in two rather similar countries, Malaysia and Singapore. The comparison shows that in both countries the level of intervention is high in the areas of education, health and housing, and low in that of income maintenance. Examination of policy outcomes shows that the policies have been most successful in instances when the governments have directly provided a service rather than merely funded its provision by the private sector. The finding undermines the currently fashionable 'liberal' view that governments would be better off promoting the private sector to assume social policy functions currently performed by the state.

When we speak of state intervention in a policy sector, we are referring to two separate but related aspects: provision and financing. The state may be involved in either, neither, or both, as shown in Table 8.1.

When the state is involved in both providing and financing a service (top left quarter of the table) there is no role for the private sector, as the state provides it at its own facilities, largely by its own employees, from funds drawn from the public exchequer. Examples of the arrangement include income assistance, healthcare, education and housing provided by the government without requiring payment by the recipient. The fact that the arrangement does not permit competition among suppliers, and services are delivered by the bureaucracy, which is viewed by many as being inherently inefficient, makes the arrangement vulnerable to attack. Critics also claim that wholly public provision and financing wastes scarce public resources unless the benefits are targeted only at the needy (van de Walle and Kimberley 1996). For the defenders of the arrangement, it promotes efficiency because of the economy of scale it allows in production of services. It is also claimed to promote equity, especially if the tax system is progressive, in that it collects taxes according to income and distributes them according to need. The social solidarity that results from meeting the needs of those unable to generate sufficient income to pay for essential services is said to be another beneficial by-product of this arrangement.

Table 8.1 Public and private provision and financing

| | *PROVISION* | |
FINANCING	*Public*	*Private*
Public	Government provision and funding. Free at point of use.	Private provision of publicly funded functions
Private	Private payment for publicly required or publicly provided service	Purchase of service either directly from private supplier or indirectly through private insurance

Source: adapted from World Health Organisation (1993: 13).

When the state is involved in neither providing nor financing a service (bottom right quarter of the table), the functions are undertaken by private agents acting as suppliers and consumers. Private education, housing and healthcare not subsidised or prescribed by the government and fully paid for by individuals are instances of such arrangements, as are private pension and health insurance funds. This is an efficient mechanism for providing a service, provided the rather stringent conditions for an efficient market, including full competition, are met. Mainstream neo-classical economists recommend this arrangement when dealing with goods or services that are excludable and divisible, that is to say, private goods. The self-serving activities of consumers and suppliers are believed not only to deliver best prices (static efficiency) but also to promote innovation (dynamic efficiency) whereby suppliers are constantly launching new products to meet customer demand and devising new ways of reducing production costs. There are, of course, a host of market failures which make it difficult for the expected efficiencies to be realised: monopoly, lack of competing buyers and sellers of identical goods, high entry barriers, public good characteristics, and so on. The political unacceptability of distribution based on the market alone – whereby benefits accrue in proportion to factor ownership, thus perpetuating inequality – also reduces the arrangement's political appeal. The state may correct these failures through appropriate intervention, though in reality this is a more difficult task – for technical and political reasons – than may appear.

Once the state decides to intervene in a social welfare goods market without wanting to produce the welfare good directly and finance it entirely, it may do so either in the realm of production or financing. If the state provides a service but requires recipients to totally or partially pay for it, we have a situation as in the bottom left quarter of the table. Examples of the arrangement include social insurance schemes to which both employers and employees contribute, user charges levied at public hospitals, tuition fees charged by public schools and rents charged for public housing. The fact that consumers must pay is believed to lead them to restrain consumption. It also enables the state to recover a portion of the cost of providing a service, thus releasing funds for other purposes. On the down side, the charge may put the service beyond the reach of those without the means, thus defeating the purpose of state intervention. Moreover, setting an optimal charge is a complex task, compounded by the fact that social policies are intended to serve multiple objectives.

If, on the other hand, the state pays for a service provided by private suppliers, we have the situation represented in the top right quarter of Table 8.1. The arrangement is recommended by economists for providing desirable social goods that the market would not voluntarily provide in adequate quantities, because it ensures adequate supply while maintaining competition among suppliers, which not only reduces cost but also gives consumers choice. The proponents of this arrangement, however, typically ignore the cost of maintaining multiple suppliers in areas such as health, where competition leads to higher rather than lower costs because of information asymmetries. The arrangement also involves significant adverse consequences for equity, because of the potential of schools and hospitals located in prosperous neighbourhoods to attract better pupils and more well-off patients from surrounding areas, thus undermining the competitiveness of the suppliers in poorer neighbourhoods. Moreover, monitoring and enforcing compliance on private suppliers receiving public funds involves significant administration costs, which may well make the arrangement more expensive than when the state produces and provides the service directly.

The four alternative arrangements are thus not entirely equivalent in their operation and effects. In this chapter we will see that social welfare policies in both Malaysia and Singapore have been moving away from government-provided to privately provided services since the mid-1980s. While the implications of the shift are yet to be fully comprehended, preliminary evidence suggests that this may be undermining their past achievements and eventually will worsen social conditions in the region.

Provision

The level of state intervention in social affairs in both Malaysia and Singapore increased substantially in the final days of British rule, and the trend continued after independence, until it began to be wound back in the mid-1980s. As the Malaysian government's planning document put it: 'During the Seventh Plan period, the privatisation program will be accelerated, covering projects ... in the services sector, particularly, education and training, health services, and research and development' (Malaysia 1996b: 199). The level of involvement in some areas, however, continues to be substantial despite efforts to reduce it. Intervention in both countries has taken the form of direct provision by the state, without necessarily financing it, in an arrangement resembling the scenario represented in the bottom left quadrant in Table 8.1.

Education in both Malaysia and Singapore – unlike their counterparts in South Korea, Indonesia and the Philippines – is provided primarily in the public sector. Approximately three quarters of primary and secondary school pupils in Singapore, and a yet higher proportion in Malaysia, attend public schools. The proportions are even larger at higher education level, although it should be noted that 30,000–60,000 Malaysian and about 15,000 Singaporean students go abroad for study every year (Selvaratnam 1994: 47; Yee and Lim 1995: 186). The large number of students going abroad is the result of a shortage of university places in their home country, as only 40 per cent of applicants to universities in Malaysia and 50 per cent in Singapore are accepted. Of the limited places at universities available in

Malaysia, close to 75 per cent are reserved for the Malays ('Bumiputras') as part of the government's affirmative action policy (Pong 1993: 247).

Following the economic recession of the mid-1980s, and the widespread market liberalisation that followed, the Malaysian government began to reduce its involvement in economic and social affairs. The Seventh Malaysia Plan clearly expressed its commitment to 'encouraging more private sector investment in education and training to complement public sector efforts' (Malaysia 1996b: 322). The objective was sought to be realised through award of greater autonomy to private schools, and promotion of the domestic education industry by encouraging twinning, distance learning, and credit transfer arrangements with foreign universities. In 1998, all public universities were 'corporatised', which enables them to operate as private institutions, though they continue to receive public subsidies and are not expected to make profits. The long-term policy goal is to promote an indigenous, and largely private, education industry attracting students from the entire region.

In Singapore, the government has been promoting elite schools in both private and public sectors by according them greater operational autonomy and additional funds, on the grounds that such measures reward effort and promote innovation (Tan 1998). At the higher education level, the Singapore government recently established the Singapore Management University which, when enrolment commenced in mid-2000, was run as a private firm. Despite its 'corporatisation', the university receives significant public funds.

A remarkable feature of the health systems in the two countries is the concentration of hospitals, the most expensive component of healthcare, in the public sector: 75 per cent of all hospital beds in Malaysia and 79 per cent in Singapore. However, in recent years both governments have been trying to reduce the size of the public sector and correspondingly expand the private sector. The Malaysian government's privatisation plan identifies health as one of the target areas, and it is projected that the size of the private sector will equal that of the public sector by early in the twenty-first century (Malaysia 1996b: 533). In Singapore, too, the government is involved in expanding the private sector and making the public sector operate more like its private counterpart. Since the mid-1980s, the government has 'corporatised' public hospitals and increased out-of-pocket payments for health services (Phua 1990). In recent years the government has been working towards implementing the Health Review Committee's report of 1992, which argued that the government's share in providing healthcare was 'unduly large' and recommended a greater role for private hospitals. To roll back the public sector, the committee proposed that the government build hospitals and lease them to private hospital and charitable organisations, or give grants to private hospitals that provide services to the poor. The report also suggested that competition among providers coupled with government control would maintain efficiency in both the public and private sector.

As a part of its policies to improve Malays' living conditions, the Malaysian government increased its involvement in the provision of housing in the early 1970s. However, its achievement in building low-cost housing was rather modest, despite the fact that it spent huge resources. Recognising its failings, the government began to shift its housing responsibility to the private sector in the 1990s. As the government's planning document confirmed, 'The private sector will play an increasingly important role in meeting the housing needs of the population' (Malaysia 1996b: 573). As a part of the shift, the government began to require private developers to reserve 30 per cent of their new housing stock for low-income families in order to receive building approval. While this appears to be an ingenious way of directing the private sector to use profits from expensive homes to cross-subsidise low-income housing, in practice it has been a failure as builders find clever ways of getting around the requirement. As a result, Malaysia is now in a situation where low-cost housing is being neglected by both public and private sectors. The private sector is clearly the dominant provider of housing in Malaysia, as only 30 per cent of all housing is built by the state (*New Straits Times* 1998: 9). What is particularly unfortunate is that there is a glut of expensive housing in urban areas at the same time as there is unmet demand for inexpensive housing.

The importance accorded public housing in Singapore is perhaps unparalleled in the world. Almost 90 per cent of the Singaporean population lives in public housing. The government owns all vacant land on the island and has the statutory authority to acquire privately held land at below market prices. It acquits its vast responsibilities in the sector through the Housing Development Board (HDB), which is in charge of all aspects of housing on the island: the agency develops land, builds and maintains houses, and finances their purchase through inexpensive loans. The centralised administration in Singapore is unlike Malaysia, where the responsibility for public housing is split between different levels of governments and across different bureaucratic agencies which are often at loggerheads. The distortionary, and often contradictory, regulations they impose on the housing industry is cited as the most important reason for the high housing prices in Malaysia (Malpezzi and Mayo 1997: 388).

In contrast to their heavy involvement in the social policy sectors discussed so far, Malaysia and Singapore maintain a rather light intervention in the provision of income maintenance. The notable exception is the treatment accorded to government employees. Both countries have two separate income maintenance systems: one for state employees and another for the rest, with the former providing far more generous benefits. In Malaysia, the full monthly pension for civil servants is set at one half of the last drawn monthly salary, and eligible dependents are offered survivors' benefits in the event of the member's death during employment or retirement. In 1994, pension payments cost the government M$2.018 billion, or nearly 8 per cent of its total current expenditures (Malaysia 1995). The pension scheme for civil servants in Singapore is even more generous: the scheme provides tax-free monthly pension equivalent to two thirds of the last-drawn monthly salary to those who complete at least 400 months in public service (*Straits Times* 1994: 1). In 1996, the scheme paid out S$11.5 million to 17,000 pensioners each month.

Neither governments directly provide income protection to private sector workers. These are covered by a provident fund, which is a compulsory savings arrangement whereby employees and employers contribute a set percentage of salary to the former's account and the accumulated balance is returned to the member at a specified date. In Malaysia the scheme is called the Employee Provident Fund (EPF), whereas in Singapore it is called the Central Provident Fund (CPF). Both EPF and CPF compulsorily cover all private sector employees, except those in informal, domestic, casual and seasonal employment. The exclusions leave out a lot of people, as active contributors form only half of the labour force in Malaysia and two thirds in Singapore (Asher 1994).

The public assistance schemes that exist in both countries are largely for the aged or sick poor. They are subject to severe means tests and the amount of benefits they bestow is small. Unfortunately, little is known about the schemes and the profile of their beneficiaries.

Financing of social programmes

Turning to the financing of social policies, we find that the governments are not as tight-fisted as popular characterisation suggests, as shown in Table 8.2 below.

Table 8.2 Share of government expenditure on social policies, annual average, per cent

	Gross domestic product			Total government expenditure		
	1972–9	1980–9	1990–5	1972–9	1980–9	1990–5
Malaysia						
Education	5.63	5.88	5.39	22.45	19.20	20.03
Housing	0.17	1.79	1.55	0.69	5.97	5.79
Health	1.68	1.52	1.46	6.71	4.82	5.49
Income maintenance	0.77	1.25	1.47	3.11	3.99	5.51
TOTAL	8.25	10.44	9.87	32.96	33.98	36.82
Singapore						
Education	3.00	4.73	4.08	16.63	18.62	21.89
Housing	1.27	2.09	1.18	6.86	7.99	6.59
Health	1.45	1.42	1.12	8.05	5.72	6.30
Income maintenance	0.28	0.37	0.53	1.56	1.47	3.04
TOTAL	6.0	8.61	6.91	33.1	33.8	37.82

Source: World Bank 1998a.

As a percentage of GDP, the Malaysian government spends considerably more on social programmes than its Singaporean counterpart. However, in both countries the social programmes' share of the total has decreased in recent years, rather substantially in the case of Singapore. When we look at individual policies, Table 8.2 shows that education receives by far the largest share, followed by housing and health, with income maintenance receiving the smallest share. In fact, the 0.5–1.5 per cent of GDP spent by the two governments on income maintenance is a fraction of the 9.2 per cent spent on average in the OECD countries (World Bank 1994a: 358). The proportion of total public expenditures devoted to social policies, except for income maintenance and health, in Malaysia and Singapore compares favourably with the levels found in the industrialised countries (Mundle 1998). Their low expenditure on social security – which is usually the most expensive item for governments in the industrialised world – is hardly surprising considering that their population is still young, though ageing rapidly.

Public spending on education as a percentage of GDP in both Malaysia and Singapore is among the highest in the world. More significantly, their public expenditure on education as a percentage of GDP grew when the size of their economies was expanding at a remarkable rate. In recent years, however, the share of GDP spent on education has shrunk somewhat, albeit from a very high level. Of total government expenditure on education in the mid-1980s, Malaysia devoted 36 per cent to the primary level, 34 per cent to the secondary level, and 26 per cent to higher education (UNESCO 1995). The corresponding figures for Singapore were 29, 36 and 31 per cent respectively. Malaysia charges virtually no tuition fees at any level of education, whereas Singapore levies no tuition at primary or secondary level, but recovers 25 per cent of the universities' operating costs through tuition fees.

In the area of healthcare, Malaysia has a system of financing which includes varying levels of user charges in public hospitals, government grants, some private insurance and compulsory savings, and substantial out-of-pocket expenses. Among users of government facilities, 70 per cent received free services at the government's expense, and only 23 per cent paid out of their own pockets. According to official estimates, the government pays M$14–21 towards hospital care for every dollar paid by the patient (*New Straits Times* 1995: 11).

Healthcare financing arrangements in Singapore are complex and consist of four mechanisms: direct expenditure by the government from its general revenues, out-of-pocket private expenditure, Medisave, and public (Medishield) and private insurance. Of these, only the first is a purely public source of finance. The government subsidises between 20 and 80 per cent of the cost of treatment in public hospitals, depending on the class of hospital care chosen. Those unable to pay even the 20 per cent of costs of treatment in the lowest (C) class wards may request a partial or total waiver. In 1993, the government established a modest Medifund scheme to provide public assistance toward medical costs subject to stringent means test.

Since 1984, Singapore has had Medisave, which is a compulsory saving plan that sets aside 7–8 per cent of one's monthly income, depending on age, to pay towards hospital care of the account holder and his/her immediate family. Recognising the limitations of Medisave in meeting the costs of treating certain illnesses, in 1990 the government established Medishield, which is a privately funded and voluntary insurance scheme for specified catastrophic illnesses. Insurance claims are subject to severe restrictions, including an age limit of seventy-five, and deductible and co-insurance payment by the insured. Because of the restrictions, Medishield accounts for only 0.7 per cent of Singapore's total expenditure on health (Prescott and Nichols 1997: 10). Medisave and Medishield represent the government's objective of shifting the primary burden of healthcare financing from the state to individuals and families as far as possible.

Thus, while governments in both Malaysia and Singapore are extensively involved in the provision of healthcare, it is financed largely from private sources. Of total (both public and private) health expenditures, the government's share is 44 per cent in Malaysia and only 25 per cent in Singapore (Aw and Low 1997: 60–1). Total health expenditure in the two countries is only about 3 per cent of GDP, which is below the 5 per cent that the World Health Organisation recommends for the developing countries, and considerably lower than the average of 8 per cent spent in the OECD countries.

As a percentage of GDP as well as total government expenditure, public expenditure on income maintenance in both Malaysia and Singapore is small, though growing gradually. Much of this expenditure is towards providing pensions to state employees because they are, as will be recalled from earlier discussion, the only ones who receive state-funded income maintenance. Private sector workers, in contrast, are looked after through compulsory savings schemes funded entirely from private contributions. The EPF is funded from contributions of 11 per cent of wages by employees and 13 per cent by employers, whereas CPF's contribution rate is 20 per cent of wages each by employer and employee. Because of the substantial contribution rates, the schemes have accumulated huge reserves: EPF's total fund size was M\$86.76 billion (46.72 per cent of GDP) in 1995 and the CPF's was S\$72.56 billion (54.71 per cent of GDP) in 1996.

In the area of housing, Singapore spent a considerably larger share of GDP and total government expenditure than Malaysia until the late 1980s, but the positions were reversed in the 1990s. In overall terms, however, both countries reduced the share of total public spending they devoted to housing during the 1990s. In Singapore, the main source of housing finance is the CPF, which allows members to use funds in their account to make down payments and service housing loans, which itself is largely borrowed from the HDB at an interest rate slightly lower than the market rate. It is estimated that 70 per cent of CPF members owning private properties have used CPF to finance their purchases (*Business Times* 1997). While EPF members too can use their provident fund to pay for housing, the conditions are more restrictive. Direct expenditure by the Singapore government is relatively small and largely directed towards developing housing infrastructure and providing low-cost housing, which is rented or sold at subsidised prices.

Policy outcomes

Both countries have had exemplary education policies at the primary and, to a lesser extent, secondary education levels. In Malaysia, an aggressive school-building programme, coupled with automatic promotion of pupils up to grade nine, meant the completion rate at primary education level more than doubled to 90 per cent in the 1970s. The improvement in educational performance was particularly spectacular for Malays, whose enrolment as well as completion rate began to exceed the rates for Indians and Chinese. No less impressive was the reduction in gender differentials in educational performance to a point where there is now almost no difference in the attainment levels of Malay boys and girls, though some differences remain among the non-Malays (Pong 1993: 247–8). Improvements in secondary enrolment were far less spectacular, as only 60 per cent of all children of relevant age were enrolled at this level in 1992, though this was a great improvement from 5 per cent in 1950 and 30 per cent in 1970. In 1992, 100 per cent of the relevant age group in Singapore was enrolled in primary schools and 70 per cent in secondary schools.

Both countries are poor performers at the higher education level, and their governments have done little to improve the situation. Only 8 per cent of the relevant age group in Malaysia and 22 per cent in Singapore attend higher education institutions. The shortage of university places has caused an acute shortage of skilled and technical personnel, the demand for whom has been high and growing because of rapid economic growth. As a result, those with tertiary qualifications in the two countries are able to command windfall salaries in labour markets, thus aggravating the wage disparities between university graduates and non-graduates.

Malaysia and Singapore have impressive health policy records, despite small expenditure in the area. Their populations' health status, which during the 1960s resembled those found in the developing world, now equals the levels found in the developed countries. Between 1960 and 1995, life expectancy at birth increased from 58 to 71 years in Malaysia and from 65 to 76 years in Singapore. Similarly, child (under the age of five) mortality in Malaysia decreased from 106 to 14 per 1,000 births between 1960 and 1995, whereas it declined from 47 to 6 in Singapore over the same period (World Bank 1998a).

The reasons for the two countries' low healthcare costs include a relatively young population – 94–6 per cent of the population is under sixty-five years of age – which tends to consume fewer healthcare services. Strong family support for the sick, which reduces the duration of hospitalisation, is perhaps another reason. Malaysia and Singapore also stand out as countries that placed heavy emphasis on public health and sanitation, and are now reaping the benefits in terms of reduced curative healthcare.

The extensive direct provision of healthcare by the state in both countries has played a more vital role in keeping costs down than is usually acknowledged. The public sector is able to price its services lower not just because of government subsidies, but also because of its centralised administration which keeps costs down. The governments' tardiness in purchasing the latest technology, coupled with their lack of emphasis on accommodation and service-related frills, have a similar affect on the containment of costs. More significantly, as the dominant supplier, the public sector serves as a price benchmark which affects the private sector's pricing behaviour. The overall result of the extensive state involvement in healthcare provision is lower healthcare costs for society as a whole.

Despite the similar scale of resources devoted to housing in Malaysia and Singapore, the policies have generally been more effective in Singapore. Approximately 90 per cent of the Singaporean population lives in publicly built housing, with over 80 per cent of them owning their own homes. The availability of inexpensive loans from the HDB and the ability to use provident funds to service the loans account for Singapore's superior performance. Heavy state intervention in the forms of compulsory acquisition of land at below market prices and centralised construction which yielded economy-of-scale benefits also made housing more affordable on the island.

The Malaysian government has generally fallen well short of its low-income housing construction targets: it met only 49 per cent of its overall public housing target and 37 per cent of the low-income housing target set out in the Sixth Malaysia Plan (1991–5). The private sector too fell short of its target for low-cost housing by a significant margin, though it exceeded its target for high-cost housing. Even low-cost housing that was built by both the public and private sectors did not reach the targeted population because it was either too expensive or poorly located (Malpezzi and Mayo 1997: 375–6). The Malaysian government's policy of requiring private developers to reserve 30 per cent of the proposed units for low-income families may be an inexpensive strategy, but it has accomplished little in terms of actually providing low-cost housing.

Housing policies in both countries are, of course, used for purposes other than providing shelter. In Malaysia, local officials belonging to the ruling party play a prominent role in allocating public housing, a practice used to bolster support among voters. In Singapore, the government cites its success in housing the population as evidence of its administrative skills and compassion. Having housed much of the population, the government is now financing the upgrading of the older public housing stock in order to continue to reap political benefits (Rodan 1997). More remarkably, the government's success in providing affordable housing enabled it to keep a tight rein on wages, which was essential for the success of its export-oriented industrial policy (Castells *et al.* 1990). It has also used its position as a dominant supplier in the housing market to disperse different ethnic and income groups throughout the island, thus reducing the potential for emergence of ethnic and economic ghettos.

Malaysia and Singapore's greatest shortcoming lies in their system of income maintenance. Middle and senior employees of the state – including military, political and judicial officials – are the only ones for whom the state provides adequate income protection during retirement, even though they are not the lowest-paid workers.

While the provident fund is an effective means of promoting savings – though even this has been disputed (see Hussain 1995; Mackenzie *et al.* 1997) – it is of limited use as an income maintenance mechanism. It fails to protect those with inadequate or no provident fund balance because of unemployment or low wages during their working lives. In addition to the large proportion of the population excluded from the schemes, as noted earlier, the average size of the account in both countries is rather small because of severe disparities in wages. In 1996, the average size of the provident fund amount withdrawn at age fifty-five was M$19,501 in Malaysia and S$11,838 in Singapore (Asher 1998), amounts too small to provide adequate income during the twenty or so years that one may be expected to live after retirement. It is estimated a majority of those aged forty-five and above in Singapore would not be financially independent when they retire (*Straits Times* 1996: 31). The problem is especially acute for women, who live longer, have a lower income during their working lives, and typically have a small provident fund balance.

Conclusion

In this chapter we found that state involvement in social policy sectors in Malaysia and Singapore is considerably more elaborate and complex than the minimalist role often portrayed by commentators. Moreover, contrary to what is suggested by the recent mainstream economic literature, the policies have been more effective when the state is directly involved in their provision, as is the case in education and health in both countries and in housing in Singapore. Their experience offers valuable lessons in economic and social development for policy-makers and analysts.

The heavy state involvement in the provision and financing of primary and secondary education in both countries played a pivotal role in expanding enrolment, increasing completion rate and, more significantly in the case of Malaysia, reducing inter-ethnic disparities. However, the state in both countries has been less involved in expanding opportunities at the higher education level, which has resulted in a shortage of skilled personnel. That, in turn, has adversely affected industrial development and aggravated wage inequities. Those denied admission to universities in their home country are forced to seek education abroad, provided their family has the means to pay for it. The recent efforts to marketise and privatise education are likely to aggravate the problems unless they are accompanied by appropriate safeguards. As research on China and Thailand has shown, increasing returns to higher education is a significant cause of income-growing inequality in rapidly growing economies (Tamar and Walton 1998).

The extensive state involvement in the provision, but not financing, of healthcare has been exceptionally effective in providing quality care. By directly providing the vast majority of inpatient care in the public sector, both countries have made tremendous advances in their population's health status at a relatively low cost. The recent efforts to expand the role of the private sector are puzzling considering they already have an inexpensive healthcare system. While privatisation will no doubt reduce the governments' share of health expenditures, total healthcare costs are likely to increase because of the peculiarities of the healthcare market whereby private payment and competition increase rather than decrease cost, as the American experience shows all too well.

In housing, Singapore exemplifies the difference the state can make through well designed and comprehensive intervention, without necessarily spending a great deal. By controlling all aspects of housing production and distribution, the state has ensured that housing remains affordable, while still maintaining a thriving private sector with ample opportunity for profit. The result has been immense economic and social benefits for the population and political benefits for the government. The Malaysian experience, in contrast, shows that poor programme design coupled with large private sector involvement dilutes the benefits of relatively large public expenditure on housing. The shortcomings have been accentuated by the government's recent efforts to further reduce its involvement.

Income maintenance is the area of greatest weakness in both countries, in that the existing programmes are both inadequate and inequitable. On the one hand are the unemployed and the informally employed for whom there is virtually no income maintenance programme, and on the other, state employees who are covered by generous schemes funded from the public exchequer. In between are the private sector employees who are protected primarily by compulsory savings programmes which provide inadequate protection to those in low-wage employment, precisely the people who need income protection. If there is currently no crisis in the two countries' social security systems, it is only because they have low unemployment and young populations. However, this is changing rapidly because of population ageing and increased vulnerability to global economic instability. The projected rapid increase in the proportion of the aged, coupled with the fact that significant numbers of them will have insufficient income during their old age, will make it inevitable that they will turn to the state for support.

The social policy experience of the two countries affords valuable lessons regarding privatisation and marketisation efforts underway around the world. Policy-makers must be cautious about extending the sanguine lessons of privatising steel mills and deregulating telecommunications to social policy matters. They should at least be open to the possibility that in many circumstances direct government provision may be a more efficient as well as a more effective mechanism of production and delivery. By providing a service directly, the government may save on transaction costs that are involved when the service is provided by private suppliers. It may also be a cheaper form of intervention in situations where the government is able to realise the benefits of economies of scale. And the value of political benefits in the form of voter support that accrues to governments from providing adequate social policy goods should not be underestimated.

Private provision and public funding may represent the worst possible arrangement in situations when market competition is distorted, absent, and/or the government is unable to prevent rent-seeking by suppliers or to enforce cost-saving. Yet this is the direction in which many governments are heading, especially in the area of healthcare.

The findings in this chapter are consistent with those in the economic literature suggesting that state provision of some goods and services may be both more efficient and equitable. Stern (1991: 4–5) argues that the state should produce

> goods and services in which, for some reason, it has a comparative advantage. These include at least the provision of some infrastructural services, education and health, besides pure public goods. The reasons why the government may have a social cost-benefit advantage in the supply of these particular commodities has to do with the relative importance of market failures (e.g. externalities) *vis-à-vis* government failures (e.g. rent-seeking) in their markets.

In particular, it is shown that productive public investment can alleviate inequality of opportunity even if expenditures are uniformly distributed, rather than targeted at the poor.

Yet governments in the region – supported by mainstream economists, international economic agencies and business groups – continue to call for cutbacks in states' involvement in provision of social services. As the World Bank (1997d: 53) in its report on the role of the state argued: 'Most curative health care is a (nearly) pure private good – if the government does not foot the bill, all but the poorest will find ways to pay for care themselves'. Their researchers only needed to look at the case of Malaysia and Singapore to find out why these countries have been able to deliver high health status at a lower cost than, say, South Korea where the state plays a minimal role in the provision of clinical care. Comparative studies of OECD countries certainly confirm that healthcare systems based on centralised provision by the state, as in Britain, have lower overall costs (OECD 1990).

9

INDIVIDUALISATION OF
SOCIAL RIGHTS IN CHINA

Linda Wong

For several decades, the almost universal right to work and access public and collective goods buttressed claims about the superiority of Chinese socialism. Leninist theory legitimated the deduction of part of the common product for social benefits and services before primary distribution via wages and other public expenditures. The masses, though not holding the formal status of citizens, enjoyed extensive social and economic rights. Successive Chinese constitutions guaranteed the right to work, assurance of physical survival, and assistance in old age, sickness, disability and times of adversity. Access to primary education became free and near-universal in cities and towns, although compulsory education did not become law until 1995.

Of course, there were big gaps between rhetoric and practice. This is hardly surprising given the backwardness of the economy. Nor was the system one of equality and uniformity. Social welfare was better developed in cities than on the farms, and far more generous to labourers than to people unable to work. Nevertheless, the system of public ownership and central planning, comprehensive allocation through work units and communes, and societal policies like rationing, price subsidies and income equalisation combined to create a strong web of social and economic security. In the 1980s, Chinese leaders began to argue that the provision of these social rights was harmful to the country's transition to a market economy. This reassessment built on a new political rationality of welfare provision.

This chapter compares liberal concepts of public and collective goods with the system of welfare goods in China's socialist command economy. It examines the reconceptualisation of welfare goods under China's market system and the implications of this for people's social rights. Areas under review include what are commonly conceived as major components of welfare: employment, social security, social welfare, health, housing and education. I shall argue that the marketisation process involves a gradual curtailment and reconfiguration of welfare goods, or what Zsuzsa Ferge (1997) calls the 'individualisation' of the social rights of citizenship. Finally,

I shall comment on the prospects for China's provision of welfare goods in the foreseeable future.

Collective goods: classic liberal concepts and Chinese socialist versions

There are marked differences between the terminological referents, philosophical basis and structural origins of classic liberal and Chinese socialist notions of collective goods.

The classic interpretation of collective goods suggests that in contrast to private consumption goods, collective goods are produced by and on behalf of the public to tackle issues of concern to the commonweal. They are goods that the market cannot or will not provide because they do not generate profits and consumers do not possess the means for custom. As explained in the introduction to this book, the core features of collective goods centre on joint supply, non-excludability, non-rejectability and non-rivalry.

Thus, for classic scholars such as Samuelson (1954) and Musgrave (1958), collective goods become residual products *vis-à-vis* commercial supplies. When pragmatic considerations make their provision necessary, they will be supplied at a level deemed politically, economically and ideologically acceptable in accordance with what is defined as 'the public interest' (Cerny 1990; Olson 1965). Their supply has to be demanded by, and justified to, the public. The logic of democratic politics means that the level of public provision, as well as the financial arrangements and institutions that evolve to guide their production, can only be the outcomes of a political process (Downing and Thigpen 1993; Galston 1991). This is because, although citizens want collective goods, they usually want more than they are willing to pay for. Hence, demands for collective goods are politically determined via bargaining among political parties, pressure groups, bureaucratic interests, claimants, media spokespeople and moral entrepreneurs. The end results are often uneasy compromises.

Two caveats deserve mention. The first is that the character of public and collective goods is much more complex than classic liberal notions suggest. 'Impure' public goods are aplenty. There is so much public and private interplay in the provision of many goods that it is impossible to draw neat distinctions between public and collective, or collective and private goods (Rein and Rainwater 1986). A more meaningful distinction between private, collective and public goods might be whether or not the goods are allocated according to user pays or citizenship criteria. Public and collective goods are normally decommodified products, whose consumption is not solely conditional upon the consumer's ability to pay. The second point to bear in mind is that the boundary between public, collective and private good changes. The size and contents of the public sector are constantly in flux.

This elasticity often is linked to shifting political rationalities and economic circumstances.

Collective goods under Chinese socialism had some features in common with the classic concept of collective goods. What was more remarkable were their differences. Shared traits included public provision, joint supply, non-excludability and non-rejectability. However, collective goods under the system of public ownership were not residual products. Rather they stemmed from legitimate action by the state and made up *the totality of goods available in society*. The nationalisation of ownership and elimination of markets in the mid-1950s supposedly removed the basis of human exploitation and unfair distribution. Thence everything belonged to the commonweal, with the right to access available to all, barring 'enemies of the people'.

The right to collective survival began with assured participation in labour. Once the masses were linked to the work process, the door to welfare goods opened immediately. Nominated as the formal 'owners' of common assets, the Chinese masses theoretically were elevated to the enviable status of 'masters'. The comprehensive way in which labourers and their dependants came to rely on the collective, be it the proverbial work unit (*danwei*) in cities or production brigades and teams in the countryside, denied any traces of individual autonomy: material, political and cultural. Urban work units provided a complete range of life support as an occupational package. Apart from wages and pensions, they also supplied collective amenities like housing, healthcare, canteens, nurseries, schools, bathing halls, recreational facilities and the like. Workers also received subsidised goods and services through their work unit. In a way, provision of goods in kind was necessary to supplement the cash wage, which was set at exceedingly low levels. Moreover, the ban on self-initiated job transfers effectively bonded workers to their collective, and the abolition of markets meant that there were no alternative channels to satisfy consumption needs.

In addition to assuring labourers' social rights through work units, the state directly delivered welfare goods, including education, public hygiene, health, and environmental and cultural services, to urban populations. Education and health work were regarded as tasks of great political importance: the former for the making of socialist citizens and the latter for the reproduction of labour.

In rural areas, people's communes were created to handle local investment, production and distribution as well as to supply food and agricultural raw materials for industry. The buzzword for their economic function was local self-sufficiency. Equally vital was their role in local administration and social development (Parish and Whyte 1978; Shue 1988; Selden 1993). Communes provided and funded social goods like education, health and welfare. To reinforce local self-reliance and mutual help, peasants were taught not to compare their lot with their urban brethren or make demands on the state coffer, at least until such times as the social surplus was abundant enough for all to share.

The philosophical basis of socialist collective goods was underlined by the place of the state in Chinese society. The party-state was the leading force in socialist development. It not only steered the general course but also directed ideological control and micro-management. Its powers over the masses were absolute, although in theory its mandate came from the people. In the identification/construction of social need, as well as in the determination of how needs were to be met, senior cadres held sway. After the cautionary crushing of some early expressions of dissent, such as the anti-rightist movement in the late 1950s, the masses were wise enough to see what was good for them and support the government. As a result, the only justification needed for policy decisions was the assertion of their correct nature by state leaders and party members. Those debates that took place did so between party factions rather than between the state and exogenous social groups. The end result was the suffocation of civil society and total state domination. For more than thirty years political orthodoxy, rather than democratic contest, defined the public interest and the provision of collective goods.

In short, the ways in which decisions about the provision of collective goods in Chinese socialism were reached contrasted markedly with the non-stop demands, lobbying and appeals from interest groups that classic theorists said decided collective goods provision in capitalist democratic societies. Socialist collective goods departed from the classic definition of collective goods in philosophical terms, and their practical delivery was marked by quite different interpretations of the role of the state, the people and enterprises.

From the 1980s, the provision of public and collective goods by governments across the globe was subjected to widespread criticism. Neo-liberal ideologues argued that this resulted in government overload, over-consumption and inefficient provision (King 1975; King 1987; Gamble 1988). Critics on the left pointed to fiscal and legitimacy crises and the inherent contradictions of welfare capitalism (Offe 1984). Welfare state commitments, in particular, came under fire. (Mishra 1985; Pierson 1994; Esping-Andersen 1996). Whereas state welfare was once applauded for having assured living standards, health, education and income security, state welfare goods increasingly were said to encourage dependency and irresponsibility, undermine self-reliance and the willingness to work, breed passivity and sap incentives to save and invest. Another verdict was that universal welfare goods were simply unsustainable when growth slumps and labour market, family and demographic forces multiply demand to unprecedented levels. Hard evidence, however, was not easy to come by. Research findings were mostly ambiguous and contingent (Gough 1998).

Received wisdom in the 1980s and 1990s was that the remedy for state failure in the provision of public and collective goods was to denationalise state industries and public utilities, deregulate economies, reduce the public sector and introduce markets and quasi-markets to produce and allocate goods. Strategies designed to boost nations' global competitiveness abetted the sweep of marketisation (Esping-Andersen 1996; United Nations 1999). In states undergoing structural adjustment, usually at the behest of lenders like the International Monetary Fund and the World Bank, curtailment of state expenditures, including retrenchment in social transfers and benefits, was a key requirement.

The old socialist and welfare states had all assumed responsibility for welfare provision as a means of supporting social reproduction, reducing inequality and pursuing social solidarity and integration. Their assurance of strong social rights had become a major ingredient of national identities and models of citizenship. In contrast, the new paradigm prioritised economic growth as the ultimate objective of public policy, stressed market solutions to social problems and tolerated deprivation and inequality. Market-dominated provision individualised what had formerly been a collective entitlement (Ferge 1997) and eroded existential security and social solidarity. Social security had to be assured by individuals' purchase of freely chosen instruments. Not surprisingly, the costs involved in the withdrawal of state responsibility for the provision of public and collective goods fell heavily on the poor, the unemployed and marginalised groups who were most in need of protection.

Criticisms of state provision of welfare goods, and the advocacy of the panacea of privatisation, also took place in China. So, too, did some of the adverse consequences of state withdrawal from provision.

Chinese welfare goods: new political rationalities

The pre-reform system of social rights was far from perfect. The level of goods and services was basic. There was hardly any consumer choice. Service staff attended to customers grudgingly, heedless of their duty to 'serve the people'. The award system was also governed by hierarchy and privilege, with senior cadres getting the best and rarest goods, urban workers taking up most of state resources, peasants subsisting on local self-help and skeletal services, and people with no work and family treated little better than pariahs (Wong 1998a). Constant shortages of all kinds, notably housing, childcare, bathing facilities, hospital care, repair services and consumption goods, was a hallmark of the planned economy. Nevertheless, there were benefits. Within the same work unit or residential community, access to resources was more or less equal. Entitlement to employment, education, housing, healthcare and social security, at least for urbanites, was practically universal. Above all, there was a high degree of existential security.

The official verdict on the socialist state's provision of welfare took a U-turn after the reformers took charge. In the words of Deng Xiaoping, if socialism only meant poverty, what would be its appeal? Social levelling and egalitarianism had been useful in wiping out past injustices. However, the planned economy was increasingly blamed for keeping China backward. It was said to have been inefficient, wasteful, destructive of incentives and unable to respond to emerging needs. The goal of reformers was to enliven the economy by opening it to the outside world, diversifying ownership to tap new sources of capital and jobs, creating incentives and devolving powers to enterprise managers to respond to market signals. A critical insight was that markets and private ownership were not an anathema to socialism. They could perform equally well in capitalist and socialist systems.

Over the course of two decades, there was a pronounced shift towards introducing market principles in all spheres of public life, including the critical sector of social policy. The remoulding of social rights and welfare provision was premised on limited state provision, greater community production, individual responsibility for financing and consumption and the introduction of private markets in social goods.

The old notion of 'big state, small society' was said to have produced unbearable 'burdens' for the state in catering to the insatiable demands of the masses on the one hand, and directing a society that was passive and dependent on the other. On resource grounds alone, the state reckoned it could no longer afford to feed its subjects from the 'iron rice bowl'. Moreover, state failure had led to loss of confidence, which could only be redeemed by revising people's expectations. Heavy reliance on the state by enterprises was another problem. Firms were encouraged to stop behaving as appendages of central and local governments, and start producing goods and services to satisfy the taste of consumers and to make profits. At the same time, the state accepted the need to grant more autonomy to social groups, individuals and enterprise managers.

The critique of work unit welfarism was central to new conceptions of welfare. First, it was claimed that life tenure and workers' 'organised dependence' (Walder 1986) had prevented the mobility of labour, a key requirement of the market economy. Second, rewarding employees equally without regard for their performance had resulted in laziness and poor productivity. Third, state enterprise welfare was too costly. The bills for pensions, healthcare, housing and collective amenities accounted for one third to a half of total payroll, which reduced the competitiveness of state enterprises in comparison with private and village enterprises which offered none of these perks. These considerations rationalised a shift of employee welfare functions to other agencies under the policy to 'socialise' or share responsibility with private assurance firms, residents' organisations, non-profit agencies, families and philanthropic associations (Zhang 1990; Wong 1994; 1999).

The pluralisation of social responsibility was premised on a reassessment of state/society relationships. In the past, the state's monopoly of social product had necessitated its assurance of social rights. By the 1990s, the vast majority of goods and services were being allocated through markets. The distribution of national income belonging to individuals and enterprises had greatly increased, while the proportion taken by the state had declined. Many people had the ability and freedom to fund their own education or training, find their own jobs, choose their level of healthcare and decide where they wanted to live. The contraction of state functions was inevitable.

Greater contribution from communities and individuals was also expected. In the past, collective agriculture had financed the provision of local welfare by communes and brigades. In the new era, villagers had to bear the cost of running local schools, clinics, old age homes and relief schemes for the indigent. City neighbourhoods had run and funded amenities such as nurseries, baths, reading rooms and first aid stations. From the 1980s, state civil affairs departments urged residents' organisations to save state money, harness local initiative and resources and take over collective amenities run by besieged work units. It was assumed that individuals and families would provide for many of their own needs. User payment became a mark of responsibility in families' consumption of housing, education, pensions, healthcare and unemployment insurance.

While market supply of social goods was banished under the command economy, it was now seen as desirable and necessary. Given the government's shortage of revenue, the state pointed out it could no longer satisfy needs and wants in the quantities and of the quality required by the people. Market provision would not only augment the deficiency of collective goods, it would offer better choice, quality and efficiency. Although the wholesale commodification of goods like education, health and welfare would not be feasible, the state insisted that, henceforth, provision should be driven by consumer demands and providers should heed market signals. All in all, the above messages contributed to the emergence of a powerful pro-reform discourse. The rationality was explained, or rather pontificated, to the people through the usual channels. These included propaganda via the state-run media, patient explanation by party and government leaders and the mass organisations, and an avalanche of publications and films bent on selling the inevitability and the advantages of reform.

The new welfare rights paradigm

Labour rights

The right to work had once been guaranteed by the state to everyone who was capable of work, including women long used to exclusion from paid employment. Socialist China claimed to have wiped out unemployment, a common fate for working people in the capitalist system. The reality was rather more complex. There was substantial under-employment and un-employment.

To the post-Mao reformers, long-standing practices like the state's alloca-tion of life-long jobs and tied occupational benefits were anachronisms in a market economy. Firms, like humans, would face natural cycles of life and death. Unemployment would be inevitable. The interests of enterprises and the national economy would have to take precedence over the rights of labour: *the right to work no longer would be absolute*. Moreover, reformers reckoned that a growing economy would provide more jobs and more freedom to choose work compatible with individuals' interests and abilities. Therefore, the state no longer would accept responsibility for finding work for everyone. In 1994, the term 'unemployment' (*shiye*) came into the official lexicon (Wong and Ngok 1997). Unemployment benefits, *daiye baoxian*, were instituted in 1986, at the same time as enterprises were granted powers of open recruitment and dismissal.

Active labour market policies aimed at raising employability and easing job search were embraced. Access to labour markets for rural residents was entirely privatised. Labour relations became more diverse. State and collec-tive firms still adhered to past practices, as far as they were capable. The private sector, in the meantime, was exempted from requirements to provide welfare and, because of legal loopholes and lax administration, evaded many regulations designed to ensure workers' health and safety (C. K. Lee 1998). At the end of 1998, employees in the private sector and firms of other types of ownership made up 20.3 per cent and 10.5 per cent of all urban employees, while the state and collective sectors accounted for 56.9 per cent and 12.3 per cent of urban employment respectively (*China Labor Statistical Yearbook 1999*). In rural areas, almost all non-agricultural employment was in private, shareholding and collective firms.

However, old ideological commitments remained to haunt the reformers. In the 1980s, the state was very cautious in handling requests for bank-ruptcy, dismissal and redundancy. Enterprises had to cope with their labour problems as best they could. Further opening of the economy and wors-ening of operating conditions for the state sector in the 1990s caused an explosion in unemployment. At the end of 1997, roughly one tenth of employees in state-owned enterprises had been laid off informally (*xiagang*) and close to six million became openly unemployed (Wong 1998a). One year later, there were 6.5 million *xiagang* personnel who had not found work (*Hong Kong Economic Journal* 2000) and 5.71 million registered unemployed (*China Statistical Yearbook 1999*). The state responded by strengthening efforts to re-employ urban workers, setting minimum wages, instituting living allowance for redundant workers, refining unemployment insurance and expanding social relief (Wong 1998a). Nevertheless, unemployment became the number one social problem in urban China, creating grave

hardship, discontent and instability. The employment situation in the countryside was even more serious. Although more than 100 million people left
the countryside in search of temporary work, estimates of the remaining
surplus labour force ranged from 100 to 200 hundred million (Wong 1998a).
Regrettably, rural unemployment did not advance to the state agenda.

Social security

Social security became the responsibility of state enterprises in the early
1950s. Resources for social security came from the operating funds of firms;
there was no accumulation for pension and other benefits. Funding was not
a problem as long as the state remained the ultimate backer. That changed in
the 1980s, when direct state allocation to enterprises was gradually replaced
by bank loans. Increased social security and welfare costs for firms were
partly attributed to the growing numbers of pensioners. Besides, lack of
portability reduced worker mobility and increased the danger of default
when firms became insolvent. Such considerations convinced the state that
social security must be separated from enterprises and transferred to a
public agency. Henceforth, workers would be required to contribute to their
own protection instead of relying on their employers.

The administration of social security by a municipal or provincial-level
agency was a definite improvement on the pre-existing system. Worker
contribution did not necessarily mean a retraction of social rights. However,
from the angle of social rights, social security reform caused considerable
concern. First, in the urban areas alone, up to half of the workforce were
not insured. Non-state firms were not compelled to insure their workers.
Nor were the self-employed, migrant workers and employees in firms that
could not maintain subscriptions covered by social security schemes. In
other words, the great majority of the non-agricultural labour force was
uninsured. Eventually, the state intended to make social security mandatory
for all firms and employees. Without effective sanctions and with so many
firms experiencing financial hardship, however, implementation was fraught
with difficulty. In the short term, the uninsured are likely to increase in
numbers.

Second, many social security schemes were in danger of insolvency (C. K.
Lee 1998). Default rates rose. Some municipal social insurance funds were
rapidly used up. Fund exhaustion was also true of pensions and unemployment insurance. Even if coverage remained intact in theory, many
enterprises were so hard pressed that they could not pay up (Li 1998; Zhu
1999). Non-payment and arrears in honouring pensions and even wages
were widely reported in the media, spurring worker protests and appeals for
central government intervention across the country.

Third, much of the rural population was left out of the safety net altogether. Except in the more affluent places and villages adjacent to big cities,

such as those described by Zhang in Chapter 6 of this volume, rural residents could only fall back on themselves and their families in facing the challenges of old age, sickness, unemployment and poverty.

Finally, the social assistance system was woefully inadequate. Previously state and local relief was confined to people who could not work and had no family support. The increase of urban poverty, mainly due to in-migration, enterprise insolvency and rising unemployment, exposed the gap between the social insurance and relief systems. The expansion of social assistance in the late 1990s managed to plug loopholes in a feeble way. However, eligibility was still too strict. At the end of 1998, only 1.84 million poor city residents were receiving assistance (*Zhongguo Minzheng Tongji Nianjian* 1999). In the countryside, subsistence protection programmes had scarcely begun.

Social welfare

The 'socialisation' of welfare and relief had been an avowed policy of the government since the mid-1980s. While policy content was rather fuzzy, the aim was clear: to reduce dependence on the state and share responsibility for welfare among all strata of society including community groups, mass organisations, work units, families and individuals. Participation could take a number of forms. Groups and individuals should voluntarily take part in service provision, financing and management. The scope of services should be widened beyond the traditional targets of childless elders, orphans and people without any means of livelihood. In short, joint effort and diversification would be the foundation stones on which a sustainable welfare system would be built.

Various initiatives were taken to extend the scope for collective social involvement. Many wealthy rural communities increased their role in financing and running welfare schemes. However, the majority of villages could barely support the elderly and the local poor. In city areas, the 'socialisation' policy gave rise to new practices. Eligibility criteria were relaxed. Formerly confined to the homeless indigent, most state-run welfare institutions began to admit fee-paying clients. Neighbourhood social services were expanded. Lack of government support, however, plunged community organisers into a quandary: running free services became more and more difficult, but charging fees deprived needy users of aid. Bowing to economic reality, many residents' organisations concentrated on profitable ventures, like restaurants, shops, karaoke bars and agencies for home-help. Another mark of state withdrawal from welfare provision was the state's embrace of philanthropy. In the past, *cishan* or charity was maligned as class patronage, social control and foreign imperialism. In the 1990s, the country's welfare bureaucracy, the Ministry of Civil Affairs, openly promoted charitable work. The Ministry planned to transfer programme administration to non-profit organisations, which were praised for their lack of profit motive and ethic of service. Even proprietary projects like private nursing homes, schools and clinics gained legitimacy as welfare goods providers.

Healthcare

Marketisation was even more prominent on the health front. The death of communes resulted in the collapse of many rural health programmes. Local schemes like cooperative health insurance and barefoot doctors virtually disappeared. Moreover, the countryside received fewer health resources from the state, aggravating the pre-existing urban/rural gap. The World Health Organisation estimated that at the turn of the century, China had one of the least equitable health systems in the world (*South China Morning Post* 2001). To a limited extent, the vacuum was filled by privatised arrangements. The vast majority of the rural population had to pay out-of-pocket to get treatment. Rapid inflation of costs followed. More than one third of rural households could not afford to pay for medical attention. Often, contracting a major disease not only proved to be fatal to a farmer, it also ensured that their family remained poor for a few generations.

Regression was also evident in urban areas. The old system of public health insurance for government workers and labour health insurance for enterprise staff was condemned as wasteful and inefficient. State enterprises steadfastly cut back their health commitments by requiring higher co-payments, restricting treatment, drugs and procedures, and dispensing with their obligation altogether by paying employees a miserly health allowance. Non-state employees were even more exposed: they did not get subsidised coverage at all. Consumption of healthcare depended crucially on whether or not one received insurance coverage, the solvency of one's work unit, and possession of family savings. As in the countryside, a common view was that getting sick was a curse.

At the end of 1998, the state announced a new health insurance scheme to cover all urban employees, to be contributed to jointly by employers and workers. This will take years to bear fruit. In the meantime, the separation of providers (hospitals and clinics), insurers (enterprises) and consumers (patients) produced a system of stakeholders working at cross purposes. One of the major fallouts was runaway cost. A key underlying factor was insufficient funding of hospitals. With state allocations making up 30 per cent or less of day-to-day operational costs, hospitals were forced to put up fees, prescribe expensive drugs, and encourage unnecessary, often harmful treatment and procedures in order to maximise income. Coupled with the fact that doctors' pay and bonuses were often tied to the profits they earned for hospitals, the space for patient exploitation was immense.

Even the normally pro-market World Bank became concerned enough to sound this warning:

China since the 1980s has been moving towards less government support for priority public health activities for all and clinic services for the poor, and greater reliance on a fee-for-service delivery system. If present trends persist, China will move into the 21st century with a poorly performing but nonetheless costly health system.

(Cited in Cheung 1999)

Education

In the field of education, the traces of marketisation were unmistakable. According to one view, educational marketisation is 'a process whereby education becomes a commodity provided by competitive suppliers, educational services are priced and access to them depends on consumer calculations and ability to pay' (Yin and White 1994: 217). Marketisation of education took two forms in China: educational institutions began to price their academic wares, and institutions adopted business principles and practices (Mok 1999; Buchbinder and Newson 1990). The reduction of state provision of education, marketisation and decentralisation of management to local governments, communities and educational institutions was justified by the claim that the state was financially unable to meet the people's pressing needs (Cheng 1995).

Despite that fact, the state stipulated that children should receive free tuition until junior high school. In rural areas where people-run (*min-ban*) primary schools predominate, funding came from multiple sources: the local community, tuition fees and donations, and limited state or local government subsidies. In urban areas too, schools turned to fee-charging as a way of compensating for inadequate budgets and improving facilities and teacher bonuses. As parents greatly value education for their children, single children being the norm since the 1979 one-child policy came into effect, big sacrifices were borne stoically. Urban parents could expect to spend up to half of the family income on schooling, private tutoring and sundry expenses on their child. Poor parents, especially those who had lost their jobs, were placed in desperate straits.

State leaders view higher education as a key instrument in producing skilled personnel for the programme of modernisation that will make China's economy globally competitive. Yet again, budget constraints convinced them that students and parents should pay more for what they began to describe as a privilege. After all, a higher education would enhance an individual's career and income prospects. At the same time, under-provision of university places also translated into vast numbers of families that were prepared to bring their political and social connections to bear, and to pay hard cash, to ensure that their children had the opportunity to gain a degree. Tuition fees skyrocketed. There was a proliferation of 'ultra-plan' or 'self-supporting' students and sponsored or 'commissioned' students, who sometimes made up as much as 25 per cent of student intake according to state policy. Capable but poor students thus suffered from diminished opportunities to pursue tertiary studies. Hence the meritocratic principles that had governed access to higher education were eroded.

The development of private education, in which ability to pay determines access, likewise received a boost from the government. Private schools, which offered a modern curriculum, superior facilities, smaller classes and highly qualified teachers, and which charged expensive tuition fees and/or debentures, quietly mushroomed in many big cities. Non-state institutions at the higher education level expanded just as quickly. Vocational courses were especially popular. Admittedly, most of these schools received some support from local governments, often in the form of school buildings and financial aid. Hence they are better described as the product of mixed public-private auspices rather than springing from a pure market parentage (Mok and Wat 1998).

Even state-run universities and institutes began to operate according to marketised principles. This was evident in the encouragement of competition, the merger of institutions to achieve economies of scale, curriculum reform (trimming small courses and expanding courses meeting market demands), pedagogical innovation, and the pressure to tailor academic research to industry needs. Especially noteworthy was the drive for revenue generation. The money craze affected teachers as much as institutions. In many universities, the more capable teachers either left to join the high-paid private sector or were too busy servicing industry, doing private tutoring, writing books and organising consultancy work, to attend to their teaching duties. The fee-charging principle, in particular, curtailed commitment to public education. In sum, marketisation reduced access without producing demonstrable improvements in the quality of education.

Housing

In the socialist economy, housing ceased to be a commodity. For most urban families, work-unit housing at nominal rent was the only source of housing. On the supply side, state policy discouraged spending on consumption goods and services. This translated into overall shortages, with families waiting for years for housing. Different endowments of individual enterprises led to substantial inequality in access and standards. Moreover, assignment of housing was affected by seniority, political patronage and good personal networks as much as by family size and need. Because of these reasons, housing rights never attained the status of pure public goods open to all in equal measure.

To tackle the acute shortage, Chairman Deng Xiaoping issued a directive in 1980. This directive shaped the housing reforms that ensued in the following decades:

> Urban residents should [be allowed to] buy their own houses, or to build their own houses. Not only can new houses be sold, old houses can be sold as well. They can be paid in one go or in instalments over ten to fifteen years. Public sector rentals must be adjusted; otherwise no one will buy their own home. Different rents must be charged for houses in different locations. When rents are increased, extra rent subsidies should be given to low wage earners. New houses could be jointly developed between the public and private sectors, or by the private sector alone.
>
> (Deng 1984)

Urban housing reform incorporated three strategies: rental reform, sale of public sector housing, and market housing. The aim of rental reform was to increase rents for work-unit housing to levels that would at least cover the costs of construction and maintenance. Low rents, averaging 1–2 per cent of worker salaries, were blamed for a number of deficiencies: they induced privileged persons to occupy excessive space, dampened enterprise incentive in building more housing, and failed to recover money for maintenance and repair. Several waves of rent increases took place, but as of 2001, these had met with limited success. Rent adjustments had encountered worker resistance since wages remained low and, without additional state appropriations, pay rises were impossible.

The sale of public sector housing had three objectives. It was intended to speed up the return of capital needed to build new housing. It was expected that home ownership would encourage better maintenance. And it was supposed to satisfy families who desired better quality accommodation. Yet experiments with the sale of public sector housing hit similar snags to rental reform. Workers' wages and savings were too low to meet the high costs of home purchase. As a result, work units came under great pressure to offer huge discounts or grant loans and subsidies. Their dilemma was stark: if they succumbed, they would defeat the purpose of encouraging home ownership and individual responsibility, but a failure to do so would result in lack of custom. Selling flats on the cheap also raised serious equity issues.

The latest reform package, announced in mid-1998, aimed at stopping the allocation of housing by work-units (Lau and Lee 1999). Instead, housing subsidy would be monetarised, that is, paid to workers in a one-off lump sum or monthly instalments for a period of up to twenty to twenty-five years. Work units could include the cash subsidy in workers' monthly remuneration or deposit it into workers' housing provident fund accounts. As soon as the new scheme was announced, however, a rampage ensued as work units and employees competed to 'catch the last train'. This resulted in many abuses, such as work units overspending to buy as many flats as possible for allocation, senior cadres grabbing multiple apartments for themselves and their families, and 'allocating' flats which had not been built.

The third component of urban housing reform involved the development of private real estate markets. The state reasoned that supply of private housing would allow people to solve their housing problems without queuing or being subsidised. It would enable affluent consumers, like foreigners, entrepreneurs and high-income earners, to choose housing according to their preferences. Additionally, knock-on growth would stimulate related industries: construction, banking, home decorating, electronics and other sectors. The volume and variety of private housing expanded rapidly after 1980, particularly in the major metropolises of Shanghai, Beijing and Tianjin, and in coastal cities.

However, marketised housing was not a panacea for the housing problems of ordinary people. Relative to the average wage, prices were astronomical. Few but the rich could afford private houses and apartments. Many privately built flats were bought by state units to distribute among senior cadres. This compounded the problem of inequality, especially because the chosen were already privileged and the cost to enterprises was so high. Besides, wave upon wave of property speculation throughout the 1990s produced a glut of unsold luxury flats. The central government responded by freezing investments. Not infrequently, these investments had been made by local governments and companies in poor areas, whose desire for quick profits had cost them huge sums of public money.

The experiments with housing reform mirrored the aims, methods and consequences of reforms in social security and welfare, healthcare and education. They were designed to increase individual responsibility. Provision and funding were pluralised. Marketisation was a core feature, whether through promotion of home purchase or the inflation of rental charges. In the process, goods and services such as housing were transformed from welfare goods into commodities. To the credit of reformers, some of these reforms brought significant improvements: a quantum leap in supply, enhanced quality, and expanded choice. On the other hand, they were inadequate responses to the needs of most Chinese people. The erosion of public commitment widened inequality and, in some cases, reduced the quality and increased the cost of goods and services. The problems of how to allocate responsibility for provision and funding and how to ensure fair access for poor people became especially acute, as market forces began to determine distribution.

Conclusion

I have argued elsewhere that Chinese-style 'socialisation', which is associated with a reduction in state provision, funding and regulation, is similar in spirit and in practice to Western-style 'privatisation' (Wong 1994; 1998b). It hinges on the 'individualisation' of social rights.

The above survey of the transformation of Chinese welfare goods provision demonstrates that there is a marked similarity to developments elsewhere over the last two decades of the twentieth century. Indeed, in its reform of some welfare goods, China appears to have travelled further along the route of 'individualisation' than some of the former welfare states of the West. The provision of social rights and welfare was marked by a gradual retreat of the state from fulfilling its old responsibility for ensuring the right to survival for its subjects. The state no longer guaranteed the right to work, and demanded the involvement of individuals and social groups in the provision and financing of welfare, health, education and housing. In the process, individual citizens, like their counterparts in Eastern and Central Europe and the Western liberal democracies, had to assume greater responsibility for their needs by buying welfare goods in the market.

This survey also suggests that the post-Mao reforms erased the philosophical and structural distinctions that once marked classic liberal concepts of collective goods, and the notion of collective goods in socialist China. In many instances, the provision of collective goods in China is viewed as a residual activity, one that the state sometimes performs to compensate for market failure. The commodification of collective goods shrank the size and content of the public sector.

However, the wholesale commodification of welfare goods has not yet occurred in China. As long as the government professes that China is 'socialist', its abnegation of all responsibility for welfare provision will be difficult. The hold of old ideological commitments, political pressures and pragmatic concerns for social stability might prevent the Chinese government from continuing to navigate the market route. Low per capita incomes make the wider purchase of welfare goods impossible. Nor have markets in these goods become mature.

In particular, it is apparent even to the government that the 'individualisation' of social rights in China has resulted in a host of adverse consequences, including an escalation of costs, inadequate coverage, inefficient services and increased inequality. The government is also aware that protests against these changes have been far from absent. Objections have come largely from disgruntled workers who have been laid off and have no means of livelihood, pensioners who have been denied the goods that they were promised and, to a lesser extent, farmers who pay an immense array of taxes, fees and charges and receive almost no collective goods. However, these are diffuse demands from unorganised groups. Nor are there any professional lobbies to take up the cause for the excluded or downtrodden. The Chinese state does not tolerate the formation of autonomous groups devoted to interest representation and lobbying. In the absence of citizen participation and open bargaining, then, the definition of 'the public interest', as well as the ability to construct the political rationality that underpins the changing state/society interface, continues to lodge firmly with the state.

The government's faith in the power of welfare markets remains strong, stronger than either the reality in China or spectacular examples of the failure of welfare markets in developed economies warrants. But notwithstanding its predilection for market strategies, there is reason to believe that the government, obsessed with the twin goals of preserving social stability and its own legitimacy, will tread cautiously to time the pace and scope of welfare reform to avoid violent shocks. The state is aware that increasing people's dissatisfaction with the provision of welfare goods will affect their support for the political regime. And the last thing that the government wants to see is the emergence of a lumpen proletariat, composed of disenfranchised groups like the unemployed, the poor and displaced migrant workers, and armed with a righteous mandate from 'the masses'. Therefore, I advance the following predictions. The marketisation of welfare goods will grow. The individualisation of social responsibility will steadily increase. But China's government will try to strike a balance, with a shared public/private responsibility that is socially supported and economically viable.

10

URBAN DEVELOPMENT AND THE SEARCH FOR CIVIL SOCIETY IN CHINA

A view from Quanzhou

Michael Leaf

Urban space as a collective good

In its most basic sense, a city is a collection of people. As such, it is intrinsically an important locus for the provision of collective goods and for the organisation of collective consumption. The city historically is a centre for the provision of a broad number of classic collective goods. The production of physical infrastructure, education, healthcare and other forms of social welfare are integral aspects of urban life in many cultures. The social contract of urban life requires participation in the production of those collective goods by the urban dweller, either indirectly through their payment of taxes and fees for state-provided collective goods, or through their direct personal involvement in non-state associations and voluntary activities. The meaning of the term 'collective good' that I will emphasise here is broader, however – that is, that urban space itself is a collective good.

The collective goods nature of urban space is most obvious in such 'true' public spaces as streets, parks, and squares that are jointly supplied and which individuals have the right to freely enter merely by dint of their citizenship. For argument's sake, such spaces contrast sharply with the private spaces within individual homes. Any city, however, exhibits a wide range of grey areas between the seeming black and white of public and private. The distinctions between public and private may derive as much from human psychology and social relations as from legal strictures. A few examples will suffice to illustrate this point: neighbourhood spaces, those semi-public spaces in which 'outsiders' might feel excluded or at least uncomfortable, despite their legal status as fully public space; the commercial spaces of shops, which are private from the point of view of the law, yet must maintain a distinct public nature for the sake of commerce; the legally public spaces of sidewalks which are taken over to serve the private concerns of

179

shopkeepers or café owners for exhibiting their goods or serving their customers; the array of public institutional spaces to which public access is nonetheless restricted, such as courthouses, government offices and hospitals; and those private institutional spaces, such as places of worship, to which the citizenry may be freely welcomed.

The dual nature of urban space

Further complicating the possibility of a black and white distinction between public and private in an urban setting is the perspective from urban land economics, which argues that there is no such thing as purely private space in the city, thereby adding another layer to the interpretation of urban space as a collective entity. The argument is often stated in terms of the 'dual nature' of urban land (Doebele 1983). Due to the non-substitutability of urban land (that is, the geographical uniqueness of each parcel in a city) and the existence of externalities arising from specific land uses, there are always public impacts arising from even the most privately defined uses of urban land. This shapes the urban spatial economy, although such impacts are by no means limited to the operations of property markets. The classic example is that of homeowners who choose unpopular paint colours for their houses, thus lowering the value of their neighbours' houses. Yet examples need not be so frivolous, as the dual nature of urban land (and by extension, urban space in general) has far-reaching implications for how cities are built and inhabited. Dual nature arguments underlie the many restrictions on private property, such as land use zoning, construction codes, fire safety regulations, building height and set-back requirements and other development laws. The dual nature of urban space also affects the role of urban land in public finance (Dunkerley 1983) and, by extension, the function of urban governance.

The separation of public and private space in the context of the city is indeed problematic: the streetscape of private houses gives form to the public space of the street itself. Such considerations have intergenerational implications as well, as argued by historical preservationists. As a result, a move has been made in recent years to go beyond the 'monumental' interpretation of historic patrimony in cities, in order to include the 'fabric' of the historic city as a characteristic worth protecting.

Governments, civil society and the production of urban space

The collective goods associated with the production and use of urban space are not limited to the physical entity of space itself. In every city, one will find a range of institutional and associational structures – from informal interactions among neighbours, to community groups, to private sector organisations, to local governments – which determine the formation and maintenance of urban space. Such institutional and associational structures are themselves collective goods.

A critical distinction in consideration of these structures is with regard to the interrelationships between the local state and non-state structures. The production of urban space is achieved in some instances through the direct intervention of the state (typically local government), most commonly through the provision of public infrastructure and public institutional buildings, although possibly also through the construction of public housing. The more common intervention of the local government in shaping urban space, however, is indirect. Local government agencies regulate individual households and firms through their design and implementation of building and land use regulations, urban development controls, and the guarantees of property ownership and occupation.

Collective production of urban space is clearly not the exclusive reserve of the state. In the analysis of 'third world' urbanisation in recent years, much attention has been given to the production of urban space that occurs even outside of the regulatory frameworks of local states. This has been referred to by a number of terms, most commonly as the 'popular sector', the 'informal sector' or, more pointedly, the 'illegal city' (Fernandes and Varley 1998).

The distinction between state and non-state provision of collective goods is an important one, as it raises the question of the function of civil society in the provision of collective goods. Civil society – that is, the composite of social organisations and institutions which function outside of the direct control of the state – is critical to both liberal and 'new social movement' views of collective consumption. From the normative perspective of liberalism, a vibrant civil society is healthy in that it is the firmament which accommodates the diverse interests of the citizenry and gives rise to the self-organisation of certain collective goods, thereby reducing social demands on the state. On the other hand, civil society is looked upon by neo-Marxian analysts as the means toward progressive change, as it can provide the mechanism through which pressure is brought to bear upon the state. Thus civil society can be perceived as either an alternative to the state or a venue for the expression of societal needs *vis-à-vis* the state. Civil society therefore underlies arguments both in favour of reducing the role of the state in civil life and of expanding the state's responsibility. In neither instance can the analysis of collective goods be fully separated from an understanding of civil society.

In this chapter, I examine these issues in a Chinese context, first, by looking at the changing processes of China's urbanisation as they have been shaped by ongoing economic reforms. I then consider two cases where spatial changes have been initiated through non-state mechanisms in the city of Quanzhou, in the southeastern province of Fujian. These are: the production of self-built housing as the principal means for both the redevelopment of the old inner city and the expansion of the city at its periphery, and the restoration of the neighbourhood temples which historically had been crucial to the socio-spatial structuring of the city. The case of Quanzhou, an ancient and once prominent port city, raises critical questions regarding regional differentiation in the context of China's ongoing urban change. By emphasising the particularities of one locality, we may better understand the limitations of the broad models that are articulated in explaining regional (or even global) phenomena. For, as with all cities, the specifics of Quanzhou derive from a mix of both typical and exceptional characteristics when compared to what might be referred to as the general model of Chinese urbanisation.

Institutional transformation in Chinese cities

As a socialist polity under the domination of the Chinese Communist Party, processes of urbanisation in the period of China's centralised command economy[1] were dominated by the state. It is critical to understand the functioning of the state's principal institutions in this regard, as these institutions have continued to exert a profound influence on Chinese cities throughout the subsequent reform period. This period, from the early 1980s onward, was marked by administrative decentralisation and the increasing differentiation of localities, in contrast to the centralisation of policy in the past.[2] Yet the shift to a market economy did not result in the immediate dissolution of state institutions so much as their re-invention or local re-articulation (Shue 1995; Blecher and Shue 1996). In this section, I will briefly review the general patterns of these changes and consider their implications for urban socio-spatial development.

State institutions

China in the pre-reform past can be characterised as having had a highly collectivised regime for the provision of far more than what is considered to be the usual collective consumption items of society, due to the state's approach to central economic planning and to its ideological opposition to private property. The two most critical institutional structures for the state's regulation of urban society were – and in certain respects still are – the household registration (*hukou*) system, which closely tied all residents to specific locations within the formal administrative structure of the nation, and the work units (*danwei*), the basic organisational elements which comprised the state industrial sector.

From the early days of the People's Republic in the 1950s to the beginning of the reform era at the end of the 1970s, the *hukou* system was used to prevent internal population movement, in effect freezing proportions of rural and urban residents at 1950s levels and creating a virtually impenetrable barrier to urbanisation through migration (Chan 1994; Kirkby 1985).

Enforcement of the *hukou* controls was effected through the prohibition of open markets and the establishment of state monopolies for the allocation of virtually all goods and services, including housing. Collective provision of goods could therefore be structured separately for urban and rural societies, with collectivised agricultural production and allocation through communes in the countryside and a parallel system in cities based on state sector production, as articulated through the institution of the *danwei*.

As the primary form of urban social organisation, the *danwei* functioned as much more than just a mechanism for economic production. Ostensibly organised around various forms of urban employment – industrial, service, bureaucratic and so forth – the functions of the *danwei* and their associated organisations were all-encompassing in the lives of their members (White 1998; White 1993; Whyte and Parish 1984). The *danwei* served as the vehicle for the delivery of all types of consumption items, from food and personal services to housing and even recreation. For the urban dweller, the *danwei* was the means by which the 'iron rice bowl' of state guarantees was achieved. Each *danwei* was, and still is, under the direct control of one or another agency of the state, at one or another level of the governmental hierarchy. As such, the entire system of the myriad *danwei* should thus be understood as a critical mechanism for the ideologically driven integration of state and society under the command structure of the pre-reform socialist state. This period was characterised by the complete lack of independent associational social structures, in sharp contrast to both the preceding republican period (and the Qing period before that) and the proliferation of social groups that occurred after reforms were initiated (Pye 1996). Thus in the era of socialist central planning, state and society were seen to be coterminous (Brook 1997).

The institution of the *danwei* also had profound impacts on the spatial structure of the Chinese city. Under socialist thinking, urban land was understood to be not a market commodity with value created by location, but purely an input into processes of production. Thus land was allocated by the state to the various production units of urban society – the *danwei* – seemingly according to production needs, although in practice allocation decisions were often modified to a great degree by political considerations (Wu 1995; Tang 1994). The *danwei* thus became not only the major holders of urban land, but also the principal determinants of urban form, giving rise to the characteristic of an integrated, or even 'cellular' structure of land uses in the Chinese city (Gaubatz 1995; Leaf 1995). Typically, large *danwei* built extensive compounds containing complete facilities for production, residence and the array of goods and services needed by residents.

Institutional implications of economic reform

The move to a market economy in the early 1980s affected both the central institutions of Chinese urban life – the *hukou* and the *danwei* – and fostered the gradual dismantling of the iron rice bowl of Chinese socialism. A series of reforms in the countryside, beginning with the allowance for farmers to keep and sell excess agricultural production, followed by de-collectivisation of land and the opening up of free labour markets, unleashed an historically unprecedented wave of rural migrants into China's cities (Chan 1994). The numbers of this 'floating population' (*liudong renkou*) have been estimated in official reports to be as high as 100 million, almost one tenth of the entire Chinese population (Chang 1996).The enforcement mechanisms of the *hukou* system, which in the past kept rural dwellers apart from their city cousins, were dependent upon the centralised allocation of essential goods and services, including housing and employment, which has changed fundamentally in the reform period. The establishment of markets has thus undermined the official constraints on population movement, with the result that many of the major cities of coastal China now have migrant populations one third or more the size of their official registered populations (Solinger 1995).

The *danwei* have also responded to the stresses and new opportunities of the market economy by generating a new class of 'red capitalists' or 'bureaucratic entrepreneurs' (Hsing 1998). The economic boom of China's reform period is generally attributed to what is labelled as the 'collective sector', derived from the state bureaucratic structure of the *danwei* system.[3] As established holders of capital, fixed assets and good connections, many of the major *danwei* in both state and collective sectors were able to capitalise on new business opportunities and reduce their reliance on dwindling state subsidies. However, it is notable that throughout the early reform period many of the loss-making state enterprises, which still employed a large proportion of the urban workforce, continued to be propped up despite the lack of a market logic for doing so. This is an indication that the preservation of the state sector was driven by welfare considerations rather than economic productivity. The high costs of maintaining the state sector came to a head only at the end of the 1990s, with policy directives focused on restructuring the most costly state enterprises and opening up a larger role for private and foreign investment.

As Wong's chapter in this volume shows, the effect of all these changes has been the downloading of responsibilities for the provision of collective consumption items for both the urban and rural sectors of the population. Rural migrants must increasingly rely upon such time-tested methods as personal social networks derived from family, friends and places of origin, or turn to the burgeoning but erratic urban informal sector as the basis for their livelihoods. The typical urban dweller so far has not been cast out to fend for him- or herself in much the same way, as the institution of the *danwei* still persists, and in fact has been transformed under the market economy. Growing diversification of the *danwei*, with some profiting from the market economy while others lose out, means that social stratification among registered urban residents is less an issue of personal wealth than it is of *danwei* wealth. A household connected to a successful *danwei* will have access to good housing, good healthcare, good schools and many other allowances; a household in a poor *danwei* will not. The imminent disassembly of large portions of the state sector will put further strains on these structures.

Thus the rusting and crumbling of China's iron rice bowl that followed the move to a market economy has marked out, in general, an opposite trajectory to the collective consumption patterns of other Asian countries during their 'miracle economy' periods. In the wake of the Asian crisis, when new social forces were emerging in other countries to place new demands on the state, the social guarantees of Chinese life were being dismantled one by one. As illustrated by Zhang in Chapter 6 of this volume, in some instances this reconfiguration was driven by old vested interests, while in others it was facilitated by the emergence of new interest groups.

Urban spatial implications of institutional change

The changes to the *hukou* system have had profound implications for the urban landscape of China. Many components of the floating population find accommodation in the interstices of the urban fabric, such as construction workers who generally live on building sites, often with their entire families. It has become common as well to find new low-standard rental accommodations built by villagers on the edge of cities. The most famous case of this, because of its size, is Zhejiang cun, a settlement of migrants from Zhejiang province on the southern boundary of Beijing.[4] In Zhejiangcun, as elsewhere, local villagers have transformed their agricultural lands into a mix of housing and small-scale garment factories that have been rented out to migrants. The immigrant population at times has outnumbered the local villagers by more than three to one. The peculiarities of Chinese land law placed such settlements in a legal grey area, because until 1999 village committees retained the right to determine the use of village land, even when its conversion to housing contradicted municipal-level planning stipulations.

The urban spatial implications of the *danwei* are of even greater consequence, as the *danwei* have been the principal beneficiaries of state-allocated urban lands. Despite the attention given in recent years to the establishment of formal land markets, it should be noted that the vast majority of urban lands are still under the control of various *danwei* that are not active in either the formal 'primary' or 'secondary' land markets of Chinese cities (Yeh and Wu 1996). Their continuing role is based on both their receipt of land in the pre-reform period, and the fact that the bulk of land-use control (technically not ownership under the socialist state) is still granted by the state through administrative allocation rather than by the market.

Nevertheless, unregulated 'grey' markets have emerged as powerful *danwei* trade lands with one another or otherwise utilise their assets by setting up their own collective sector property development companies. The boom in inner city redevelopment in the major cities of China throughout the 1990s was precipitated by large *danwei* developing and speculating with their land holdings.

To summarise, the particularities of urban change in China today arise from the persistence of specific institutions from China's state socialist past and their transformation in the face of rapid moves from administrative allocation to a market-oriented system. The impacts of this have been many (Leaf 1998), including: rapid economic growth in urban areas, which underlies accelerated programmes of infrastructure upgrading and physical modernisation; the devolution of fiscal responsibility to local levels and the development of new mechanisms of urban finance; the resulting shifts in urban form, particularly the rebuilding of inner city areas after decades of neglect and the deconcentration and outward expansion of old urban areas (Naughton 1995); and the inward movement of migrant rural populations.

Civil society in the Chinese context

Clearly, the impact of the market economy is not limited to changes in the physical fabric of the city. A growing diversification within Chinese society has been concomitant, and underlies discussion of the various meanings that civil society might have in China today. The current preoccupation with civil society among both Western observers and Chinese scholars is often driven by a search for the potential for democratic development, or by a desire to measure the extent to which the country has passed along a linear path in its transition to democracy. The assumed interconnections between civil society and democratisation derive, in part, from the experiences of Eastern Europe in the late 1980s, and have certainly acquired greater resonance in the Chinese context since the events surrounding 4 June 1989 (Brook and Frolic 1997). A contrary line of argument, however, dismisses the linearity of the liberal developmentalist perspective in the search for an indigenous alternative, leading to the identification of such new creatures in the civil society bestiary as 'semi-civil society' (He 1997) and the seemingly paradoxical 'state-led civil society' (Frolic 1997).

In attempting to understand this 'search for civil society' in China, Gordon White has drawn a useful distinction between two basic competing definitions of civil society. The first derives from political analysis, and emphasises the articulation and defence of human rights and the development of independent (non-state) political structures. The other displays a sociological orientation by focusing on the associational structures in (non-state) society. Often these two conceptualisations are linked, as demonstrated, for example, by Robert Putnam's study of Italian political traditions

(Putnam 1993). In Putnam's study, it is the horizontal linkages inherent in social organisations that allow for the development of trust or 'social capital'. This acts as a counterweight to the verticality of traditional political structures. The 'choral societies and soccer teams' that proliferate in northern Italy created the fundament in which the region's democratic traditions flourished, in sharp contrast to the clientelistic relations that suppressed social organisation in the south.

Autonomous (i.e. non-state) social organisations have long characterised Chinese society, as, for example, the craft guilds, literary societies and native place associations of the late Qing period (Brook 1997; Skinner 1977). This observation should be tempered, however, by the understanding that such social organisations in China's past were nonetheless typified by strongly hierarchical, clientelistic structures – a factor to be kept in mind when the search for modern civil society in China looks for historic progenitors. The meaning of autonomy in reference to such social organisations must therefore be understood in relative terms.

Looked at from this perspective, the precise correspondence of the Chinese state with society in the period of centrally planned socialism should be understood as an historic anomaly, an interpretation which is reinforced by the flourishing of new organisations since the 1980s. The Chinese government sought to have a comprehensive registry of social organisations only after 1989, and within a few years hundreds of thousands of business and professional associations, academic societies, and recreational and cultural clubs had been officially recognised (He 1997). It is a point of contention as to whether this trend is indicative of an emergent civil society, as it remains to be seen whether many of these organisations actually possess any autonomy from the local governments and offices that created them, much less have the capacity to affect political change. However, an examination of urban development in the city of Quanzhou gives an indication that this is a useful line of inquiry for understanding processes of urban change.

Quanzhou: an exceptional city

The above discussion of processes of Chinese urban change during the reform period implies a particular model or a set of norms. Like all models, this is an abstraction based upon a series of observed general patterns. Making the connection between the abstract model and on-the-ground reality requires that specific attributes of the locality be compared to the assumptions of the general model. This is an argument for regionalism, or attending to the fundamental differences between various parts of the country. A regionalist view of Chinese urbanism is hampered by the country's recent history of centralisation and by the growth of Chinese nationalism. Uniformity is implied as well by the nation-wide promulgation of urban policy. With this in mind, one can say that processes of development that are in accordance with national policy tend to support the generalisations; exceptions to policy therefore help to articulate regional or local differences. Locally acting associations, and even components of local government that act contrary to state policy, further accentuate differences from the norm.

Like all cities, Quanzhou, a medium-sized city in the southern province of Fujian, is a unique place.[5] Its uniqueness derives from its own set of particular historically rooted characteristics, combined with present patterns of change. As is common with current measures of urbanism in China, there is a great deal of ambiguity around the meaning of what is urban in Quanzhou. This arises from multiple definitions of the municipal limits and population of the city. The Quanzhou municipality, first of all, has been administratively assigned the surrounding six-county region, giving it a total population, in 1997, of 6.5 million. At that time, the built-up areas within this region that officially are classified as urbanised contained approximately half a million residents. However, the total non-agricultural population (according to *hukou* classifications) was only just over 280,000. The core of the municipal region, the old city district of Licheng and its adjacent suburbs, had a population of around 200,000. In addition to estimates of the registered population, there were some 200,000 rural migrants in the built-up areas of the municipality. With all these caveats and approximations, it is reasonable to think of the urban core of Quanzhou municipality – the area under discussion here – as containing around 300,000 people, one third or more of whom are categorised as 'temporary' migrants.

In addition to the influx of floating population, the other major urban characteristics of the reform era are also evident in Quanzhou. The opening up of the market economy has prompted accelerated economic growth, as indicated by a twenty-two-fold increase in municipal GDP between 1980 and 1997. This wealth has accrued to the local government as well as to the citizenry. Devolution of fiscal responsibility from central government since the late 1980s – allowing for a greater proportion of locally retained revenues – coupled with the introduction of new municipal financing techniques utilising land market value, have given the municipality robust budgets in recent years. The budget deficit was reduced from 16 per cent in the mid-1980s to 2 per cent in 1990 and, following the land market boom of the early 1990s, the municipality had achieved a 1997 budget surplus of 44 per cent. This economic boom underlies ongoing investments in infrastructure upgrading and physical modernisation, with major programmes of inner city redevelopment and rapid suburbanisation.

Elements of an exceptional city

Perhaps the broadest generalisation that can be made about the current processes of urbanisation in China is that there is now tremendous diversity compared to the near-monopoly position of the state in the past, diversity derived from the inclusion of new social actors in the city's development. In this respect, Quanzhou is a typical Chinese city. Considering the specific mix of new actors and new processes affecting change, however, it is more appropriate to describe Quanzhou as an exceptional city.[6] Quanzhou's exceptionality derives from the particular historic and geographic circumstances that have given rise to current forces of change. In this, we can identify three basic factors:

1   the relative lack of state investment in the region during the period of the centrally planned economy, due to what was seen as Quanzhou's vulnerable position directly across the straits from Taiwan;
2   the high degree of private control of property in the city, even during the most radical periods of collectivisation; and
3   the importance of the city's *huaqiao* (overseas Chinese) connections, as Quanzhou has been a place of great out-migration and residents have actively maintained connections with their overseas relatives.

Each of these three factors is tightly intertwined with the other two, giving rise to a particular political economy of urban development that differs from what might be considered to be the Chinese norm. This underscores the need to carefully examine local factors in the Chinese polity in order to understand processes of development and change. To give an example, the position of Quanzhou at the 'front line' of the Taiwan straits meant that the central state was reluctant to channel investment into the area. In practical terms, this resulted in a lower proportion of state ownership in the local economy and the presence of relatively few *danwei*. For the same reason, unlike most governments in urban China, the Quanzhou government never carried out a programme of housing collectivisation. By the end of the 1970s, more than 90 per cent of the city's housing stock was still in private hands.

Private ownership of housing also reflects the influence of the *huaqiao*. The local government estimates that more than five million *huaqiao*, mostly in Southeast Asia and Taiwan, trace their roots to the Quanzhou area. City officials have always worked to maintain good relations with these expatriates, and have been careful not to implement policies that would disenfranchise members of the local community who have relatives overseas. The investment and development implications of the *huaqiao* connection are historically rooted,[7] with major initiatives for development and change originating from returned expatriates in the 1920s and 1930s and a special district of elegant mansions (the *Huaqiao xincun*) set aside in the 1950s to reward the wealthiest overseas supporters of the Revolution. In short, the *huaqiao* connection has long been seen to be crucial to the local economy. Indeed, in the context of low levels of central government investment it provided the local government with some degree of leverage vis-à-vis the Beijing leadership.

These three factors combine with a fourth characteristic that has had a major influence on the city's development policies in recent years. This is the conflict between Quanzhou's position as a city of historic importance and the city's rapidly expanding urban land market. Quanzhou's designation as China's third most historic city (after Beijing and Xi'an) is based on the number of nationally registered historic structures in the city and the recognition that it was China's major seaport during the Song period (Schinz 1989). Mindful of the city's 1,300 years of continuous history and its distinctive local building style, local planners and historians understand that the character of the city is due not only to its historic monuments, but also to the overall built fabric of the urban core. Planning for development and modernisation has thus proceeded with an emphasis on contextual sensitivity and historic conservation.[8] The attempted marriage between conservation and modernisation, however, has been an uneasy one. In dealing with irreconcilable goals, the city's planners have adopted local solutions that, in certain instances, have conflicted with the urban planning regulations promulgated by central government.

It is within this context that we can consider the impacts that the various non-state social and economic actors have on shaping the collective built environment of the city. Two important examples of the creation of urban space outside of the purview of the local state are the self-built housing which has proliferated in the city and its environs, often in direct contradiction to the stipulations of urban development policies, and the restoration since the 1980s of the extensive network of neighbourhood temples throughout the city. Examination of these two forms of change in the urban environment not only gives us a sense of the local particularities of urban change in Quanzhou, but suggests as well the vitality of local 'self-organising' associations. The idea that so much of the new development of collective urban space in Quanzhou is occurring in spite of, rather than because of, local government planning could be interpreted as an indication of the strength of civil society in Quanzhou, when compared to other Chinese cities. Both these forms of urban physical change – self-built housing and local temple restoration – are also of great concern to local officials who are seeking new means of managing these changes. One might see this as a response to a perceived threat to the state arising from the dynamism of non-state actors. It is more likely, however, that this is more an expression of what is understood to be the proper function of local administrators in their supervision of the public sphere.

Self-built housing

A recent study of forms of self-built housing in Quanzhou by scholars from Qinghua University and the University of British Columbia reveals a diversity of processes resulting in a variety of built environments. This self-building has not produced the 'squatter slums' that the term 'self-built housing' connotes in other developing country contexts. Most are sound constructions, typically with concrete frames and brick infill walls. Nonetheless, self-building in Quanzhou does exhibit many of the same attributes of self-building elsewhere in the world (Leaf 1993), such as incremental construction, the use of low-cost rural migrant labour, *ad hoc* financing techniques instead of formal bank loans, and a general disregard for official planning and building codes.

The study identified six different typologies of self-built construction in and around the historic core of Quanzhou. The major distinctions were according to location – whether inner city or peripheral – and, linked to this, whether the structures were built by long-time urban residents or by villagers on the urban periphery. The current boom in inner city self-built construction can be interpreted in certain respects as the resurrection of an historic practice, as it bears similarities to a previous construction boom in the 1920s and 1930s. As with the previous boom, the larger, multi-storied houses proliferating in the residential neighbourhoods of the city owe much to remittances from overseas relatives and stylistic cues taken from Malaysia, the Philippines, Hong Kong and elsewhere. For good reason, the planners of the city are concerned that this onslaught of four- and five-storey white-tiled buildings is compromising the character of the city by obscuring the previous generation of one- and two-storey redbrick houses. It is small consolation that what are now looked upon favourably as the old 'Nanyang' (South Sea) style houses of the 1920s and 1930s were considered to be controversial imports in their time.

The self-built houses on the urban periphery are something quite different, however, as these are built by erstwhile farmers on what is officially designated as agricultural land. Typically, these houses are built with funds obtained from selling off use-rights to village lands and then rented in whole or in part to rural migrants at informal market rates. The village that we examined contained a population of more than four thousand migrants, primarily from the inland provinces of Sichuan and Gansu, in addition to the two thousand officially registered residents. A noteworthy point is that local village committee leaders view the migrants as only temporary and therefore as not playing an important role in the future of the village, despite the fact that the ongoing urbanisation of the village, and indeed its economic viability, are dependent on their presence.

The migrant population exerts a profound influence on the public sphere in this village. A tight intermixing of residential and occupational activities, with small- or medium-scale production facilities for shoes, clothing, packing materials, metal products and so forth can be found on the ground floors of the ostensibly residential buildings, with workers' dormitories above. Overall, residential space is a low priority for the migrants, most of whom are saving their wages to remit to their families back home. The result is a high density of occupation among the migrants and an intensive use of public space for recreational and commercial activities. In the early evening, the streets and shops are filled with people, with billiard tables and makeshift badminton courts crowding the small alleyways. The transformation that has occurred in this village in such a short span of time is not only a transformation in the physical sense, with networks of roads and other infrastructure linking a series of distinctive urban spaces. It is also a fundamental change in social composition, with a new residential diversity – by social class, by economic function and by place of origin – much more in keeping with an urban setting than with a village of farm families.

The process of self-building or 'grassroots' urbanisation observed on the periphery of Quanzhou is similar, in some respects, to the growth that has occurred in Beijing's Zhejiang cun. The important difference here, however, is that in contrast to the history of periodic repression and demolitions that Zhejiang cun has experienced, the urbanisation of the village in Quanzhou is welcomed by municipal authorities. Indeed, as one of the goals of the municipal authorities is to expand the urban limits of the city, they have cooperated with the village committee to carry out a programme of road widening and drainage improvement. It is anticipated that the village will be transformed into an urban neighbourhood by the early years of the twenty-first century.

Temple restoration

An examination of the ongoing restoration of temples in Quanzhou also gives us a sense of the non-state forces driving development in the city. In order to appreciate the complexities of current restoration activities, it is useful to point out a few aspects of the role of religion in China's pre-revolutionary past. In his interpretation of late imperial China's religious life, Stephan Feuchtwang (1977) stresses the distinction between the temples of official religion and those of popular religion. Official religion, incorporating elements of Daoism and Buddhism, utilised a system of temples and rites closely paralleling the formal administrative hierarchy of the state and designed to reinforce the leading agency of the imperial throne. In contrast, the various sects and temples of popular religion were locally initiated and developed into non-centralised networks of similar temples through the ritual referred to as the 'division of incense' (fenxiang), which allowed for a non-hierarchical propagation of new temples. In this distinction between official and popular temples, very different respective roles can be observed, with the temples of the official religion focused on maintaining the legitimacy of the imperial state, and the temples of popular religion playing a critical function in the construction of local community mores.[9]

In contrast to the hierarchy and exclusivity of the temples of the official religion, a 'popular temple's area is defined purely territorially – all those

within a given territory, whatever their rank or class, are expected to participate in its major festivals, at least by paying the ritual maintenance tax'
(Feuchtwang 1977: 591). This relative egalitarianism promoted the creation
of locally based social capital (i.e. horizontal social ties, in contrast to the
verticality engendered by the official religion), and has no doubt been an
important factor in the proliferation of *fenxiang* temples wherever *huaqiao*
Chinese have settled (Schipper 1977). *Fenxiang* temples served local communities in multiple ways, by functioning as points of focus for a number of
different social services and collective undertakings, such as the organisation
of small-scale rotating credit associations (Y. Zhuang 1996).

In its pre-revolutionary past, the city of Quanzhou contained well over
one hundred temples.[10] These were closed down or converted to other uses
in the 1950s, with many destroyed as relics of feudalism during the Cultural
Revolution in the 1960s and early 1970s. In response to both the interests of
local residents and the increasing influence of *huaqiao* Chinese after the
opening up of China in the early 1980s, a priority list of major temples to be
restored was drawn up in the mid-1980s. An important criterion for prioritisation was that the buildings to be restored had to be recognised as
belonging to one of the five religions defined as 'official religions' of China:
Buddhism, Daoism, Catholicism, Protestantism and Islam. Other criteria
included historical importance and an expression of interest in undertaking
restoration by the relevant religious authority. Twenty-seven temple structures were put on this list, including the only Arab-built mosque extant in
China today.

As they are not part of any officially recognised religion, the neighbourhood temples and altars to local deities that abound in Quanzhou were not
included in the list of buildings to be restored.[11] Despite the government's
disregard, it is estimated that more than one half of these local places of
worship had been restored or rebuilt by 1999. The restoration work was
funded by donations from local residents and *huaqiao*, and carried out by
informal neighbourhood groups. This resurrection of local temples has
occurred alongside a resurgence of interest in the practices and landscapes
of traditional popular religion. The city government is at a loss as to how to
react to this phenomenon, as there are no official instructions coming down
from Beijing. There is, however, recognition on the part of the government
that since this is something that will influence both the social and physical
development of the city, there is a need for a management response. Local
officials and city planners are beginning to study the situation.

Conclusions

I began this essay with an admittedly liberal definition of collective goods in
order to encompass the production and maintenance of urban space itself
as a collective good, and to distinguish this from the myriad other collective

goods which are delivered through the milieu of the city. In this, the distinction between collective goods delivery through the local state and through non-state agencies was seen as critical in that it brings to the fore the question of the vitality of civil society. The purpose here was to examine these issues in the context of one particular Chinese city, and in order to do so, it was necessary to review first the basic patterns of Chinese urban development overall. In taking this approach, I emphasised how the institutions of the Chinese state, as articulated at local levels, give rise to a particular structure of urban governance.

A consideration of urban change in Quanzhou shows how variations within the general model of Chinese urbanisation may arise from the peculiarities of local histories and geographies. By looking in particular at the incipient development of non-state spaces, I sought to expose the urban development implications of certain elements of civil society. By way of illustration, I explained how, in the village on the periphery of Quanzhou, local residents collectively decided to transform their settlement into an urban neighbourhood by taking advantage of the economic opportunity accorded by the region's burgeoning migrant population. In doing so, they necessarily have taken a position contrary to the planning policies of central government, although their actions are in the interest of, and approved by, the municipal government. Similarly, despite the state's stricture on popular religion, urban space in Quanzhou is being transformed by the many small, unofficial associations that have sprung up to work towards the restoration and construction of neighbourhood temples.

Another salient local characteristic that underpins the vitality of civil society components such as these is the strength of Quanzhou's *huaqiao* connections. The influence of the *huaqiao* on the physical and social development of the city is deep rooted and multi-layered. One can easily point out the tremendous impacts of the capital flows into the region due to these connections, not only in terms of the official channels of foreign direct investment, but in the many significant charitable donations and in the myriad and unmeasured capital transfers of comparatively small-scale family remittances. But such influence is felt not only in monetary terms, as one can discern as well the impacts of overseas connections in the actions of local associations, and beyond that, in the means of engagement between the local state and the citizenry. All of this is expressed in the production of the urban built environment, which in its totality is an aspect of collective consumption for the people of Quanzhou. It also points to the specificity, if not uniqueness, of how civil society is expressed in this locality.

These comments must be coupled with a caveat, as care should be taken not to generalise from the situation in Quanzhou to other cases of urban change in China, or to the emergence of a civil society in other Chinese cities. Instead, this should be taken as an argument for recognising the importance of a regionalist perspective. The case of Quanzhou should be seen as only one of many attempts to articulate the diversity of local experiences within China.

One general observation that does arise from the points explored here, however, is with regard to future developments in the provision of collective goods in China. As the reform era continues into its third decade, with its policy orientation towards privatisation and social safety net reductions, it can be expected that Chinese urban dwellers will be forced to rely even more on such traditional non-state social support systems as familial and personal networks and informal livelihoods. This observation highlights the importance of more careful study of non-state mechanisms of collective goods provision in Chinese cities. The examples given here of non-state production of urban space – the channelling of *huaqioa* remittances into self-built 'modern' city housing, the village committee operating outside of its formally specified mandate and the informal self-organisation of neighbourhood temple associations – have been presented only in a rudimentary fashion. It is insufficient to emphasise the non-state nature of these activities without examining in detail the internal dynamics of these associational forms and the intricacies of their interactions with the state. Further study along these lines is therefore necessary for a full understanding of the urban spatial implications of changing state/society relations in the cities of China.

Notes

1 This may be defined broadly as the period from the founding of the PRC in 1949 to the beginning of economic reforms as initiated at the Third Plenum of the Eleventh Party Congress in 1978.

2 This view of the strong central state has been increasingly challenged in recent years by careful studies of local political practices in the recent past. See for example Wolf 1996.

3 The collective sector is interpreted by some to be a 'disguised private sector', since tax laws and other punitive policies create disincentives for firms to establish themselves as true private enterprises.

4 For more on Zhejiang cun and other settlements in Beijing, see Ma and Xiang 1998; Liu and Liang 1997; C. Wang 1995; Leaf 1995. For discussions of the different urban spatial impacts of migrant populations in Shanghai, see Wu 1999; White 1998.

5 Basic statistics and other information on Quanzhou are taken from interview notes and other written documentation gathered during field visits in 1994 and 1999. Additional material may be found in Leaf *et al.* 1995, which reports on the results of a field study collaboration between students and faculty of Qinghua University, Beijing, and the University of British Columbia, Vancouver. Further results of collaborative work undertaken in 1999 (which also included students from McGill University, Montreal) are presented in Abramson *et al.* 2001. I gratefully acknowledge the instrumental role of Daniel Abramson in establishing these collaborative linkages between UBC, Tsinghua, McGill and the Quanzhou Municipal Planning Bureau.

6 'New' in this regard should be understood in contrast to the previous centralised socialist period, as the point can be made that many of the new actors and new processes of urban change are in actuality the re-emergence of older forms, as

can be seen in the role of Overseas Chinese interests or in the strengthened position of local property owners.

7 The scale of these impacts in the early twentieth century is well illustrated by historic analyses of the *huaqiao* influence in the region, such as those by G. Zhuang 1996; Dai 1996.

8 In its application, the emphasis on historic conservation in Quanzhou raises questions about the political and symbolic uses of history. The historic designation of the city by the Beijing government arises from consideration of the various historic structures found within the city and its surroundings, undergirding a 'monumental' interpretation of conservation which has found favour among certain of the city's elites. Others, however, stress the historical importance of the overall character of the urban core, an alternative view which has prompted ongoing debate over the application of the large-scale redevelopment practices which typify urban construction elsewhere in coastal China.

9 It should be pointed out, however, that when viewed historically, these two aspects of Chinese religion cannot be seen as mutually exclusive. Feuchtwang (1977) emphasises the overlaps between the official and popular religions. As the gods of popular religion were almost invariably once living beings who were canonised through the popular religion, good administrative practices from time to time required their official recognition, resulting in the co-optation of certain of the *fenxiang* temple networks into the administrative hierarchy of the official religion. The Tien Hou Temple in Quanzhou is a good example of this. In contrast, the practices surrounding the City God (Cheng Huang) Temple illustrate a downward appropriation: this temple is characteristically part of the official religion, yet its ceremonies allowed for broader popular participation than would be necessitated by formal ritual. As it was at the lowest end of the official religious hierarchy, the City God Temple was thus closest to the citizenry, a factor resulting in adaptive ritual practices over time.

10 In addition to the city's *fenxiang* temples, a good many of the neighbourhood temples were those associated with what are locally referred to as *pujing* (wards or precincts), the socio-spatial divisions which characterised Quanzhou in the late imperial period (1368–1911) and possibly before. In his analysis, C. Wang (1995) emphasises the ambiguity of Quanzhou's *pujing* structure, as simultaneously an apparatus for imperial administrative rule and a vehicle for the practice of local folk rituals in the popular religion.

11 It is notable that three of the major *fenxiang* temples, including the Tien Hou Temple, mentioned in note 9 above, were included in the list for restoration despite their roots in popular religion.

11

PROVIDING PUBLIC SPACES

Singapore and Taibei[1]

Chua Beng-Hua

Singapore and Taiwan have followed similar developmental paths. Although Taiwan industrialised earlier than Singapore, both experienced very high rates of economic growth as a result of government-directed credit and export-oriented industrialisation. For much of the last four decades of the twentieth century, both had authoritarian governments. Taiwan was under the military rule of the Guomondang (KMT) until 1989, when the democratisation process was instituted under a reformed KMT – a process that subsequently led to the replacement of the KMT by the Democratic Progressive Party (DPP) in the presidential election of 2000. At that date, Singapore was still under the single-party dominance of the People's Action Party (PAP).

To accommodate rapid economic growth, the city-state of Singapore and the cities of Taiwan had to undergo massive physical transformation. Yet despite the similarities in their political and economic organisation, the two countries adopted very different strategies in the provision of collective consumption goods that have resulted in marked differences in their spatial and social organisation. The profusion of public spaces beneath the lush green urban landscape of Singapore and the dusty and confusing streetscape of Taibei are immediately obvious to anyone who is even slightly familiar with the two cities. Taiwan's current DPP President, Chen Shuibian, openly recognised the divergence when he was Mayor of the city of Taibei. He expressed undisguised admiration for Singapore as a model of Asian urban planning.[2]

The differences between the public spaces in Singapore and Taibei are examined in this chapter. After surveying the visible contrasts between public spaces in the two cities, this analysis will focuses on contestation over the creation of green spaces and over the historical readings that are imposed on public spaces.[3]

Visible differences

The use and regulation of the space surrounding the shop-houses that front the streets of Singapore and Taibei is symptomatic of contrasts between the two cities. In both cities, shop-houses have a sheltered public corridor that runs the length of the block along the shop front. In Taibei, shop-owners usually colonise the footpath for private use, either as an extension of the retail space or as a place on which to park motor scooters and cars. Even big department stores will use the space close to their entrances for retail purposes. Indeed, frequently the shop owner simply grills or walls up the space, incorporating it into the 'interior' of the shop and thus disrupting the pedestrian flow in the corridor of that particular block. An example of such colonisation can be found in the older section of Ximendin district, just behind the gentrified, pedestrianised shopping area. Colonisation of public space is even more unrestrained in the back streets, where portions of public space are frequently incorporated into houses as private spaces. These colonising activities, combined with the narrow streets that were developed according to Japanese colonial planning sensitivities, give segments of the city the appearance of unruly congestion that is suitable, even 'cosy', for pedestrians. However, it impedes vehicular traffic.

Singaporeans who recall the pre-industrial period find Taibei visually reminiscent of their own city's past.[4] Similar corridors, locally called 'five-foot ways', can be found throughout older commercial sections of the island; this is because these were a planning feature dictated by Raffles, the British colonial 'founder' of Singapore. As in Taibei, these spaces once were either appropriated by shop owners who used them for display or storage, or leased to people such as barbers, letter-writers and fortune-tellers. The presence of these sidewalk activities and the general congestion of the streets both attracted and repelled foreign and local visitors to Singapore's Chinatown (Savage 1992).

However, since the early 1970s, sidewalk commerce in Singapore has been prohibited. The public corridor spaces have been policed by the Ministry of Environment and the Fire Department. In contrast to Taibei, the five-foot ways have reverted to their originally planned function as footpaths for pedestrians, sheltering them from the tropical sun and rain. Similarly, the back lanes have been cleared to facilitate the collection of domestic refuse. The enforced 'tidying up' of the five-foot ways and the back lanes has been so successful that it has bled street life out of parts of Chinatown. Consequently, roadside vendors have become icons representative of Singapore's 'colourful' past, feeding the nostalgia of older Singaporeans and tourists alike (Siew 1999). The plan by the Singapore Tourist Board to revitalise the dead streets and rebuild their pastel façades is examined later in this chapter.

In Taibei, noted public spaces tend to be expanses of hard surface that surround and enhance grandiose national monuments and exhibition halls, including those that commemorate the late Jiang Jieshi (Chiang Kai Shek), founding President of the Republic of China or Taiwan. There has been an attempt to delegate the responsibility for providing public green spaces to the private sector. Owners of large edifices are permitted to increase their floor area if they offer public space at ground level. However, in almost every instance, the 'public' space provided is incorporated into the design of the building itself, thus inhibiting public use. For example, in the Regent Hotel, a very well designed 'public' garden is framed at one edge by the large windows of the coffee shop, which simultaneously transform any member of the public using the garden into either a part of the view of the hotel customers, or a 'voyeur' of activities within the coffee shop. In another instance, the Hotel Forum has audaciously absorbed a small park planted with trees into the design of its semi-circular driveway. It could be argued that the mountains that surround Taibei supply ample greenery and parks, but this is cold comfort in the daily life of city dwellers.[5]

Whereas Taibei is dusty and exposed to the elements, Singapore appears to be a veritable garden city, where it is rare to find a street unprotected by trees and where small green parks provide visual relief to the hard concrete of the city centre. Parks developed during the colonial days, such as Central Park, which was once King George V Park, and the Padang, in front of the colonial edifice of the City Hall and the Supreme Court, are kept as green areas in spite of the high real estate values of their locations.[6] In addition to the urban parks, the entire stretch of reclaimed land along the east coast of the island from the edge of the city to the airport is designated parkland.

Polluted rivers are the norm for cities in Asia. The Danshui River runs through Taibei. Not surprisingly, pollutants were emptied unchecked into the Danshui River until 1988, when a concerted government effort to clean up the river was initiated. Compared to the Danshui River and the rivers that run through many large cities in the region, the Singapore River is a mere tributary. In contrast to other polluted rivers, however, the Singapore River was cleaned up by a ten-year environmental project that began in 1977. During this period, human settlements and all economic activities along the river that caused pollution were either moved or phased out (Hon 1990). The quays on both banks became highly priced entertainment sites. The warehouses once owned and operated by immigrant Chinese businesspeople, and which accommodated the entrepôt commodity trade that was the city's lifeline, were converted into bars, restaurants and other entertainment outlets where locals and tourists mingle, soaking in the tropical nights and the reinvented ambience of the colonial and immigrant past, *al fresco*.[7]

Shopping facilities further differentiate the appearance of the two cities. Strictly speaking, shopping centres are privately owned places. Nevertheless, in urban areas these spaces have become public leisure spaces, in spite of their not-so-hidden surveillance cameras and security guards. A simple interest in purchasing constitutes the necessary condition to wonder through shopping centres, and so they become a place for all and sundry to hang out – particularly youth. In Singapore, shopping complexes are ubiquitous and are found in symbiotic clusters that combine to form shopping districts. As sociologist Mike Featherstone observes, 'To walk through the centre of Singapore represents a movement through a series of air-conditioned shopping centres' (1998: 917).

By contrast, in Taibei shops continue to line street fronts and seldom go higher than the second floor. Large shopping complexes are still a relatively new phenomenon. For example, the Sogo shopping complex on Duenhua South Road was only built in the late 1990s. One of the new enterprises that stands out in this respect is the Eslite chain owned by local entrepreneur, Wu Cin Yuo, which combines high-culture commodities, such as an art gallery, bookshop, vintage wine shop, middle-range fashion shops and a high-price café. It is, in short, a consumer lifestyle centre. Shopping districts are largely absent in Taibei. The very first such configuration, the Ximendin Pedestrian District, opened in 1999, thirteen years after the idea was initiated. Since the beginning of the century, Ximendin had been an entertainment area, particularly for movie houses. In the early 1980s, it declined as a result of disruptions from public infrastructure construction. Shopping facilities moved to the eastern part of the city. This led to the idea of reviving and developing the place as a pedestrian district. In Ximendin itinerant hawkers are banned, streets pedestrianised and new shops, movie houses, restaurants and other entertainment outlets are housed in the renovated buildings. Not surprisingly, the place has quickly become the 'happening' place for the young. The new street life is brought into relief by traces of the place's decline, such as the very observable and disproportionate presence of old men hanging out in the McDonald's that stands at the entrance the renovated district.

The highly visible contrast between Taibei and Singapore, in terms of provision of public spaces, can be explained by a single word: planning. Singapore is an excessively planned space. The island is so comprehensively planned that even remnant patches of natural vegetation require the planners' permission to exist. This intensity of planning is largely motivated by a very keen sense of the smallness of the island and the need to maximise its land use in order to accommodate all the demands of a modern nation-state. It has had a concept plan in place since 1971. Since then, the long-ruling PAP government has adhered closely to this plan, with periodic reviews for 'fine tuning'. Initiated by Lee Kuan Yew himself, the 'garden city' concept has been in place since the mid-1960s. This garden city concept is tied to the general aspiration for a clean city that surpasses the standards of the developed world.

The growth of Taibei has not been overseen by urban planners. In fact, a recent attempt to clear an illegal squatter settlement, established after the arrival of the KMT army in 1949, was legitimised by reference to the designation of the area as parkland in the 1930s plan that was left behind by the Japanese colonial administration – a plan that was re-adopted in 1966 in the very first urban planning review carried out by the KMT government. The Taibei City Comprehensive Plan was initiated as late as 1992, and further amendments were finalised only in 1996.[8] The difference in the presence and absence, or, to put it more generously, the timing of the implementation of urban space planning in the two cities, is all too obvious. The question is, why?

The greening of city spaces

The reason why the PAP regime has planned Singapore is explained in the chronicles of the ministries of National Development and Environment and the various agencies under their auspices, such as the Urban Redevelopment Authority, the Housing and Development Board, the Parks and Recreation Board, the Environmental Health Department and the Hawkers, Sewerage, Drainage and Pollution Control Division.[9]

On the other hand, the question of why Taibei was not more stringently planned under the KMT is difficult to answer. One Taiwanese commentator suggests that 'until the political and social liberalisation of the 1980s, "public space" was neither a conceptual nor an experiential reality in Taibei City' (Martin 2000: 87). A commonly cited explanation is that the leaders of the KMT were so convinced that they would regain the mainland that they saw little reason to elaborate on the plans left behind by the Japanese admin-istration. Popular and psychologically satisfying although this 'explanation' may be to those who are critical of the KMT regime, it ignores the fact that the KMT did execute a successful rural land reform programme. A second line of 'reasoning' is that a stringent policing of urban zoning and other bylaws would have been very unpopular during the marshal law period because the government was already deficit in legitimacy. Consequently, it decided to let violations and deviations from planning guidelines pass without disciplinary action. In the absence of definitive answers, the ques-tion about the absence of planning will have to be deferred.[10]

For now, it is to be noted that Chen Shuibian, once DPP Mayor of Taibei and then President of Taiwan, viewed Singapore as both a model and a refer-ence point for rationalising the changes that he proposed for Taibei. Elected Mayor in 1994, it is argued that Chen had a mission to improve the environ-mental life of Taibei's population as a means of showing up the negligence and corruption of the KMT regime in the country as a whole. Certainly, those who voted for Chen were likely to have harboured frustrations with the KMT and to have had high expectations for environmental improvements and, indeed, several improvements were achieved during Chen's single term as Mayor.[11] The most obvious of these was the development of dedicated bus lanes to improve public transport. Less obvious were attempts to maintain zoning bylaws. The most controversial change was undoubtedly the DPP's attempt to clean up the city in an effort to push Taibei into the ranks of 'international cities'. It is to this final ambition that I now direct my analysis.

Taibei: Parks 14 and 15

The 'green' space located on Nanjing East Road, Section 1, and Linxing North Road was once a squatter settlement inhabited by some of the poorest people in Taibei. Many were old soldiers who had come with the retreating KMT army in 1949. They levelled and occupied an old Japanese graveyard and incorporated salvageable materials, such as marble gravestones, into dwellings of otherwise impermanent building materials. In the 1960s, the first wave of rural immigrants, displaced by the industrialisation process, joined the existing inhabitants. Also included were members of the aboriginal population who drifted into the city. Such a community of the poorest strata, living in apparent over-congestion in a settlement built with found and impermanent materials, would be considered a 'blight' by most city governments. Moreover, the settlement was built on a location of very high real estate value that the KMT government had acquired in the late 1980s. Thus the settlement was not only illegal, it was also considered an unsightly obstacle to development.

In September 1996, Chen announced that the squatter settlement would be demolished to make way for a park. The determination of the city government was underpinned by a perceived need for recreational space in the city centre. Further, it was thought that a sprawling squatter settlement in the urban centre was unbecoming of a Taibei that aspired to world city status. The Mayor argued that during his tour of Taibei, pop star Michael Jackson had been aghast at the view of the 'offending' settlement from his hotel window.

Resettlement of the squatters was to be completed by mid-1997. Contrary to the Mayor's earlier promise that resettlement would take place before the destruction of existing residences, as is the practice in Singapore, no replacement public housing was provided. Affected individuals and households had to wait for the completion of public housing, the date of which was uncertain. Furthermore, anyone who resisted the destruction of the squatter settlement was threatened with denial of compensation and with prosecution.

On 14 March 1997 bulldozers levelled the settlement. In its place now stand two small adjacent parks. Both are completely lacking in character, as reflected in their names, Park 14 and Park 15.[12]

This simple narrative glosses over the conflicts and negotiations that occurred between squatters, their civil society supporters and city hall. The site turned into a test case for new social movements under the DPP government. Until the election of Chen as Mayor, however, the DPP had been on the same side as the new social movements in their common opposition to the KMT regime.

As it happened, a student from the Institute of Building and Planning at National Taiwan University was conducting fieldwork at the site before demolition of the settlement began. The ideological orientation of the Institute has always been towards the promotion of 'grassroots' democracy – a democracy in which citizens are conceived as active participants in the process of planning and planning offers an opportunity to engage in the democratic process.[13] When the demolition was announced, this student mobilised fellow students to help organise the affected residents. He also enlisted the help of professors, who had been politically associated with the Mayor, to negotiate with city hall and to lobby other politicians, including members of the KMT. Other professional individuals and organisations became involved in the 'Coalition Against the Bulldozer of City Hall'. The coalition and the residents requested that demolition be postponed until the resettlement of all affected people had been properly executed; that is, they argued that re-housing should precede demolition.

Unfortunately, as the resistance movement progressed, the squatter residents became less and less directly involved in the negotiation process. Professionals, particularly the Institute's professors, mediated and represented the residents' interests to city hall. These interventions received much attention in the media, which in turn became one of the sites in which the Coalition's representatives met spokespersons from city hall. Each side attempted to influence public opinion in its favour. During the protracted period of resistance and negotiation, an elderly resident, unable to contemplate a future away from the squatter settlement, committed suicide. In addition, on the day before the bulldozers were to move in, a fire broke out in the settlement, leaving many of the residents homeless. Perhaps coincidentally, the fire facilitated the demolition of the squatter housing. The bulldozers moved in on the appointed day.

Significantly, the demolition and the clearance of squatters to make way for Parks 14 and 15 were carried out by an avowedly pro-citizen municipal government headed by a mayor who supported an increasingly democratising polity. Among Chen's many electoral promises had been the promotion of two-way communication between citizens and city hall. Yet once elected, pressures from competing interests and his own vision of the future of the city began to impinge on that commitment. In relation to Parks 14 and 15, he was able to invoke the need of the 'larger' citizen body in general for a 'clean and green' environment against the 'self-serving' interests of the squatter residents. In this way he appealed to the interests of the expanding middle class.

The social movement activists appear to have gained little from their protests, except perhaps tangible experiences of organisation and strategies of engagement; experiences which may be increasingly useful now that the DPP is in political ascendancy rather than on the margins. In addition, the collective memory that the social activists' interventions have etched symbolically into Parks 14 and 15 should not be underestimated. Perhaps because of the memory of the residents' struggle, the parcels of land will remain as parks instead of being sold to the highest bidder for construction – a strong possibility given their very high value and consequent capacity to generate municipal revenue.

Ironically, despite the admiration that Chen expressed for the PAP's achievement in Singapore, he seems to have missed a critical lesson regarding squatter resettlement; that is, to provide better quality housing for affected residents before the impermanent structures that they call home are demolished. In the history of the reconstruction of Singapore, tens of thousands of residents were moved from different forms of housing into high-rise flats in planned housing estates. Since the inception of the housing estates in the early 1960s, resistance against resettlement has been minimal. By the early 1980s it was a rare occurrence. What was obvious to squatters, especially those who were renting spaces in the settlements, was that the housing estates offered them a better environment, improved sanitation and health, and the chance to own a flat for ninety-nine years.

The only drawback for Singapore's resettled squatters was a sharp increase in the cost of living. In spite of national economic expansion, the cost of living was a concern to about ten per cent of households that rented from the public housing authority.[14] However, the early participants in the national mass housing programme were those that benefited disproportionately from the constant inflation of property prices. Between the 1960s and mid-1990s, every household in public housing, including those that had been resettled into modest apartments, made a capital gain. In 1997 the Asian economic crisis radically lowered property prices in Singapore. This deflation probably signalled the end of assured capital gains in public housing ownership, rendering such ownership a speculative activity, just like private housing. Nevertheless, by then all resettlement had long since been completed, and any political costs incurred in the process compensated for in full.

Gardening Singapore

As for the provision of public green spaces in Singapore, the lushness of the overall cityscape is undoubtedly the result of a concerted effort by the PAP government, which initiated the 'garden city' concept in the early 1960s. Tree planting by the roadside had also been a practice of the colonial administrators, for whom the benefits of shaded streets in the tropical heat were more than apparent.[15] In the late 1990s, the Housing and Development Board, the Urban Redevelopment Authority and the Jurong Town Corporation (responsible for the development and leasing of industrial spaces and estates) were each responsible for their own green programmes. The Parks Board took care of the rest of Singapore, including the maintenance of major public parks such as the Botanic Gardens and the Central Park at Fort Canning.[16] In its enthusiasm to green the city, the Parks Board 'invented' the 'instant tree', in which trunks of fast growing trees were planted to accelerate the development of green coverage.[17] The greenness of Singapore has since become a source of civic and official pride and an abiding concern of government. Indeed, according to Goh Chok Tong, he and his predecessor Lee Kuan Yew are two Prime Ministers who unfailingly read the reports of the gardening activity of the Parks Board (Goh 1999).

Nevertheless, in spite of the obvious greenness of Singapore, problems have occurred. First, the plants used in the greening of Singapore are almost all imported from other tropical or sub-tropical areas for their ornamental and exotic values. In some locations, exotics have crowded out indigenous flora. Second, government agencies simultaneously have destroyed Singapore's natural environment for development purposes. For example, almost all of the coastline vegetation was destroyed by land reclamation. Up to 40 per cent of the mangrove species are extinct, and only residual groves of the original mangrove swamps are left in various parts of the island (Turner and Yong 1999: 5). Even Bukit Timah Hill, a nature reserve since the mid-nineteenth century, was subjected to constant encroachment. Only the natural environment that surrounds the reservoirs in the centre of the island is exempt from such appropriations because destruction of the secondary forest for human settlement would pollute the valuable water resource. The central concern of environmentalists in Singapore, therefore, is to conserve what little remains of the natural environment.

In this context, the Nature Society, particularly its conservation committee, emerged as one of the most vocal civic groups to contest the government's plans for land use. The Society had some victories and some defeats. For example, in spite of its effort to gather a petition of more than 25,000 names, including those of prominent Singaporeans, a bird sanctuary was lost to public housing development. A high point of the group's work was its participation, in 1992, with the Ministry of the Environment in formulating a national Green Plan. In the Green Plan, 5 per cent of the land was set aside for nature conservation, and nineteen sites suggested by the Nature Society were incorporated within these designated areas. Unfortunately, these 'conserved' areas were not protected by legislation and remained vulnerable to encroachment. As recently as 1999, a major riverine conservation area was threatened by highway straightening, despite an earlier plan to bypass the reserve (Ho 1999). Until the areas designed on the Green Plan are legally demarcated and protected, the struggle for nature conservation will remain the major task of the Nature Society. Furthermore, as encroachments are quietly approved by government authorities (in the example offered, the Urban Redevelopment Authority), the Nature Society has good reason to reconsider its strategy of negotiating with authorities behind closed doors. Public debate in the media might be the only way to protect conservation areas.

Recovering collective memories

In both Singapore and Taibei, by 2000 the frenzied race for economic and physical growth had slowed. Satisfied with their relatively high level of economic development, state leaders turned their attention to political and cultural issues, including the recovery or the reinvention of the collective past and its commemoration as national history. The need for an historical consciousness assumed particular urgency for Singapore's long-ruling government. In its own assessment and apprehension, the absence of a sense of history among the younger population who were born and grew up in relative economic affluence apparently had allowed the young to take success for granted, and to be ignorant of the difficulties that the nation had faced in the past and continued to face in the competitive, globalised present. The government therefore instituted informal mass education in the official 'Singapore story' through multi-media exhibitions. Furthermore, it introduced Singapore's history into the formal education curriculum at all levels up to tertiary education.

A corresponding process of national historical construction took place in Taiwan after the presidency was transferred in 1987 from the Jiang Jieshi 'dynasty' to Li Denghui, a Taiwanese born during the Japanese colonial occupation. As the Jiang 'dynasty' was identified with the population from 'outside provinces', referring to descendants of the generation that accompanied the defeated KMT from mainland China, this transfer is commonly read as the indigenisation of KMT politics. Indigenisation involves jettisoning the idea of 'recapturing the motherland', and instead investing ideological energy into the creation of a Taiwanese nation. This led Li, the first popularly elected President, to suggest on the eve of his retirement from office in 1999 that future negotiations between Taiwan and the People's Republic of China be conducted as negotiations between two states. The discursive struggle to create a Taiwanese nation advanced several steps with the election to the presidency of Chen Shuibian, because the DPP espoused Taiwan's independence.

In both countries, official attempts to recover the past as a part of a national ideology unavoidably come up against publics with memory constructions of their own. The historicised public spaces that emerge from these confrontations are often determined by political power or the audibility of public protests, rather than being emblematic of any 'authentic' historicity.

228 Park[18]

An example of the ideological investment in Taiwanese nationalism is the construction of '228' monuments across the island, including one in Taibei. The '228' refers to February 28 1947, the day on which the KMT military government, as it repossessed Taiwan from the Japanese colonial government, massacred Taiwanese protesters in Taibei. The 228 Incident remained a suppressed but never erased memory among the local population under the authoritarian rule of the KMT. Until the lifting of martial law, commemoration of the Incident was prohibited. In 1987, public demand for historical redress and commemoration of the event began to build. This reached a peak in 1992, when urban communities in different parts of Taiwan began to build their own '228' monuments which included gardens, museums and statues.

Under Li Denghui's presidency, the central government was anxious to capitalise on public sentiment and establish its own Taiwanese identity by commemorating the 228 Incident. In Taibei, the KMT city government also set up a committee to construct a commemorative monument. The Mayor's office wanted to control the entire process, but as a demonstration of its newly acquired democratic credentials, it opened up public discussions about proposals for a monument and found itself at loggerheads with the descendants of the 228 martyrs. The project was soon mired in competing interests, competing voices and competing discourses over the design and siting of the monument. Indeed, the project mirrored in microcosm the complexity of social memory, and illuminated 'nation' as a site of contested hegemony.

In February 1992, the Mayor proposed several sites for the Taibei monument, but expressed a preference for the existing Xinsheng Park. The site was in the city centre, easily accessible, of sufficient size and, as it was already parkland, construction could start immediately. However, Xinsheng Park was rejected by the descendants of the 228 Incident and their representatives. They objected that because the area was on a flight path and exposed to the sonic boom of passing airplanes, it was unsuitable for the solemnity that befits ritual commemoration. In turn, the 228 descendants proposed New Park as the best location for a monument. New Park enfolded layers of Taiwan's 'national' history although, since the 1980s, it had become a gathering place for gay men.[19] 'New' in the park's name referred to the 1908 reconstruction of the park by the Japanese colonial regime. In the course of that reconstruction, symbols of the Qing Dynasty's formal annexation of Taiwan, including a temple, were demolished. In February 1947, New Park had housed the Chinese broadcasting station. Consequently, it was the setting for many demonstrations during the 228 Incident. In the decade after the massacre, the KMT regime built several structures in New Park, all of which drew on the architectural idioms of the northern Han Chinese in the expectation that these might erase the significance of the site for indigenous

Taiwanese. Finally, several government buildings are located in the vicinity of the Park, including the Presidential Office. In the early stages of negotiation, the government argued that this made the park unsuitable because demonstrations over the 228 Incident could easily spill over into the grounds of the Presidential Office.

These opposing views reflected the two most clearly identifiable factions in the debate that followed, with other individuals or groups lining up behind them according to their political sentiments and ethnic affiliations. Eventually, the government conceded and agreed that the monument would be constructed in New Park. The siting of the monument at New Park was thus a victory, spatially and symbolically, for the descendants of the 228 Incident.

However, if the descendants' interests in the memorial were principally in the commemoration of their massacred relatives, the political and ideological investments by governments lay elsewhere. For example, the first urban authority to complete a 228 monument was Peng Tung County, where the opposition DPP was in power. Its governor suggested that Peng Tung County's pyramid-shaped memorial symbolised an iceberg in which the 'truth' of the 228 Incident was submerged as part of the 'dirty' history of the KMT (Wu 1994: 856–86). But as Wu (1994) points out, in building its own memorials, the KMT was seeking to transform its own ignominious history as a colonising outsider into a tragic episode in the history of Taiwan-as-a-nation. This ideological sleight of hand allowed the KMT government to simultaneously both capitalise on, and disown, an event in the history of Taiwan; to embody it through its construction of the monument and disown it by intentionally distancing the present KMT from its own past.

To a wider audience, the construction of all 228 monuments was an integral step in the post-1989 construction of a nation called Taiwan – a nation that has been shedding its past pretence and ideological encumbrance as part of the larger China. The 228 monuments, along with other 'Taiwanese' historical narratives and cultural institutions, contribute toward a new national discourse that has prepared the grounds for Li Denghui's announcement of his 'two states' stance in international relations and Chen Shuibian's efforts to assert Taiwan's identity as a nation-state.

The thematisation of Singapore's 'Chinatown'

The history of a nation is unique unto itself; consequently, it would be futile to look for an event that has the same cache of political sentiments for Singaporeans as the 228 Incident has for the Taiwanese. Without a similar history of marshal law whose removal instantiated the democratisation process in Taiwan, Singapore's political institutions have always lived within the procedures of democracy. Thus civil society/state relations are not subject to similar processes of negotiation and contestation as those of Taiwan have been since 1989. In Singapore, administrative activities continue to be top-down, with the government initiating almost all policies, which are then executed by an efficient bureaucracy. Public participation is kept to a minimum and within the confines of government-organised feed-back sessions. However, the issue of conservation shows that differences and contests between the state and concerned citizens on specific issues go on, without necessary reference to the changing of government. In this way a level of political activity continues to exist beneath the absence of contesta-tion for state power. One of the more significant instances concerning collective memory in recent urban development is the proposal, by the Singapore Tourist Board (STB), to redevelop Chinatown.

Faced with declining tourist numbers from the usual sources in Asia, the STB had been hard pressed to increase the number of arrivals. An obvious, though not necessarily foolproof strategy, was to create tourist attractions by exoticising local cultures and cultural sites. Thus the entire island was demarcated into several theme areas including, of course, the so-called 'traditional' ethnic areas such as Chinatown, Little India and Kampung Glam. The latter refers to the area of early Malay and Arab settlement. Of these, Chinatown was the first to be selected for redevelopment, with a substantial fund of just under S$100 million. A local architectural firm DP (Design Partners) Architects was engaged, with American consultants who had experience in the development of Boston's Chinatown.

The STB's proposal, entitled 'Enhancing the Chinatown experience' (1998), published between appropriately red covers,[20] was widely circulated, indicating the pride and confidence of the STB and its hired agencies in their product. But the proposal immediately met with protests. Individuals who had an association with Chinatown, professionals who used their knowledge and position to state their cases as concerned citizens and organ-ised associations such as the Singapore Heritage Society (SHS), channelled their remarks through the newspapers, from letters to the editor to detailed arguments for an 'authentic' historical preservation of Chinatown for Singaporeans. They saw the STB proposal as the destruction-as-renovation of Chinatown as a theme park. Local historical experiences would be effaced by generic, archaic architectural motifs.

This unexpected barrage of criticism caused the STB to hold a public forum at which its architects, planners and management staff were available to answer all public queries. This was unprecedented, and may well have been prompted by the government's recent rhetoric on public participation and feedback. The forum was well attended by members of the SHS and its sympathisers, and current and past residents of Chinatown. Scheduled to last two hours, it went on for four, leaving the STP and its hired agencies embattled. Subsequently, the then Minister for Information and the Arts, George Yeo, said in Parliament, with no apparent sense of contradiction, that the high level of public discussion on the STB's proposal showed the cultural and emotional significance of Chinatown to Singaporeans at large and that the criticisms constituted no more than 'inconveniences' with which the STB had to deal.

In the end, the STB withdrew some of its proposals. All street furniture and other street ornamentations that mimic American Chinatown kitsch were deleted, as was the proposal to include three 'elemental' – earth, fire and water – gardens. What remained to be built was a 'village' theatre, with its Southern Chinese, rather than Southeast Asian Chinese, architectural elements, and an interpretative centre that would showcase Chinatown's history. The centre was to be placed under the authority of the National Heritage Board, which is responsible for all museums in Singapore, rather than the STB. Finally, of far greater significance in policy-making, all future STB proposals for large-scale redevelopment would be subject to regular reviews by a watch committee comprised of individual professionals drawn from the private sector. On the other hand, the SHS's next step was to try to focus the STB's efforts onto the few 'dead' streets in area. The street life in these areas had been bled out of them about a decade ago, when the streets were cleared of hawkers, the residents resettled into public housing, and the old shop houses tendered off, by the Urban Renewal Authority, to the highest bidder in order to conduct commercial activities from the subsequently rebuilt structures. The SHS hoped to distract the STB from reconceptualising Chinatown in its entirety to prevent the latter from further 'Disneyfication'.

Protests against the thematisation of Chinatown clearly did not have the same political significance as the conflicts over the 228 monuments in Taiwan. Nor were the sentiments that surrounded it as clearly crystallised. The struggle for the collective memory of Chinatown was more multiple and diffused, with each participant carrying their own memories of biographically significant events. In the end, what the unorganised contestants against the STB managed to obtain was the prevention of certain elements or modes of redevelopment, without specifying what was 'appropriate' to the spirit of Chinatown's past and present. This was, however, but a staying of the hands of destruction without any guarantees for the future.

Conclusion

Compared to collective goods that are necessary for the functioning and continued productivity of capitalist societies, such as public transport and mass education, the provision of public spaces usually takes a back seat in spite of the generalised recognition that they contribute to the quality of life of a population. Public spaces are viewed at best as aesthetic additions to everyday life; luxuries that might be supplied once the requirements of security and economy are met and people's stomachs filled. This largely explains why, in the rush to industrialise, water and air pollution and deforestation are allowed to continue, as in contemporary China.

In this respect, Singapore is an exception.[21] But viewing Singapore as a model, as politicians elsewhere in Asia, from the late Deng Xiaoping to Chen Shuibian to Xanana Gusmao, have recommended, will never result in the duplication of Singapore's urban development. It can only mean that Singapore's example suggests that things can be done through concerted public action: 'If Singapore could do it, so can we'. Neither can the extensive provision of public space in Singapore, nor its under-provision in Taibei, be explained by any intrinsic or compelling logic of industrialisation and economic growth, let alone theories of the authoritarian state.[22]

The *ad hoc* character of public space provision is, in part, both a reflection and a consequence of the difficulties of providing a fixed, substantive definition of the idea of 'the public', which is logically necessary in order to assess demands for provision. The concept 'public' is a poor guide to planning because, as Calhoun (1998: 26) points out, 'the public' is not found but forged by the competing discourses of different communities with different interests, which together constitute it. 'The public' is not outside the discursive process. It is the product of the process in which it is constituted; a conceptual point clearly substantiated by the local histories of the specific public spaces discussed in this chapter.

Definition of 'the public' defines and draws boundaries between groups of people, as indeed does the provision of collective goods. Consider how the creation, use and transformation of public space in Taibei and Singapore that has been discussed in this chapter helped to forge different 'publics'. In Taibei, in realising their locational preference for the 228 monument, the descendants of those killed in the 228 Incident displaced the gay community that previously had occupied New Park. The KMT government appropriated and invested in 228 monuments to stake its own claim to be a 'public' in the history of Taiwan-as-a-nation. In the creation of Parks 14 and 15, the squatter settlers and their student sympathisers were displaced by the city government's discursive appeal to the desires of the expanding middle class for green open space and its vision of Taibei as achieving 'world city' status. In Singapore, the SHS, the Nature Society and their sympathisers, constituted as communities of shared interests, spoke against development and the thematisation of Chinatown on behalf of a future generation of Singaporeans. Yet their goals certainly differed from the interests of the businesspeople whose firms were languishing in Chinatown. So, too, did the interests of the Singapore Heritage Society and the Nature Society run counter to the purported interests of 'the public' of future apartment owners, which were invoked to justify the development plans of government agencies.

In all these instances, the form and character of public spaces are the products of the histories of contestation, negotiation and strategic alignment. Contestants were organised as communities of shared interests, but not necessarily communities in spatial propinquity,[23] for the specific purpose of establishing a 'public' space. In each case, governments entered the debates as champions of an homogeneous, inclusive 'public', 'nation' or 'majority' for which they claimed to speak. This imagined sameness served to justify the exclusion of 'minority' groups that had different interests and which, in pursuit of their interests, were selfishly denying the realisation of 'the public good' or 'the national interest'. The concept of 'the good' is thus always a discursive claim of inclusion that is simultaneously a mechanism of exclusion.

In sum, the history of the creation of the public spaces in Taibei and Singapore discloses that 'the public' is not a substantive, consensual social entity but rather is constituted in and through the discursive engagement of different, and often conflicting, communities of shared interests. 'The public' for which space is provided is thus unavoidably both a process and a product of negotiations in the public sphere. Public spaces, historical monuments and parks in Asian cities are emblematic of the local 'public' histories of interaction between significant individual and organised players, interests and ideas. As such, public space is politicised space.

Notes

1 I am indebted to Huang Li-ling for showing me and telling me the stories behind different significant locations in Taibei city, without which this essay would be impossible. Much detail has had to be excised in the interests of space. Any mistakes in the interpretation of Taibei's conditions are entirely due to my own continuing unfamiliarity with the city, in spite of repeated visits.
2 The physical development of Singapore, in terms of urban planning, has emerged as a rhetorical 'model' for many Asian cities, such as Bangalore in India, Colombo in Sri Lanka, and Taibei. It is rhetorical because these cities do not aspire to duplicate Singapore physically, but to suggest that Singapore makes orderly urban development imaginable in an Asian city. Singapore is thus an empty signifier for each of these cities to fill in the substance.
3 I have avoided discussing the urban planning of public housing estates, in which more than 80 per cent of Singaporeans reside, because there are no comparable developments in Taiwan. Readers interested in Singapore's public housing estate planning should consult Chua (1997) and Wong and Yeh (1985).
4 As an aside, many of the street foods sold in Taiwan are also reminiscent of the hawker foods once found in Singapore, particularly those comprising pigs' offal, such as braised pig's ear. Such items are still available in Singapore but their popularity has declined particularly among those who are under forty years old.
5 In 1995, a neighbourhood improvement programme was initiated by the city's Urban Development Department, which aims to increase the number of small urban green spaces substantially in the long term.
6 The Padang is symbolically perhaps the most important public space in Singapore. Being in front of the neo-classical City Hall, it works with the high steps of the building and the latter's formal features to symbolise the power of the colonial administration. It was on the Padang that the Duke of Edinburgh reviewed the assembled colonised population. The formality and symbolism of the Padang and the City Hall was adopted by the PAP government, in the first

decade of independence, as the podium from which to review the march-past of military contingents and civilian groups on National Day (Chua 1992). Since the mid-1980s, National Day celebrations have been moved to the national sports stadium, and the programme for the celebration includes fireworks, mass choirs and coordinated mass theatrical performances that narrate different aspects of the nation's history under the PAP (Rajah 1999).

7   Chinese coolies carrying heavy sacks of rice in jute sacks or bales of smoked rubber sheets have become an icon of the Chinese immigrant life of past Singapore. Such scenes were ubiquitous along the banks of the river, where the Chinese traders had their warehouses, in immediate proximity to the boats that plied the river, transferring the cargo from sea-going vessels to the warehouses.

8   Development plans for Taiwan are on three levels: the Comprehensive Development Plan for the Taiwan Area; the City and County Comprehensive Development Plan; and the Taibei City Comprehensive Plan, in descending order.

9   Since the physical planning of Singapore is a story already well covered in existing literature, I will not be concerned with the details. For a brief review of the processes, see Chua (1996b).

10 My informal interviews with academics in urban studies drew no satisfactory answers.

11 In the general attempt to 'clean up' the city, he not only disciplined land use, but also attempted to discipline the sex trade by forcefully removing the licences from sex workers who had hitherto been legitimate prostitutes. These moralising acts contributed much to his failure to be elected for a second term as Mayor, forcing him to stand as the DPP candidate in the up-coming presidential election of 1999.

12 Details of the social movement history of Parks 14 and 15 are drawn heavily from Huang (1997).

13 The pivotal intellectual influence in the school is its current director, Hsia Chu-Joe. For a sample of his reflections on urban public space and the public sphere, see Hsia (1994; 1998).

14 For detailed accounts of the resettlement process, see Chua (1997: ch. 3).

15 Although, strictly speaking, the term 'garden city' as used in Singapore does not correspond to the British 'garden city' planning movement of the nineteenth century conceptualised by Ebenezer Howard, it is nevertheless possible that Lee Kuan Yew may have picked up the concept informally during his time as a university student in Britain. In any event, the term has also undergone significant conceptual change in Singapore. It has been transformed from 'a garden within the city' to Singapore as a 'city within a garden' (Lee 1993).

16 Of course, to survive the green environment has to be supported by other environmental control measures such as pollution and air quality control. For a comprehensive survey of all these measures in Singapore, see Ooi (1993).

17 Such trees are selected for the following qualities: 'ability to grow fast even under poor soil conditions, to be readily propagated from sizeable stem cuttings, and to be easily transplanted even as a fairly large tree' (Yeh 1985: 818).

18 All details in this section are borrowed from Wu (1994).

19 For a discussion of the gay community's response to the re-dedication of New Park and the surrounding area as public space, see Martin (2000).

20 The Chinese have a preference for red as one of the auspicious colours.

21 Significantly, even in the Singapore case, the economic benefit of public spaces is only conceived 'symbolically' rather than materially, in Lee Kuan Yew's explanation for the greening of Singapore: 'Well kept trees and gardens were a subtle way of convincing potential investors in the early crucial years that Singapore

was an efficient and effective place' (1 August 1996, on the 35th anniversary of the Economic Development Board).

22 An urban planner at the conference held in 1999, unwittingly perhaps, confirmed and endorsed this *ad hoc* character by claiming that it is as simple as some cities plan and some do not, and often because of a single powerful individual, such as Lee Kuan Yew of Singapore.

23 Calhoun (1998: 29) attributes the term 'community without propinquity' to Melvin Webber.

12

EPILOGUE

Collective goods for collective futures

Sally Sargeson

The case studies contained in this volume underline the point that an array of customs, ideologies, organisational forms, strategic and economic interests, political alliances and social relations influence the provision of collective goods. Moreover, the decision to produce goods collectively, as opposed to publicly or privately, is always open to contestation, even in inter-state interactions and authoritarian societies in which there are significant disparities of power, resources and capacity. Our case studies also show that collective goods provision frequently has a greater impact than originally intended. It overturns old ideational, regulatory, organisational productive and redistributive systems; distinguishes new groups of beneficiaries from non-beneficiaries; and precipitates collective actions at various levels of geo-political scale.

Struggles to find new ideologies to legitimate collective goods provision, innovative methods of supplying collective goods and mechanisms for accessing those goods, were significant features of the turbulent landscape of East and Southeast Asia at the end of the twentieth century. In the neo-liberal programme for collective goods provision that was propagated by international agencies, and adopted by many political leaders, bureaucrats, civil associations and 'responsible' citizens in countries as diverse as China and Malaysia, the privatisation of collective goods and deregulated markets became core rhetorical components not only of arguments about how best to provide the instrumental goods necessary for achievement of 'the good', but also in conversations about the content of 'the good'.

To date, the full implications of the neo-liberal programme remain unclear. Nevertheless, two significant trends are evident, particularly in the old developmental and socialist states. On the one hand, the organisational capacities of some segments of society have been enhanced. Opportunities exist for limited civilian participation in national, municipal and local governance. Debates over the management of spatial welfare and cultural goods and common pool resources have modified the media and discursive content of the public sphere. The formation of NGOs, activist groups and global networks and the availability of new communications systems have allowed people to work together to define common goals and learn the skills necessary to pursue those goals. Concepts of responsible 'self-rule' discursively have empowered groups that had been politically marginalised and socially disadvantaged, and new fiscal and legal arrangements have provided them with the means with which to produce goods collectively. Of course, many kinds of collective goods, such as autonomous trade unions in China and legal protections for indigenous peoples' resource rights, remain undersupplied. But there is little doubt that these emergent organisational and institutional goods have the potential to allow new 'publics' to communicate about their shared wants and needs.

On the other hand, the ability of national governments to regulate markets, nurture domestic industries and collect taxes has been undermined. Consequently, access to a wide array of collective goods has been commercialised, and public expenditure, especially on welfare goods, has been reduced. The introduction of neo-liberal programmes for funding economic and social infrastructure has sparked conflicts over distributive inequity and inter-generational transfers. Knowledges have been commodified. Proposals to create new property relations have pitted market advocates against communities concerned about resource sustainability and retention of their traditional cultural and institutional entitlements. While there is little doubt that a larger percentage of the population of East and Southeast Asia has the wherewithal to purchase the goods and services it desires, it is also clear that considerable numbers of people are suffering from the dismantling of collective goods regimes that once offered them some measure of protection from dispossession, exploitation, poverty, environmental degradation, disease and natural disasters.

In the context of these dual trends, what framework could the future provision of collective goods take? Recognition of the increasing impact of cross-border problems has prompted one influential group of scholars to sketch a plan to internationally coordinate public policy (Kaul et al. 1999). The plan, published under the aegis of the United Nations Development Programme and inviting the participation of an expanded G-8, centres on the principle of subsidiarity. Vertical subsidiarity entails agencies at all levels of geo-political scale becoming involved in the design and implementation of policy. Horizontal subsidiarity refers to a tripartite arrangement in which, at each level of scale, representatives of government, business and civil society participate equally in decision-making. The organisational model implied would nest these three kinds of actors in international, regional, national and local forums, with each forum exercising jurisdiction over its own affairs. The publication of national 'externality profiles' would facilitate a trade in negative and positive externalities, while market pricing would provide incentives to participating countries, businesses and civil groups.

We concur with the authors of this plan that policy coordination is necessary to overcome cross-border problems. We agree that more communication should take place about the collective wants, needs and interests that drive collective goods provision, and proposed strategies to produce the goods required. However, on the basis of our findings we do not think that the plan is either feasible or, indeed, desirable. Our aim in expressing these reservations is to advance an argument not for one, but rather for a multiplicity of frameworks for providing collective goods.

Consider, first, the universalising agenda contained in the proposed plan. Like many that have preceded it, it is predicated on an assumption that a carefully articulated, corporatist organisation could collate a universally appealing description of 'the good' and determine which instrumental collective goods should be produced to assist in realising 'the good'. But as we have shown, the achievement of consensus as to 'the good', and about how best to pursue that 'good', is rare. 'The good' envisaged by political, bureaucratic, business and technocratic elites often turns out to be disadvantageous to some of the people on whom their policy visions are visited.

We also suspect that the plan is politically impracticable. Governments in East and Southeast Asia would be wary of participating in the kind of structure and procedures that Kaul *et al.* propose. What seasoned political leader would be prepared to relinquish their policy-making authority to an organisation that, the lessons of recent history suggest, would be dominated by Northern interests and committed to the pursuit of Anglo-American objectives? Despite the proliferation of new associational and institutional forms in their jurisdictions, governments in the region lack the will and capacity to observe principles of vertical and horizontal subsidiarity. Indeed, the neo-liberal celebration of efficiency and competitiveness, which allows reigning politicians to recast themselves in the heroic role of nationalist CEOs, and domestic firms to pose as standard-bearers in the nation's struggle for global market share, re-legitimises the continued prioritisation of government and business interests in the design of public policy.

Nor do many of the civil associations that currently exist in East and Southeast Asia provide the kind of inclusive, equal foundation on which to conduct the communication, negotiation and coordination procedures recommended by Kaul *et al.*. Their hierarchical structure, elite composition and circumscribed goals means that their policy interventions may be more likely to reinforce, rather than erase, inequalities of power over, and access to, collective goods. Associations whose membership is restricted by ethnicity and religion are increasing in size and influence in at least some countries. And, as with governments and businesses, the appeal of many associations is limited by the individualistic vocabulary in which their aims and strategies are couched.

We recall that the most eminent scholar in this field, Elinor Ostrom (1998), found that even in single municipalities it was impossible to predict one set of arrangements that would result in the economically optimal provision of all types of goods. Why, then, attempt to impose one set of arrangements on a globalised arena of dramatically different physical environments, states and peoples? The complex mix of interests, regimes, developmental models, public and private ventures, associational forms and institutions described in this book, in themselves artefacts of former patterns of collective goods provision, need not be viewed as impediments to the provision of collective goods. In fact, they might offer a rich suite of ideas, rules and structures from which people can choose to devise new methods for the provision of collective goods. The proposal to create one overarching regime that has the authority to design, produce and distribute collective goods threatens not only to undermine this source of inventiveness, but also to forestall the more fundamental ideological, political and cultural changes thereby engendered.

Finally, then, what this book demonstrates is that there needs to be greater support for the multiplicity of arrangements through which people act collectively to resolve their common problems. The challenge for international organisations and funding agencies, governments, NGOs, community associations and enterprises is to enable people, both within and across the many boundaries that divide them, to design, produce and allocate the collective goods they want. That requires genuine commitment towards information dissemination, the creation of inclusive, equitable participatory forums, and funds and resources for production of collective goods and their sustainable management. If some of the resulting arrangements eventually prove to have economically sub-optimal outcomes, others undeniably will be superior to the current fad of private provision and individualised consumption. At the least, they will comprise mechanisms for accommodating the ideals, interests and needs of different groups of people, and offer a contribution towards the creation of collective futures.

BIBLIOGRAPHY

ABARE (Australian Bureau of Agricultural and Resource Economics) (1988) 'Fishing industry', in *Japanese Agricultural Policies: A Time for a Change*, Canberra: ABARE.

Abdurrahman, S. H. (1983) *Masalah Pencabutan Hak-Hak atas Tanah dan Pembebasan Tanah di Indonesia* [The Problem of Extinguishing Land Title and Land Resumption in Indonesia] Bandung: Penerbit Alumni.

—— (1984) *Kedudukan Hukum Adat dalam Perundang-undangan Agraria Indonesia* [The Place of Customary Law in Indonesian Agrarian Law] Jakarta: Akademika Pressindo.

Abramson, D. B., Leaf, M. L. and Tan Ying (2001) 'Social research and the localization of Chinese urban planning practice: some ideas from Quanzhou, Fujian', in John Logan, (ed.) *Globalization, Market Reform, and the New Chinese City*, London: Blackwell.

ADB (Asian Development Bank) (1996) *Country Operational Strategy Study, Lao PDR*, Manila: Asian Development Bank.

—— (1997a) *Co-financing: A Strategy for Resource Mobilization*, Manila: Asian Development Bank.

—— (1997b) *Commercial Co-financing and Guarantees*, Manila: Asian Development Bank.

Aditjondro, G. (1998) 'Large dam victims and their defenders: the emergence of an anti-dam movement in Indonesia', in P. Hirsch and C. Warren (eds) *The Politics of Environment in Southeast Asia*, London: Routledge.

Agnew, J. and Corbridge, S. (1995) *Mastering Space: Hegemony, Territory and International Political Economy*, London: Routledge.

Anderson, B. (1991) *Imagined Communities: Reflections on the Origin and Spread of Nationalism*, London: Verso.

Angelsen, A. (1995) 'Shifting cultivation and "deforestation": a study from Indonesia', *World Development*, 23, 10: 1713–29.

Anheier, H. K. and Seibel, W. (eds) (1990) *The Third Sector: Comparative Studies of Non-profit Organizations*, Berlin: de Gruyter.

Ansell, C. K. and Weber, S. (1999) 'Organizing international politics: sovereignty and open systems', *International Political Science Review*, 20, 1: 73–93.

Arrighi, G. (1998) 'Globalization and the rise of East Asia', *International Sociology*, 13, 1: 59–77.

Ascher, W. (1993) *Political Economy and Problematic Forestry Policies in Indonesia: Obstacles to Incorporating Sound Economics and Science*, Durham NC: Center for Tropical Conservation, Duke University.

Ashenden, G. P. and Kitson, G. W. (1987) 'The Japan tuna market', in D. Doulman (ed.) *Tuna Issues and Perspectives in the Pacific Island Region: An Analysis of Options*, Hawaii: East-West Center.

Asher, M. G. (1994) *Social Security in Malaysia and Singapore: Practices, Issues, and Reform Directions*, Kuala Lumpur: Institute of Strategic and International Studies.

—— (1998) 'Investment policies and performance of provident fund in Southeast Asia', unpublished paper presented at conference on Economic Development Institute of the World Bank Organized Workshop on Pension System Reform, Governance and Fund Management, Yangzhou, Jiangsu Province, China, 13–15 January.

Aspinall, E. (1996) 'The broadening base of political opposition in Indonesia', in G. Rodan (ed.) *Political Oppositions in Industrialising Asia*, London: Routledge.

Australian Fisheries (1989) 'The state of the environment', August, 10–11.

Australian SBT fishers and officials (1998) interview, February.

Aw, T. C. and Low, L. (1997) 'Health care provisions in Singapore', in T. M. Tan and S. B. Chew (eds) *Affordable Health Care: Issues and Prospects*, Singapore: Prentice-Hall.

Bachriadi, D. (1997) *Reformasi Agraria: Perubahan Politik, Sengketa, dan agenda Pembaruan Agraria di Indonesia* [Agrarian Reform: Political Change, Cases and Agrarian Reform in Indonesia] Jakarta: Lembaga Penerbit Fakultas Ekonomi Universitas Indonesia and Kionsorsium Pembaruan Agraria.

Bangkok Post (1998) 2 July.

Banjarmasin Post (1999) 11 March.

—— (2000) 10 March.

BAPPENAS (1993) *Biodiversity Action Plan for Indonesia*, Jakarta: Ministry of National Development Planning/National Development Planning Agency.

Barber, C. V. (1998) 'Forest resource scarcity and social conflict in Indonesia', *Environment*, 40, 4: 4–20.

Beeson, M. (1999a) 'Reshaping regional institutions: APEC and the IMF in East Asia', *The Pacific Review*, 12, 1: 1–24.

—— (1999b) *Competing Capitalisms: Australia, Japan and Economic Competition in the Asia Pacific*, London: St Martin's Press.

—— (2000a) 'Globalization and trade: the end of the national interest?', in P. Boreham, R. Hall and G. Stokes (eds) *The Politics of Australian Society: Political Issues for the New Century*, Melbourne: Addison Wesley Longman.

—— (2000b) 'Mahathir and the markets: globalisation and the pursuit of economic autonomy in Malaysia', *Pacific Affairs*, 73, 3: 335–51.

—— (2002) 'Theorising institutional change in East Asia', in M. Beeson, (ed.) *Reconfiguring East Asia: Regional Institutions and Organisations After the Crisis*, London: Curzon Press, 7–27.

Beeson, M. and Jayasuriya, K. (1998) 'The political rationalities of regionalism: APEC and the EU in comparative perspective', *The Pacific Review*, 11, 3: 311–36

Beeson, M. and Robison, R. (2000) 'Introduction: interpreting the crisis', in R. Robison, M. Beeson, K. Jayasuriya and H-R. Kimet (eds) *Politics and Markets in the Wake of the Asian Crisis*, London: Routledge.

Bello, W. (1998) 'East Asia: on the eve of the great transformation?', *Review of International Political Economy*, 5, 3: 424–44.

—— (1999) ' "The Iron Cage": the WTO, the Bretton Woods institutions, and the South', *Focus on Trade*, 42.

Benda-Beckman, F. von, (1979) *Property in Social Continuity*, The Hague: Martinus Nijhoff.

Benda-Beckman, F. von and Benda-Beckman, K. von. (1999) 'A functional analysis of property rights with special reference to Indonesia', in T. van Meijl and F. von Benda-Beckmann (eds) *Property Rights and Economic Development: Land and Natural Resources in South East Asia and Oceania*, London: Kegan Paul.

Benda-Beckmann, F. von and Velde, M. van der (eds) (1992) *Law as a Resource in Agrarian Struggles*, Wageningen: Agricultural University.

Benjamin, R. (1980) *The Limits of Politics: Collective Goods and Political Change in Postindustrial Society*, Chicago: University of Chicago Press.

Bennet, L. A. (1980) *International Organizations: Principles and Issues*, Englewood Cliffs: Prentice-Hall.

Benoit, P. (1996) 'Mitigating project risks – World Bank support for government guarantees', *Public Policy for the Private Sector*, note 79, Washington DC: World Bank.

Bergin, A. (1994) 'Recent development and announcements: conservation and management of highly migratory species', *Ocean and Coastal Management*, 24: 139–44.

Bergin, A. and Haward, M. (1996a) *Japan's Tuna Industry: A Setting Sun or New Dawn?*, New York: Nova Science Publishers.

—— (1996b) *Trends in Tuna Fisheries: The Republic of Korea and Taiwan*, unpublished report, Unitas Consulting Limited.

Berkes, F. (ed.) (1989) *Common Property Resources: Ecology and Community-Based Sustainable Development*, London: Belhaven.

Berkes, F. and Farvar, M. T. (1989) 'Introduction and overview', in F. Berkes (ed.) *Common Property Resources: Ecology and Community-based Sustainable Development*, London: Belhaven.

Bhagwati, J. and Patrick, H. T. (eds) (1990) *Aggressive Unilateralism: America's Trade Policy and the World Trading System*, New York: Harvester Wheatsheaf.

Birdsall, N. and Lawrence, R. Z. (1999) 'Deep integration and trade agreements: good for developing countries?', in Inge Kaul, Isabelle Grunberg and Marc A. Stein (eds) *Global Public Goods: International Co-operation in the 21st Century*, New York: Oxford University Press.

Bisnis Indonesia (1997) 18 September.

—— (1999) 19 April.

Blau, P. M. and Scott, W. R. (1962) *Formal Organizations: A Comparative Approach*, New York: Chandler Publishing Co.

Blecher, M. and Shue, V. (1996) *Tethered Deer: Government and Economy in a Chinese County*, Stanford: Stanford University Press.

Boli, J. and Thomas, G. M. (1997) 'World culture in the world polity: a century of international non-governmental organization', *American Sociological Review*, 62: 171–90.

Borgstrom, G. (1964) *Japan's World Success in Fishing*, London: Fishing News Books.

Bourchier, D. (1999) 'Magic means, collusion and judges with attitude: notes on the politics of law in contemporary Indonesia', in K. Jayasuriya (ed.) *Law, Capitalism and Power in Asia*, London: Routledge.

Bowen, J. R. (1986) 'On the political construction of tradition: *Gotong Royong* in Indonesia', *Journal of Asian Studies*, 45, 3.

Boyer, R. and Hollingsworth, J. R. (1997) 'From national embeddedness to spatial and institutional nestedness', in J. R. Hollingsworth and R. Boyer (eds) *Contemporary Capitalism: The Embeddedness of Institutions*, Cambridge: Cambridge University Press.

BPN (1993) 'Project preparation report: land administration project', Badan Pertanahan Negara and Land Administration Systems Australia.

Broadbent, J. (1998) *Environmental Politics in Japan: Networks of Power and Protest*, Cambridge: Cambridge University Press.

Bromley, D. W. (1991) *Environment and Economy: Property Rights and Public Policy*, Oxford: Blackwell.

Brook, T. (1997) 'Auto-organization in Chinese society', in T. Brook and B. M. Frolic (eds) *Civil Society in China*, Armonk NY: M. E. Sharpe.

Brook, T. and Frolic, B. M. (eds) (1997) *Civil Society in China*, Armonk NY: M. E. Sharpe.

Brookfield, H. and Byron, Y. (eds) (1992) *Southeast Asia's Environmental Future: The Search for Sustainability*, New York: United Nations University Press.

Bruce, J. W. and Fortmann, L. (1991) 'Property and forestry', *Journal of Business Administration*, 20, 1–2: 471–98.

Bryant, R. C. (1995) *International Coordination of National Stabilization Policies*, Washington: Brookings Institution Press.

Buchanan, J. M. (1965) 'An Economic Theory of Clubs', *Economica*, 32: 125.

Buchanan, J. M. and Tullock, G. (1965) *The Calculus of Consent: Logical Foundations of Constitutional Democracy*, Ann Arbor: Chicago University Press.

Buchbinder, H. and Newson, J. (1990) 'Corporate/university linkages in Canada: transforming a public institution', *Higher Education*, 20, 4: 355–79.

Bullard, N. with Bello, W. and Malhotra, K. (1998) 'Taming the tigers: the IMF and the Asian crisis', in K. S. Jomo (ed.) *Tigers in Trouble: Financial Governance, Liberalisation and Crises in East Asia*, London: Zed Books.

Burchell, G. (1996) 'Liberal government and the techniques of the self', in A. Barry, T. Osborne and N. Rose (eds) *Foucault and Political Reason: Liberalism, Neoliberalism and Rationalities of Government*, London: UCL Press.

Burns, P. (1989) 'The myth of *adat*', *Journal of Legal Pluralism*, 28: 1–127.

Business Times (1997) 9 April.

—— (2000) 29 February.

Buzan, B. (1995) 'The level of analysis problem in international relations reconsidered', in K. Booth and S. Smith (eds) *International Relations Theory Today*, London: Polity Press.

Byrd, W. A. and Lin, Q. (eds) (1990) *China's Rural Industry: Structure, Development and Reform*, Oxford: Oxford University Press.

Calhoun, C. (1998) 'The public good as a social and cultural project', in W. W. Powell and E. S. Clemens (eds) *Private Action and the Public Good*, New Haven: Yale University Press.

Carfuny, A. W. (1990) 'A Gramscian concept of declining hegemony: stages of US power and the evolution of international economic relations', in D. Rapkin (ed.) *World Leadership and Hegemony*, Boulder: Lynne Reinner.

Carter, A. (1989) *The Philosophical Foundations of Property Rights*, New York: Harvester Wheatsheaf.

Casson, A. (2000) 'The hesitant boom: Indonesia's oil palm sub-sector in an era of economic and political change', Centre for International Forestry Research, Occasional Paper 29, Bogor, Indonesia.

Castells, M., Goh, L. and Kwok, R. Y. W. (1990) *The Shek Kip Mei Syndrome: Economic Development and Public Housing in Hong Kong and Singapore*, London: Pion.

Caton, A. (1991) 'Commercial and recreational components of the southern bluefin tuna fishery', in R. Shomura, J. Majkowski. and S. Langi (eds) *Interactions of Pacific Tuna Fisheries: Proceedings of the First FAO Expert Consultation on the Interactions of Pacific Tuna Fisheries*, December, New Caledonia, Rome: FAO Fisheries Technical Paper 336/2, 3–11.

Caton, A., McLoughlin, K. and Williams, M. (1990) *Southern Bluefin Tuna: Scientific Background to the Debate*, bulletin 3, Canberra: Department of Primary Industry and Energy, Bureau of Rural Resources.

CCEJ (Citizen's Coalition for Economic Justice) (1997) *Civil Society*, Seoul: CCEJ.

CCSBT (Commission for the Conservation of Southern Bluefin Tuna) (1994) *First Meeting of the Commission for the Conservation of Southern Bluefin Tuna*, May, Wellington NZ.

—— (1995) *Special Meeting of the Commission for the Conservation of Southern Bluefin Tuna*, 3–6 October, Canberra.

—— (1996) *Third Annual Meeting 24–8 September*, available online at *http://www. home.aone.net.au/ccsbt/ccsbt3-2.html#REG5.5*.

—— (1997) *Resumed Third Annual Meeting 18–22 February*, available online at *http://www.home.aone.net.au/ccsbt/3rtoc.html*.

Cerny, P. G. (1990) *The Changing Architecture of Politics: Structure, Agency and the State*, London: Sage.

—— (1995) 'Globalization and the changing logic of collective action', *International Organization*, 49, 4.

Chalmers, I. (1997) 'Introduction', in I. Chalmers and V. Hadiz (eds) *The Politics of Economic Development in Indonesia: Contending Perspectives*, London: Routledge, 1–35.

Chalmers, J. (1982) *MITI and the Japanese Miracle: The Growth of Industrial Policy, 1925–1975*, Stanford: Stanford University Press.

Chan, K. W. (1994) *Cities with Invisible Walls: Reinterpreting Urbanization in Post-1949 China*, New York: Oxford University Press.

Chang, S. (1996) 'The floating population: an informal process of urbanisation in China', *International Journal of Population Geography*, 2: 197–214.

Chen, W. (1998) 'The political economy of rural industrialisation in China: village conglomerates in Shangdong Province', *Modern China*, 24, 1: 73–95.

Cheng, K. (1995) 'Education: decentralization and the market', in L. Wong and S. MacPherson (eds) *Social Change and Social Policy in Contemporary China*, Aldershot: Avebury.

Cheng, Y. and Tsang, S. (1995–6) 'Agricultural land reform in a mixed system: the Chinese experience of 1984–1994', *China Information*, 10, 3: 44–74.

Cheung, A. (1999) 'Health policy reform', in L. Wong and N. Flynn (eds) *Marketizing Social Policy in China*, London: Macmillan.

Chew, H. H. (1999) 'The Singapore green plan endangered', *Nature Watch*, 4, 3: 4–9.

China Daily (1998) 4 June.

China Labor Statistical Yearbook 1999 (1999) Beijing: China State Statistical Bureau.

China News Analysis (1994) 'Land market', 1503.

Chua, B. H. (1992) 'Decoding the political in civic spaces: an interpretative essay', in B. Chua and N. Edwards (eds) *Public Spaces: Design, Use and Management*, Singapore: Singapore University Press.

—— (1996a) 'Culturalisation of economy and politics in Singapore', in R. Robison (ed.) *Pathways to Asia: the Politics of Engagement*, Sydney: Allen and Unwin.

—— (1996b) 'Singapore: management of a city-state in Southeast Asia', in J. Ruland (ed.) *The Dynamics of Metropolitan Management in Southeast Asia*, Singapore: Institute of Southeast Asian Studies.

—— (1997) *Public Housing and Legitimacy: Stakeholding in Singapore*, London: Routledge.

Clark, A. M., Friedman, J. E. and Hochstetler, K. (1998) 'The sovereign limits of global civil society', *World Politics*, 51: 1–35.

Clark, J. (1991) *Democratizing Development: The Role of Voluntary Organizations*, London: Earthscan.

Cleary, M. and Eaton, M. (1996) *Tradition And Reform: Land Tenure and Rural Development in Southeast Asia*, Kuala Lumpur: Oxford University Press.

Colfer, C. and Dudley, R. (1993) (reprinted 1997) *Shifting Cultivators of Indonesia: Marauders or Managers of the Forest?*, Rome: UN Food and Agriculture Organisation, Community Forestry Cast Study Series no. 6.

Comitini, S. (1987) 'Japanese trading companies: their possible role in pacific tuna fisheries development', in D. Doulman (ed.) *Tuna Issues and Perspectives in the Pacific Island Region: Analysis of Options*, Hawaii: East-West Center.

Commission on Global Governance (1995) *Our Global Neighbourhood*, New York: Oxford University Press.

Convention for the Conservation of Southern Bluefin Tuna (1993) available online at *http://www.home.aone.net.au/ccsbt/conventi.html*.

Conybeare, J. (1987) *Trade Wars: The Theory and Practice of International Commercial Rivalry*, New York: Columbia University Press.

Cotton, J. (2000) 'The Asian crisis and the perils of enterprise association', in R. Robison, M. Beeson, K. Jayasuriya and H-R. Kimet (eds) *Politics and Markets in the Wake of the Asian Crisis*, London: Routledge.

Cox, R. (1981) 'Social forces, states, and world orders: beyond international relations theory', *Millennium: Journal of International Studies*, 10, 2: 126–55.

—— (1993) 'Gramsci, hegemony and international relations: an essay in method', in S. Gill (ed.) *Gramsci, Historical Materialism and International Relations*, Cambridge: Cambridge University Press.

Cox, R. H. (1998) 'The consequences of welfare reform: how conceptions of social rights are changing', *Journal of Society and Politics*, 27, 1: 1–16.

Cox, R. W. (1987) *Production, Power, and World Order*, New York: Columbia University Press.

Crone, D. K. (1993) 'States, elites and social welfare in Southeast Asia', *World Development*, 21, 1.

Crough, C. J. (1987) 'The development of the Australian tuna industry', in D. Doulman (ed.) *Tuna Issues and Perspectives in the Pacific Island Region: An Analysis of Options*, Hawaii: East-West Center.

CSIS (Centre for Strategic and International Studies) (1991) 'Masalah tanah semakin meningkat' [The land question as a growing problem] special issue, *Analisis*, 20, 2.

Dai, X. (1998) ' "East Asian model": a few problems, but it works', *Beijing Review*, 41: 12.

Dai, Y. (1996) 'Overseas migration and the economic modernization of Xiamen City during the twentieth century', in L. Douw and P. Post (eds) *South China: State, Culture and Social Change during the 20th Century*, Amsterdam: North Holland.

Dauvergne, P. (1997a) 'Globalisation and deforestation in the Asia-Pacific', working paper 7, Canberra: Australian National University, Department of International Relations.

—— (1997b) *Shadows in the Forest: Japan and the Politics of Timber in Southeast Asia*, Cambridge MA: MIT Press.

—— (1997c) 'Weak states and the environment in Indonesia and the Soloman Islands', working paper 10, Canberra: Australian National University, Department of International Relations.

Davis, D. (1993) 'Urban households: supplicants to a socialist state', in D. Davis and S. Harrell (eds) *Chinese Families in the Post-Mao Era*, Berkeley, Los Angeles and London: University of California Press.

Davis, D. S., Kraus, R., Naughton, B. and Perry, E. J. (eds) (1995) *Urban Spaces in Contemporary China*, New York: Cambridge University Press.

De Bruin, G. P. (1991) *Decisionmaking on Public Goods: An Exploration into the Borderland of Politics and Economics*, Amsterdam: Hef Spinhuis.

De Swaan, A. (1994) (ed.) *Social Policy Beyond Borders: The Social Question in Transnational Perspective*, Amsterdam: Amsterdam University Press.

De-Shalit, A. (1997) 'Is liberalism environment-friendly?', in R. S. Gottlieb (ed.) *The Ecological Community: Environmental Challenges for Philosophy, Politics and Morality*. London: Routledge. .

Deacon, B. (1997) *Global Social Policy*, London: Sage.

Deng, X. (1984) 'Notes of speech to the Chinese Communist Party leaders', *Beijing Daily*, 16 May.

Department of Statistics, Malaysia (1996) *Social Statistics Bulletin: Malaysia 1996*, Kuala Lumpur: Department of Statistics Malaysia.

Dephutbun (1988) *Keputusan Kepala Kantor Wilayah Departmen Kehutanan dan Perbeunan Kantor Wilayah Propinsi Daerah Istimewa Aceh Nomor: 445/KPTS?KWL-4/1988* [Decision of the Head of Aceh Regional Forestry Office]

Departmen Kehutanan dan Perkebunan Kantor Wilayah Propinsi Daerah Istimewa Aceh.

Deyo, F. (1989) *Beneath The Miracle: Labour Subordination in the New Asian Industrialism*, London: University of California Press.

Dirkse, J., Hüsken, F. and Rutten, M. (eds) (1993) *Development and Social Welfare: Indonesia's Experiences under the New Order*, Leiden: Koninklijk Instituut Voor Taal, Land en Volkenkunde.

Doebele, W. (1983) 'Concepts of urban land tenure', in H. B. Dunkerley (ed.) *Urban Land Policy: Issues and Opportunities*, New York: Oxford University Press.

Dong-A Ilbo (1996) 12 September.

—— (1999) 22 January.

Donner, W. (1987) *Land Use and Environment in Indonesia*, Honolulu: University of Hawaii Press.

Douglass, B. (1980) 'The common good and the public interest', *Political Theory*, 8, 1.

Douw, L. and Post, P. (eds) (1996) *South China: State, Culture and Social Change during the 20th Century*, Amsterdam: North Holland.

Dove, M. R. (1983) 'Theories of swidden agriculture, and the political economy of ignorance', *Agroforestry Systems*, 1: 85–99.

—— (1993a) 'A revisionist view of tropical deforestation and development', *Environmental Conservation*, 20, 1: 17–24.

—— (1993b) 'Smallholder rubber and swidden agriculture in Borneo: a sustainable adaptation to the ecology and economy of the tropical forest', *Economic Botany*, 47, 2: 136–47.

—— (1996) 'So far from power, so near to the forest: a structural analysis of gain and blame in tropical forest development', in C. Padoch and N. L. Peluso (eds) *Borneo in Transition: People, Forests, Conservation and Development*, Kuala Lumpur: Oxford University Press.

Down to Earth (1999) 'Aman: Indonesia's new indigenous voice', 41: 3–4.

Downing, L. A. and Thigpen, R. B. (1993) 'Virtue and the common good in liberal theory', *The Journal of Politics*, 55, 4.

Dunkerley, H. B. (ed.) (1983) *Urban Land Policy: Issues and Opportunities*, New York: Oxford University Press.

EAAU (East Asia Analytical Unit) (1997) *The New ASEANS: Vietnam, Burma, Cambodia and Laos*, Canberra: Department of Foreign Affairs and Trade.

Esping-Andersen, G. (ed.) (1996) *Welfare States in Transition: National Adaptations in Global Economies*, London: Sage.

Etzioni, A. (1961) *A Comparative Analysis of Complex Organizations*, New York: Free Press.

—— (1973) 'The Third Sector and domestic missions', *Public Administration Review*, 33: 314–23.

Evans, P. (1997) 'The eclipse of the state? Reflections on stateness in an era of globalization', *World Politics*, 50, 1.

Evers, P. J. (1995) 'Preliminary policy and legal questions about recognizing traditional land in Indonesia', *Ekonesia: A Journal of Indonesian Human Ecology*, 3: 1–24.

Far Eastern Economic Review (1994) 21 January.

—— (1998a) 2 July.

—— (1998b) 1 October.

—— (1999) 21 January.

Fauzi, N. (1998) *Perlawanan Kaum Tani: Analasis terhadap Gerakan Petani Indonesia sepanjang Orde Baru* [Farmers Struggle: Analysis of the Indonesian Farmers Movement during the New Order] Medan: Yayasan Sintesa and Serikat Petani Sumatera Utara (SPSU).

Fauzi, N. and Faryadi, E. (1997) 'Penilaian terhadap peran Bank Dunia dan reformasi kebijakan dan manajemen pertanahan di Indonesia' [Evaluation of the role of the World Bank and policy reform and land management in Indonesia] KPA – Makalah pada Lokakarya Globalisasi dan Perubahan Sosial: Agenda Pemberdayaan Rakyat, Jogjakarta: Yayasan, *Lapera Indonesia*, 29: 1 October.

Featherstone, M. (1998) 'The Flaneur, the city and virtual public life', *Urban Studies*, 35: 909–26.

Ferge, Z. (1997) 'The changed welfare paradigm: the individualization of the social', *Social Policy and Administration*, 31, 1: 20–44.

Fernandes, E. and Varley, A. (eds) (1998) *Illegal Cities: Law and Urban Change in Developing Countries*, London: Zed Books.

Ferreira, D. and Khatami, K. (1996) *Financing Private Infrastructure in Developing Countries*, Washington DC: World Bank.

Feuchtwang, S. (1977) 'School-temple and city god', in G. W. Skinner (ed.) *The City in Late Imperial China*, Stanford: Stanford University Press.

Fisher, J. (1998) *Non-governments: NGOs and the Political Development of the Third World*, West Hartford: Kumarian Press.

Fitzpatrick, D. (1997) 'Disputes and pluralism in modern Indonesian land law', *The Yale Journal of International Law*, 22, 1: 171–212.

FKKM (1998) 'New era for Indonesian forestry, forest resource management reformation', available online at *http://forests.org/gopher/indonesia/newindo2.txt*, 22 September.

Foldvary, F. (1994) *Public Goods and Private Communities: the Market Provision of Social Services*, Aldershot: Edward Elgar.

Foreign Investment Advisory Service (1995) *Policy Framework for Foreign Direct Investment in Infrastructure Projects in Vietnam: A Background Paper for the Roundtable on the Business Environment for Promoting and Implementing Foreign Direct Investment in Vietnam's Infrastructure, Hanoi, Vietnam, September 14–15, 1995*, Washington DC: International Finance Corporation.

Foster, T. and Knight, A. (1997) 'Legal issues in BOT projects in Vietnam', *Journal of Project Finance*, 3, 2: 16–29.

Fox, J. (1993) 'The tragedy of open access', in H. Brookfield and Y. Byron (eds) *South-East Asia's Environmental Future: The Search for Sustainability*, Kuala Lumpur and New York: Oxford University Press.

Frolic, B. M. (1997) 'State-led civil society', in T. Brook and B. M. Frolic (eds) *Civil Society in China*, Armonk NY: M. E. Sharpe, 46–67.

Fujinami, N. (1987) 'Development of Japan's tuna fisheries', in D. Doulman (ed.) *Tuna Issues and Perspectives in the Pacific Island Region: An Analysis of Options*, Hawaii: East-West Center.

Gale, F. (1998) 'Cave "Cave! Hic dragones": a neo-Gramscian deconstruction and reconstruction of international regime theory', *Review of International Political Economy*, 5, 2: 252–83.

Galston, W. A. (1991) *Liberal Purposes: Goods, Virtues and Diversity in the Liberal State*, Cambridge: Cambridge University Press.

Gamble, A. (1988) *The Free Economy and the Strong State: The Politics of Thatcherism*, Basingstoke: Macmillan.

Gaubatz, P. R. (1995) 'Urban transformation in post-Mao China: impacts of the reform era on China's urban form', in D. S. Davis, R. Kraus, B. Naughton and E. J. Perry (eds) *Urban Spaces in Contemporary China*, New York: Cambridge University Press.

George, A. D. (1981) 'The Japanese farm lobby and agricultural policy making', *Pacific Affairs*, 54, 3: 409–30.

Gereffi, G. and Wyman, D. L. (eds) (1990) *Manufacturing Miracles: Paths of Industrialization in Latin America and East Asia*, Princeton: Princeton University Press.

Ghils, P. (1992) 'International civil society: international non-governmental organizations in the international system', *International Social Science Journal*, 133: 417–31.

Gill, S. (1992) 'Economic globalization and the internationalization of authority: limits and contradictions', *Geoforum*, 23, 3: 269–83.

—— (1993) 'Epistemology, ontology and the Italian school', in S. Gill (ed.) *Gramsci, Historical Materialism and International Relations*, Cambridge: Cambridge University Press.

—— (1995) 'Globalization, market civilization, and disciplinary neoliberalism', *Millennium*, 24, 3: 399–423.

—— (1997) 'Transformation and innovation in the study of world order', in S. Gill and J. H Mittleman (eds) *Innovation and Transformation in International Studies*, Cambridge: Cambridge University Press.

Gill, S. and Law, D. (1988) *The Global Political Economy: Perspectives, Problems and Policies*, London: Wheatsheaf.

Gills, Barry K. (2000) ' The crisis of postwar East Asian Capitalism: American power, democracy and the vicissitudes of globalisation', *Review of International Studies*. 26, 381–406.

Gilpin, R. (1987) *The Political Economy of International Relations*, Princeton: Princeton University Press.

Global Intelligence Update (1999) 25 May.

Goh, C. T. (1999) 'National rally speech', 22 August.

Gonner, Christian (1998) *Conflicts and Fire Causes in a Sub-District of Kutai, East-Kalimantan, Indonesia*, World Wide Fund of Indonesia

Goodman, R. and Peng, I. (1996) 'The East Asian welfare states: peripatetic learning, adaptive change and nation building', in G. Esping-Anderson (ed.) *Welfare States in Transition: National Adaptations in Global Economies*, London: Sage.

Goodman, R., White, G. and Kwon, Huck-ju (1998) *The East Asian Welfare Model: Welfare Orientalism and the State*, London and New York: Routledge.

Goor, C. P. V. (1982) *Indonesian Forestry Abstracts: Dutch Literature until about 1960*, Wageningen: Pudoc.

Gough, I. (1998) 'Social policy and competitiveness', public lecture at City University of Hong Kong, Hong Kong, 31 March.

Gourevitch, P. (1986) *Politics in Hard Times: Comparative Responses to International Economic Crises*, Ithaca NY: Cornell University Press.

Gray, R. D. and Shuster, J. (1998) 'The East Asian financial crisis: fallout for private power projects', *Public Policy for the Private Sector*, August, 146.

Greico, J. M. (1988) 'Anarchy and the limits of cooperation: a realist critique of the newest liberal institutionalism', *International Organization*, 42, 3: 485–501.

Gu, Xin (1998) 'Danwei fuli zhuyi yu Zhongguo de zhiduxing shiye' [Work unit welfarism and China's structural unemployment] *Jingji Shehui Tizhi Bijiao* [Economic Social System Comparison], 4: 20–7.

Guangzhou shi Tianhe qu nongwei (ed.) (1992) 'Tianhe qu nongcun hezuo jingji gufenzhi cailiao huibian' [Collection of documents on the rural shareholding cooperative system in Tianhe district in the city of Guangzhou] unpublished documents of the Agricultural Committee of Tianhe District.

Guardian Weekly (1999) 'Tuna war looms: Japanese fishermen face ban', 26 September.

—— (2000) 26 February.

Guha, R. (1994) 'Fighting for the forest: state forestry and social change in tribal India', in O. Mendelsohn and U. Baxi (eds) *The Rights of Subordinated Peoples*, Delhi: Oxford University Press.

Gujia cun (Gujia village) (1994) 'Hangzhou shi Xihu qu Gujia zhen Gujia cun cungui minyue' [The village code of the Gujia village, Gujia town, Xihu district, Hangzhou] unpublished document of Gujia village.

Gujia cun cunweihui (The village committee of Gujia) (1996) 'Guanyu zhigong tuixiu, yiliao fei deng qi xiang guiding de tongzhi' [Seven regulations regarding retirement pensions, etc.] unpublished document of Gujia village.

Guo, Z. and Zhou, D. (1997) 'Rural development and social security', in G. E. Guldin (ed.) *Farewell to Peasant China: Rural Urbanisation and Social Change in the Late Twentieth Century*, Armonk NY: M. E. Sharpe.

Guowuyuan Yanjiushi (Research Office of the State Council) (1993) 'Guanyu nongcun gufenzhi he gufen hezuozhi de diaocha baogao' [Report on the rural shareholding system and shareholding cooperative system] *Zhongguo nongcun jingji* [Journal of Rural Economy] 9: 3–7.

Ha, Y. (1997) 'Public finance and budgeting in Korea under democracy: a critical appraisal', *Public Budgeting and Finance*, 17, 1.

Habermas, J. (1989) *The Structural Transformation of the Public Sphere: An Inquiry into a Category of Bourgeois Society*, Cambridge MA: MIT Press.

Haggard, S. and Simmons, B. A. (1987) 'Theories of international regimes', *International Organization*, 41, 3: 491–517.

Hampsher-Monk, I. (1996) 'The individualist premise and political community', in P. King (ed.) *Socialism and the Common Good: New Fabian Essays*, London: Frank Cass.

Han, J. and Zhang, Q. (eds) (1993) *Zhongguo Nongcun Gufen Hezuo Jingji: Lilun, Shijian, Zhengce* [The Rural Shareholding Cooperative Economy in China: Theory, Practice, Policy] Beijing: Jingji guanli chuban she.

Handley, P. (1997) 'A critical view of the build-operate-transfer privatisation process in Asia', *Asian Journal of Public Administration*, 19, 2: 203–43.

Hanson, R. A. (1978) 'Toward an understanding of politics through public goods theory: a review essay', in W. Loehr and T. Sandler (eds) *Public Goods and Public Policy*, Beverly Hills: Sage.

Hardiyanto, A. (1998) *Agenda Land Reform di Indonesia Sekarang*, Bandung: Konsorsium Pembaruan Agraria.

Hardjono, J. (1991) *Indonesia: Resources, Ecology and Environment*, Singapore: Oxford University Press.

Hardmen, D. J. (1963) 'Economic potential of Australian tuna', *Fishing News International*, 2, 2: 138–41.

Hariadi, U. and Masruchah (1995) *Tanah, Rakyat dan Demokrasi* [Land, People and Democracy] Yogyakarta: Forum LSM-LPSM DIY.

Harsono, B. (1997) *Hukum Agraria Indonesia*, Jilid I Hukum Tanah Nasional, Jakarta: Djambatan.

Harwood, M. (1996) 'Submission 33', *Joint Standing Committee on Treaties: Inquiry Concerning the Subsidiary Agreement Between the Government of Australia and Government of Japan Concerning Japanese Tuna Long-lining 1996*, Canberra: Department of Primary Industry and Energy.

Hasenclever, A., Mayer, P. and Rittberger, V. (1996) 'Interests, power, knowledge: the power of international regimes', *Mershon International Studies Review*, 40: 177–228.

Hass, P. (1992) 'Banning chloroflurorocarbons: epistemic community efforts to protect stratosphere ozone', *International Organization*, 46, 1: 187–224.

Haverfield, R. (1998) '*Hak Ulayat* and the state: land reform in Indonesia', in T. Lindsey (ed.) *Indonesia Law and Society*, Leichhardt NSW: The Federation Press.

Hayes, A. C. (1997) 'Local, national and international conceptions of justice: the case of swidden farmers in the contexts of national and regional developments in Southeast Asia', *Resource Management Working Paper Series*, working paper 14, Canberra: Australian National University.

He, B. (1997) *The Democratic Implications of Civil Society in China*, New York: St Martin's Press.

Held, D., McGrew, A., Goldblatt, D. and Perraton, J. (1999) *Global Transformations: Politics, Economics and Culture*, Stanford: Stanford University Press.

Higgott, R. (2000) 'The international relations of the Asian economic crisis', in R. Robison, M. Beeson, K. Jayasuriya and H-R. Kimet (eds) *Politics and Markets in the Wake of the Asian Crisis*, London: Routledge.

Hirsch, P. (1996) 'Dams and compensation in Indo-China', in R. Howitt, J. Connell and P. Hirsch (eds) *Resources, Nations and Indigenous Peoples: Case Studies from Australasia, Melanesia and South East Asia*, Oxford: Oxford University Press.

Hirsch, P. and Warren, A. (eds) (1998) *The Politics of Environment in Southeast Asia: Resources and Resistance*, London: Routledge.

Ho, H. (1999) 'The Singapore green plan endangered', *Nature Watch*, 4, 3: 4–9.

Holleman, J. F. (1981) *Van Vollenhoven on Indonesian Adat Law*, The Hague: Martinus Nijhoff.

Hollingsworth, J. R. and Boyer, R. (1997) 'Co-ordination of economic actors and social systems of production', in J. R. Hollingsworth and R. Boyer (eds) *Contemporary Capitalism: The Embeddedness of Institutions*, Cambridge: Cambridge University Press.

Hon, J. (1990) *Tidal Fortunes: A Story of Change – The Singapore River and Kallang Basin*, Singapore: Landmark Press for the Ministry of the Environment.

Hong Kong Economic Journal (2000) 8 March.

Hook, B. (ed.) (1996) *The Individual and the State in China*, Oxford: Clarendon Press.

Hooker, M. B. (1978) *Adat Law in Indonesia in Modern Indonesia*, Oxford: Oxford University Press.

Horden, N. (1998a) 'Ban imposed as tuna talks break down', *Australian Financial Review*, 23 January: 3.

—— (1998b) 'Get your hands off our Patagonian toothfish', *Australian Financial Review*, 4 September: 4.

Howitt, R., Connell, J. and Hirsch, P. (eds) (1996) *Resources, Nations and Indigenous Peoples: Case Studies from Australasia, Melanesia and Southeast Asia*, Melbourne: Oxford University Press.

Hsia, C. (1994) '(Re)constructing the public space: a theoretical reflection', *Taiwan: A Radical Quarterly*, 16: 21–54.

—— (1998) 'Theorizing public space', *Environmental Theory Arena*, 5, 1: 1–5.

Hsing, Y. (1998) *Making Capitalism in China: The Taiwan Connection*, New York: Oxford University Press.

Huang, J. (1992) 'Shixing gufen hezuozhi gaige chengjiao nongcun jiti jingji jingying guanli tizhi' [Adopting the shareholding cooperative system, reforming the management system of collective assets in the suburban rural areas] in Guangzhou shi Tianhe qu nongwei (ed.) *Tianhe qu Nongcun Hezuo Jingji Gufenzhi Cailiao Huibian* [Collection of Documents on the Rural Shareholding Cooperative System in Tianhe District in the City of Guangzhou] unpublished documents of the Agricultural Committee of Tianhe district.

Huang, S. C. (1997) 'Green bulldozer: the squatters, parks, nature estate and institutionalized landscape in 90s Taipei', unpublished master's thesis, Graduate Institute of Building and Planning, National Taiwan University.

Hume, D. (1951) *A Theory of Politics*, ed. F. Watkins, Edinburgh: Nelson.

Hung, D. (1999) 'Contract for $400 million power plant won by French', *Vietnam Investment Review*, 1–7 February: 5.

Hüsken, F. and White, B. (1989) 'Java: social differentiation food production and agrarian control', in G. Hart, A. Turton and B. White, with B. Fegan and Lim Teck Gee (eds) *Agrarian Transformations*, Berkeley: University of California.

Hussain, A. M. (1995) 'Determinants of private saving in Singapore', in K. Bercuson (ed.) *Singapore: A Case Study in Rapid Development*, Occasional Paper 119, Washington DC: IMF.

IFC (International Finance Corporation) (1996) *Financing Private Infrastructure*, Washington DC: World Bank.

Ikenberry, G. J. (1998) 'Constitutional politics in international relations', *European Journal of International Relations*, 4, 2: 147–77.

Ikenberry, G. J. and Kupchan, C. A. (1990) 'Socialization and hegemonic power', *International Organization*, 44, 3: 283–315.

Indonesian Observer (2000a) 1 March.

—— (2000b) 30 March

International Labour Organization (1999) 'ILO governing body to examine responses to Asia crisis', Geneva: ILO.

Interpress Service (1997) 20 May.

IRN (International Rivers Network) (1999) *Power Struggle: The Impacts of Hydro-development in Laos*, Berkeley: International Rivers Network.

Irvine, R. (1997) 'Seeing the light', *The Vietnam Business Journal*, 5, 6: 32–3.

Jakarta Post (1998) 16 June.
—— (1999) 29 March.
—— (2000a) 4 March.
—— (2000b) 9March.
—— (2000c) 28 March.
—— (2001) 10 August.
Japan Economic Newswire (1997) 7 November.
Jayasuriya, K. (1998) 'Globalisation, authoritarian liberalism and the developmental state', paper presented to workshop on 'Globalization and Social Welfare in East Asia', Aalborg University, 12–13 March.
Jayasuriya, K. and Rosser, A. (1999) 'Economic orthodoxy and the East Asia crisis', paper presented to the Australasian Political Studies Association, Sydney, 27–9 September.
Jefferson, G. H. (1998) 'China's state enterprises: public goods, externalities, and Coase', *American Economic Review*, 88, 2: 428–32.
Jenkins, J. C. (1987) 'Nonprofit organizations and policy advocacy', in W. W. Powell (ed.) *The Non-profit Sector: A Research Handbook*, New Haven: Yale University Press.
Johnson, C. (1982) *MITI and the Japanese Miracle: The Growth of Industry Policy 1925–1975*, Stanford: Stanford University Press.
Johnson, C. and Keehn, E. B. (1994) 'A disaster in the making: rational choice and Asian studies', *The National Interest*, 36: 14–22.
Juma, C. and Ojwang, J. B. (1996) *In Land We Trust: Environment, Private Property and Constitutional Change*, Cambridge: Cambridge University Press.
Kahin, A. (1994) 'Regionalism and decentralisation', in D. Bourchier and J. Legge (eds) *Democracy in Indonesia: 1950s and 1990s*, Papers on Southeast Asia, no. 31, Melbourne: Monash University.
Kano, H. (1996) 'Land and tax, property rights and agrarian conflict', paper presented to the International NGO Forum on Indonesia Conference, Canberra.
Kapital (1999) December.
Kapur, B. K. (1996) 'Ethics, values and economic development', in M. G. Quibria and J. M. Dowling (eds) *Current Issues in Economic Development: An Asian Perspective*, Hong Kong: Oxford University Press.
Kartodihardjo, H. (1999) *Toward an Environmental Adjustment: Structural Barrier of Forestry Development in Indonesia*, Washington DC: World Resources Institute.
Kaul, I., Grunberg, I. and Stern, M. A. (eds) (1999) *Global Public Goods: International Cooperation in the 21st Century*, New York: Oxford University Press.
Kennedy, P. (1988) *The Rise and Fall of the Great Powers: Economic Change and Military Conflict from 1500 to 2000*, London: Fontana.
Keohane, R. (1982) 'The demand for international regimes', *International Organization*, 36, 2: 141–71.
—— (1984) *After Hegemony: Co-operation and Discord in the World Political Economy*, Princeton: Princeton University Press.
—— (1995) 'Hobbes's dilemma and institutional change in world politics: sovereignty and international society', in H. H. Holm and G. Sorensen (eds) *Whose World Order? Uneven Globalization and the End of the Cold War*, Boulder: Westview Press.

Keohane, R. and Nye, J. (1977) *Power and Interdependence: World Politics in Transition*, New York: Little, Brown.

Khammone Phonekeo (1993) speech by Vice-minister of Industry and Handicrafts at Conference on 'The Emerging Private Power Sector in Asia', Bangkok, March.

Kim, H. (1997) 'Korean NGOs: global trend and prospect', *Global Economic Review*, 26, 2: 93–115.

—— (2000a) 'The state and civil society in transition: the role of non-governmental organizations in South Korea', *The Pacific Review*, 13, 4: 595–613.

—— (2000b) 'Fragility or continuity? Economic governance of East Asian capitalism', in R. Robison, M. Beeson, K. Jayasuriya and H-R. Kimet (eds) *Politics and Markets in the Wake of the Asian Crisis*, London: Routledge.

—— (2000c) 'The state, civil society, and development in South Korea', manuscript submitted to the Asia Foundation.

—— (2001a) 'The dilemma of the making of civil society in democratic transition: civic coalition for the 2000 general elections in South Korea', unpublished manuscript.

—— (2001b) 'Unraveling civil society in Korea: old discourses and new insights', presented at the international conference on 'Civil Society in Asia' at Griffith University, Brisbane, 10–12 July.

Kindleberger, C. C. (1973) *The World in Depression, 1929–1939*, Berkeley: University of California Press.

King, A. (1975) 'Overload: problems of governing in the 1970s', *Political Studies*, 23, 2 and 3.

King, D. S. (1987) *The New Right: Politics, Markets and Citizenship*, Basingstoke: Macmillan.

Kirk, M. (1996) *Land Tenure Development and Divestiture in Lao PDR*, Vientiane: GTZ.

Kirkby, R. J. R. (1985) *Urbanisation in China: Town and Country in a Developing Economy 1949–2000 AD*, London: Croom Helm.

KLH/UNDP (1998) *Kebakaran Hutan dan Lahan di Indonesia. Dampak, Faktor dan Evaluasi* [Forest Fires and Land in Indonesia. Impacts, Factors and Evaluation] State Ministry for Environment Republic of Indonesia: United Nations Development Programme.

Kojima, R. (1988) 'Agricultural organisation: new forms, new contradictions', *The China Quarterly*, 116: 706–35.

Kolko, G. (1997) *Vietnam: Anatomy of a Peace*, Routledge: London.

KomNasHam (1996 s/d 1998) *Laporan Tahunan* [Annual Report] Jakarta: Sekretaris Jenderal Komisi Nasional Hak Asasi Manusia.

Kompas (1998) 22 March.

—— (1999a) 4 April.

—— (1999b) 16 April.

—— (2000a) 10 January.

—— (2000b) 3 March.

—— (2000c) 15 April.

—— (1999c) *Partai Partai Politik Indonesia: Ideologi, Strategi, dan Program* [Indonesian Political Parties: Ideology, Strategy and Programme] Jakarta: Kompas.

Kong, J. (1995) 'Nongcun gufen hezuo jingji ji qi zhidu fenxi' [Rural shareholding cooperative economy and analysis of its institution] *Jingji Yanjiu* [Journal of Economic Research] 3: 22–34.

Korea Times (2000) 13 April.

Korten, D. (1990) *Getting to the 21st Century: Voluntary Action and the Global Agenda*, West Hartford: Kumarian Press.

KPA (1998) *Usulan Revisi Undang-Undang Pokok Agraria* [Proposed Revisions to the Agrarian Act] Jakarta: Konsorsium Reformasi Hukum Nasional and Konsorsium Pembaruan Agraria.

KPA Munas (1998) 'Deklarasi konsorsium pembaruan agraria' [Declaration of the agrarian reform consortium] unpublished manuscript.

KPL (Khao San Pathet Lao) (1996) 'News bulletin', March 20, Vientiane: Lao People's Democratic Republic.

Krasner, S. D. (1983) 'Structural causes and regime consequences: regimes as intervening variables', in S. D. Krasner (ed.) *International Regimes*, Ithaca NY: Cornell University Press.

Kwon, H. (1997) 'Beyond European welfare regimes: comparative perspectives on East Asian welfare systems', *Journal of Social Policy*, 26, 4.

Lane, T., Haman, J., Phillips, S., Schulze-Ghattas, M. and Tsikata, T. (1999) *IMF Supported Programs in Indonesia, Korea and Thailand: A Preliminary Assessment*, Washington DC: IMF.

LAP (1994) 'Staff appraisal report: Indonesia', report no. 12820-IND.

—— (1999) 'Evolutionary change in Indonesian land law: traditional law (*Adat*) perspectives', draft final report, Land Administration Project, Topic Cycle 4, prepared by Arcadis Euroconsult in association with PT Pusat Pengembangan Agribisnis for the National Development Planning Agency (BAPPENAS) funded by the Government of Indonesia and World Bank.

Larner, W. (1997) ' "A means to an end": neoliberalism and state processes in New Zealand', *Studies in Political Economy*, 52.

Latin (1998) 'Reorientasi sektor kehutanan untuk mendukung pemberdayaan ekonomi rakyat' [Reorientation of the forestry sector to support the capacity of the people's economy] *http://www.latin.or.id/berita_biotrop.htm*.

Lau, K. Y. and Lee, J. (1999) 'Housing policy reform', in L. Wong and N. Flynn (eds) *Marketizing Social Policy in China*, London: Macmillan.

Leaf, M. L. (1993) 'Urban housing in third world market economies: an overview of the literature', Asian Urban Research Network, Working Paper 1, Vancouver: UBC Centre for Human Settlements.

—— (1995) 'Inner city redevelopment in China: implications for the city of Beijing', *Cities*, 12, 1: 149–62.

—— (1998) 'Urban planning and urban reality under Chinese economic reforms', *Journal of Planning Education and Research*, 18: 145–53.

Leaf, M. L. and students of Plan 545 (1995) 'Planning for urban redevelopment in Quanzhou, Fujian, China', Asian Urban Research Network, Working Paper 5, Vancouver: UBC Centre for Human Settlements.

Lee, C. K. (1998) 'From organized dependence to disorganized despotism: changing labour regimes in Chinese factories', *The China Quarterly*, 157: 44–71.

Lee, E. (1998) *The Asian Financial Crisis: The Challenge for Social Policy*, Geneva: International Labour Office.

Lee, S. K. (1993) 'Concept of the garden city', in G. L. Ooi (ed.) *Environment and the City: Sharing Singapore's Experience and Future Challenges*, Singapore: Times Academic Press.

Levy, S. M. (1996) *Build, Operate, Transfer: Paving the Way for Tomorrow's Infrastructure*, New York: Wiley.

Lewis, C. M. and Mody, A. (1998) 'Risk management systems for contingent infrastructure liabilities', *Public Policy for the Private Sector*, August, 149.

Leyshon, A. (1994) 'Under pressure: finance, geo-economic competition and the rise and fall of Japan's post-war growth economy', in S. Corbridge, N. Thrift and R. Martin, *Money, Power and Space*, Oxford: Blackwell.

Li, L. and O'Brien, K. (1996) 'Villagers and popular resistance in contemporary China', *Modern China*, 22, 1: 28–61.

Li, P. (1995) 'Zhongguo nongcun tudi zhidu gaige: shidi diaocha baogao' [The reform of the land system in rural China: field research notes] *Zhongguo Nongcun Jingji* [Journal of Rural Economy] 3: 38–44.

Li, P. L. (1998) 'Zhongguo shehui xingshi fenxi yu yuce zhongbaogao' (Summary report on analysis and forecast on China's social situation) in Yu, X., Lu, X. Y. and Shan, T. L. (eds) *1998 Nian: Zhongguo Shehui Xingshi Fenxi Yu Yuce* [1998: Analysis and Forecast of China's Social Situation] Beijing: Shehui Kexue Wenxian Chubanshe.

Lin, N. (1995) 'Local market socialism: local corporatism in action in rural China', *Theory and Society*, 24, 3: 301–54.

Little, R. (1997) 'International regimes', in J. Bayliss and S. Smith (eds) *The Globalization of World Politics: An Introduction to International Relations*, Oxford: Oxford University Press.

Liu, X. and Liang, W. (1997) 'Zhejiang cun: social and spatial implications of informal urbanization on the periphery of Beijing', *Cities*, 14, 2: 95–108.

Livingston, I. (1997) 'The experience of privatization and private investment in Lao PDR', *Journal of the Asia Pacific Economy*, 2, 2: 225–38.

Lucas, A. (1992) 'Land disputes in Indonesia: some current perspectives', *Indonesia*, 53: 79–92.

—— (1997) 'Land disputes, the bureaucracy and local resistance in Indonesia', in J. Schiller and B. M. Schiller (eds) *Re-imagining Indonesia: Cultural Politics and Political Culture*, Athens OH: Ohio University Press.

Lucas, A. and Warren, C. (2000) 'Agrarian reform in the era of Reformasi', in Chris Manning and Peter van Diermen (eds) *Social Dimensions of Reformasi and Crisis*, London: Zed Books.

Luttwak, E. (1990) 'From geopolitics to geo-economics', *The National Interest*, summer: 17–23.

Ma, L. J. C. and Xiang, B. (1998) 'Native place, migration and the emergence of peasant enclaves in Beijing', *The China Quarterly*, 155: 546–81.

Macken, M. (1981) *Environmental Protest and Citizen Protest in Japan*, Berkeley: University of California Press.

Mackenzie, G. A., Gerson, P. and Cuevas, A. (1997) 'Can public pension reform increase saving?', *Finance and Development*, 34: 46–9.

Macpherson, C. B. (1978) *Property: Mainstream and Critical Positions*, Oxford: Blackwell.

Mahathir, M. (1996) 'Business partnership a success story', *New Straits Times*, 30 July.

Mahathir, M. and Ishihara, S. (1995) *The Voice of Asia: Two Leaders Discuss the Coming Century*, trans. Frank Baldwin, Tokyo: Kodanshu Institute.

Mai, H. (1999) 'Construction set to begin on first local BOT project', *Vietnam Investment Review*, 11–17 October, 417: 11–17.

Majolelo, Y. (1980) *Pepatah Petitih Minangkabau*, Jakarta: Mutiara.

Malaysia (1995) *The Public Sector Pension Scheme in Malaysia*, Kuala Lumpur: Public Service Department.

—— (1996a) *Social Statistics Bulletin: Malaysia 1996*, Kuala Lumpur: Department of Statistics.

—— (1996b) *Seventh Malaysia Plan, 1996–2000*, Kuala Lumpur: Economic Planning Unit, Prime Minister's Department.

Malpezzi, S. and Mayo, S. K. (1997) 'Getting housing incentives right: a case study of the effects of regulation, taxes, and subsidies on housing supply in Malaysia', *Land Economics: Journal of Planning, Housing*, 73: 372–91.

Mann, M. (1997) 'Has globalization ended the rise and rise of the nation-state?', *Review of International Political Economy*, 4, 3: 472–96.

Mansbridge, J. (1998) 'On the contested nature of the public good', in W. W. Powell and E. S. Clemens (eds) *Private Action and the Public Good*, New Haven: Yale University Press.

Martin, F. (2000) 'From citizenship to queer counter-public: reading Taipei's New Park', *Communal/Plural*, 8: 81–94.

Mayer, J. (1996) 'Environmental organizing in Indonesia: the search for a newer order', in R. D. Lipschutz with J. Mayer (eds) *Global Civil Society and Global Environmental Governance: Priorities from Place to Planet*, Albany: State University of New York.

Mayer, P., Rittberger, V. and Zürn, M. (1993) 'Regime theory: state of the art and perspectives', in V. Rittberger and P. Mayer (eds) *Regime Theory and International Relations*, Oxford: Clarendon Press.

McCarthy, D. D., Hodgkinson, V., Sumariwalla, R. and associates (eds) (1992) *The Non-profit Sector in the United States*, San Francisco: Jossey-Bass.

McCarthy, J. (2000) 'The changing regime: forest property and reformasi in Indonesia', *Development and Change*, 31, 1: 91–129.

McKay, B. and Acheson, J. M. (1990) 'Human ecology of the commons', in B. McKay and J. H. Acheson (eds) *The Question of the Commons: the Culture and Ecology of Communal Resources*, Tucson: University of Arizona Press.

Mearshimer, J. J. (1990) 'Back to the future: instability in Europe after the Cold War', *International Security*, 15, 1: 5–56.

Meyer, C. A. (1996) 'NGOs and environmental public goods: institutional alternatives to property rights', *Development and Change*, 27.

Miller, P. N. (1994) *Defining the Common Good: Empire, Religion and Philosophy in 18th-century Britain*, Cambridge: Cambridge University Press.

Milner, H. (1992) 'International theories of cooperation among nations: strengths and weaknesses', *World Politics*, 44: 466–96.

—— (1997) *Interests, Institutions, and Information: Domestic Politics and International Relations*, Princeton: Princeton University Press.

Mingat, A. (1998) 'The strategy used by high-performing Asian economies in education: some lessons for developing countries', *World Development*, 26: 695–715.

Ministry of Agriculture, People's Republic of China (1992) '1992 nian nongcun gufen hezuo zuzhi fazhan baogao: quanguo 75 ge xian de diaocha fenxi' [Report on the development of the rural shareholding cooperative organisations in 1992: a national survey of seventy-five counties] in *Zhongguo Nongcun Jingji* [Journal of Rural Economy] 3: 47–9.

Mishra, R. (1985) *The Welfare State in Crisis: Social Thought and Social Change*, Brighton: Wheatsheaf.

Mody, A. and Patro, D. K. (1996) 'Methods of loan guarantee valuation and accounting', in A. Mody (ed.) *Infrastructure Delivery: Private Initiative and the Public Good*, Washington DC: World Bank.

Mok, K. H. (1999) 'Education policy reform', in L. Wong and N. Flynn (eds) *Marketizing Social Policy in China*, London: Macmillan.

Mok, K. H. and Wat, K. Y. (1998) 'Merging of the public and private boundary: education and the market place in China', *International Journal of Educational Development*, 18, 3: 255–67.

Moon, S. (1999) 'Partnership between government/non-profit sector in social services of Korea', paper presented at the Asia Third Sector Research Conference, Bangkok, Thailand, 20–2 November.

Morris, L. (1997) 'Eastern distributor faces Federal Court roadblock', *Sydney Morning Herald*, 10 October, 8.

Mubyarto (1992) *Desa dan Perhutanan Social: Kajian Social-antropologis de Prop. Jambi*, Yogyakarta: Aditya Media.

Mundle, S. (1998) 'Financing human development: some lessons from advanced Asian countries', *World Development*, 26: 659–72.

Musgrave, R. A. (1958) *The Theory of Public Finance*, New York: McGraw Hill.

Myers, N. (1980) *Conversion of tropical moist forests: A report prepared for the Committee on Research Priorities in Tropical Biology of the National Research Council*, Washington DC: National Academy of Sciences. Accessible online at *http://www.ciesin.org/docs/002-106/002-106a.html*.

Nababan, A. (1996) 'Pemerintahan desa & pengelolaan sumberdaya alam: kasus hutan adat Kluet-Menggamat di Aceh Selatan' [Village government and natural resource management; the case of the Kluet Menggamat *adat* forest in South Aceh] paper presented to the *Analyisis Dampak Implementasi Undang-Undang*, no. 5 Tahun 1979 tentang Pemerintahan Desa terdadap Masyarakat Adat: Upaya Penyysybab Kebijakan Pemerintahan Desa Berbasis Masyarakat Adat, Wisma Lembah Nyiur – Cisarua.

Naughton, B. (1995) 'Cities in the Chinese economic system: changing roles and conditions of autonomy', in D. S. Davis, R. Kraus, B. Naughton and E. J. Perry (eds) *Urban Spaces in Contemporary China*, New York: Cambridge University Press.

Neave, P. (ed.) (1995) *The Southern Bluefin Tuna Fishery 1993, Fisheries Assessment Report*, compiled by the Southern Bluefin Tuna Fishery Stock Assessment Group, Canberra: Australian Fisheries Management Authority.

Nee, V. (1989) 'Peasant entrepreneurship and the politics of regulation in China', in V. Nee and D. Stark (eds) *Remaking the Economic Institutions of Socialism: China and Eastern Europe*, Stanford: Stanford University Press.

Nee, V. and Lian, P. (1994) 'Sleeping with the enemy: a dynamic model of declining political commitment in state socialism', *Theory and Society*, 23, 2: 253–96.

New Straits Times (1995) 21 June.

—— (1998) 9 October.

New York Times (1999) 26 June.

Newsweek International (1999) 13 December.

North, D. C. (1990) *Institutions, Institutional Change and Economic Performance*, Cambridge: Cambridge University Press.

North, D. C. and Weingast, B. R. (1989) 'Constitutions and commitment: the evolution of institutions governing public choice in seventeenth century England', *The Journal of Economic History*, 49, 4.

NSW Auditor General's Office (1994) *Private Participation in the Provision of Public Infrastructure: The Roads and Traffic Authority*, Sydney: NSW Auditor General's Office.

OECD (1990) *Health Care Systems in Transition: The Search for Efficiency*, Paris: OECD.

Offe, C. (1984) *Contradictions of the Welfare State*, London: Hutchinson.

Office for Government Coordination, South Korea (1998) 'The 198th National Assembly National Policy Committee: data requested for inspection and audit (I-1)', Seoul: Office for Government Coordination.

Oi, J. C. (1986) 'Commercialising China's rural cadres', *Problems of Communism*, 35, 5: 1–15.

—— (1990) 'The fate of the collectives after the commune', in D. Davis and E. Vogel (eds) *Chinese Society on the Eve of Tiananmen*, Cambridge MA: Council on East Asian Studies, Harvard University.

—— (1995) 'The role of the local state in China's transitional economy', *The China Quarterly*, 144: 1132–49.

—— (1998) 'The collective foundation for rapid rural industrialisation', in E. B. Vermeer, F. N. Pieke and Woei Lien Chong (eds) *Cooperative and Collective in China's Rural Development: Between State and Private Interests*, Armonk NY: M. E. Sharpe.

Oi, J. C. and Walder, A. (eds) (1999) *Property Rights and Economic Reform in China*, Stanford: Stanford University Press.

Olson, M. (1965) *The Logic of Collective Action: Public Goods and the Theory of Groups*, Cambridge MA: Harvard University Press.

Olson, Robert G. (1967) 'The good', in P. Edwards (ed.) *The Encyclopedia of Philosophy*, New York: Macmillan.

Onuf, Nicholas (1995) 'Intervention for the common good', in G. M. Lyons and M. Mastanduno (eds) *Beyond Westphalia: State Sovereignty and International Intervention*, Baltimore: Johns Hopkins University Press.

Ooi, G. L. (ed.) (1993) *Environment and the City: Sharing Singapore's Experience and Future Challenges*, Singapore: Times Academic Press.

Ostrom, Elinor (1990) *Governing the Commons: the Evolution of Institutions and Collective Action*, Cambridge: Cambridge University Press.

—— (1998) 'The comparative study of public economies', *American Economist*, 42, 1: 3–18.

Ostrom, E., Berger, J., Field, C. B., Norgaard, R. B. and Policansky, D. (1999) 'Revisiting the commons: local lessons, global challenges', *Science*, 284, 5412: 278–89.

Otto, J. M. (1996) 'Implementation of environmental law in Indonesia: some administrative and judicial challenges', *Indonesian Law and Administration Review*, 2, 1: 32–71.

Owen, A. D. and Troedson, D. A. (1993) 'The Japanese tuna industry', The Japanese Tuna Industry and Market Research Project no. 8928, Canberra: Australian Centre of International Agricultural Research.

Oxford Analytica (1998a) 18 September.

—— (1998b) 9 October.

Pahlman, C. (2000) 'Australia and the Asian Development Bank in the Mekong region', *Focus on Trade*, 50.

Parish, W. L. and Whyte, M. K. (1978) *Village and Family Life in Contemporary China*, Chicago: University of Chicago Press.

Parlindungan, A. P. (1996) 'Apakah perlu UUPA direformasi?' [Does the basic agrarian law need reform?] *Prisma*, 25, 9: 51–6.

—— (1997) 'Hukum pertanahan dalam hubungannya dengan pembangunan perhutanan' [Land law in connection with forest development] *Hutan Rakyat. Hutan untuk Masa Depan*, D.V. Barus: Jakarta, Penebar Swadaya: D. V. Barus, 199–220.

Pass, C. and Lewis, B. (1993) *Collins Dictionary of Economics*, New York: Harper Collins.

Pauly, L. W. (1997) *Who Elected the Bankers? Surveillance and Control in the World Economy*, Ithaca NY: Cornell University Press.

Pei, M. (1995) 'Creeping democratisation in China', *Journal of Democracy*, 6, 4: 65–79.

Pei, X. (1998) 'Township–village enterprises, local governments, and rural communities: the Chinese village as a firm during economic transition', in E. B. Vermeer, F. N. Pieke and W. L. Chong (eds) *Cooperative and Collective in China's Rural Development: Between State and Private Interests*, New York: M. E. Sharpe.

Peluso, N. L. (1990) 'A history of state forest management in Java', in M. Poffenberger (ed.) *Keepers of the Forests: Land Management Alternatives in Southeast Asia*, Manila: Ateneo de Manila University Press.

—— (1992) 'The ironwood problem: (mis)management and development of an extractive rainforest product', *Conservation Biology*, 6, 2: 210–19.

Pempel, T. J. and Tsunekawa, K. (1979) 'Corporatism without labor? The Japanese anomaly', in P. C. Schmitter and G. Lehmbruch (eds) *Trends Toward Corporatist Intermediation*, Beverly Hills: Sage.

Peoples Republic of China (1998) *The Land Management Law of PRC*, Beijing: Zhongguo fazhi chuban she.

Phua, K. (1990) *Privatization and Restructuring of Health Services in Singapore*, Singapore: Institute of Policy Studies.

Pierson, P. (1994) *Dismantling the Welfare State? Reagan, Thatcher and the Politics of Retrenchment*, Cambridge: Cambridge University Press.

Poffenberger, M. (ed.) (1990) *Keepers of the Forests: Land Management Alternatives in Southeast Asia*, Manila: Ateneo de Manila University Press.

Polanyi, K. (1957) *The Great Transformation: The Political and Economic Origins of Our Time*, Boston MA: Beacon Press.

Pong, S. L. (1993) 'Preferential policies and secondary school attainment in peninsular Malaysia', *Sociology of Education*, 66: 245–61.

Potter, L. (1996) 'Forest degradation, deforestation, and reforestation in Kalimantan: towards a sustainable land use?', in C. Padoch and N. L. Peluso (eds) *Borneo in Transition: People, Forests, Conservation and Development*, Kuala Lumpur: Oxford University Press.

Powell, W. W. (1987) *The Non-profit Sector: A Research Handbook*, New Haven: Yale University Press.

Powell, W. W. and Clemens, E. S. (eds) (1998) *Private Action and the Public Good*, New Haven: Yale University Press.

Prescott, N. and Nichols, L. (1997) 'International comparison of medical savings accounts', paper presented at conference on Financing Health Care and Old Age Security, Institute of Policy Studies and the World Bank, Singapore, 8 November.

Price, M. D. (1999) 'Nongovernmental organizations on the geopolitical front line', in G. J. Demko and W. B. Wood (eds) *Reordering the World*, Greenwood: Westview Press.

Probert, J. and Young, S. D. (1995) 'The Vietnamese road to capitalism: decentralisation, de facto privatisation and the limits to piecemeal reform', *Centre for Research into Communist Economies*, 7, 4: 499–525.

Psota, T. (1998) 'Changes in land use and economy in Upper Lebong', in V. King (ed.) *Environmental Challenges in South-East Asia*, Richmond: Curzon.

PSPD (1999) *The 5th Annual Meeting Reference Book*, http://www.pspd.org/structure.html.

PTUN (1991 s/d 1998) *Laporan Keadaan Perkara Tahun 1991* [Annual Situation Report for Cases] Jakarta: Pengadilan Tata Usaha Negara.

Putnam, R. D. (1993) *Making Democracy Work: Civic Traditions in Modern Italy*, Princeton: Princeton University Press.

Pye, L. W. (1996) 'The state and the individual: an overview interpretation', in B. Hook (ed.) *The Individual and the State in China*, Oxford: Clarendon Press.

Quan, M. (1998) 'Electricity prices set to increase sharply next year', *Vietnam Investment Review*, 30 Nov.–6 Dec., 372: 6.

Ragayah, H. M. Z. (1998) 'Poverty alleviation in Malaysia: achievements and challenges', paper presented at International Conference on Economic Growth, Poverty and Income Inequality in the Asia Pacific Region, 19–20 March.

Rajah, A. (1999) 'Making and managing tradition in Singapore: the National Day Parade', in K. W. Kwok, K. C. Guan, L. Kong and B. Yeoh (eds) *Our Place in Time*, Singapore: Singapore Heritage Society.

Ramli, R. and Ahmad, M. (1994) *Rente Ekonomi Pengusahaan Hutan Indonesia* [Economic Rent for Indonesian Forestry Companies] Jakarta: WALHI.

Rein, M. and Rainwater, L. (eds) (1986) *Public/Private Interplay in Social Protection*, London and New York: Routledge.

Reinicke, W. H. (1998) *Global Public Policy: Governing without Government?*, Washington DC: Brookings Institute.

Reisman, D. (1990) *Theories of Collective Action: Downs, Olson and Hirsch*, Houndmills: Macmillan.

'Report of the Seventh Meeting of Australian, Japanese and New Zealand Scientists on Southern Bluefin Tuna' (1988) unpublished report, 15–19 August, Wellington.

Republika (1998) 28 December.

—— (2000) 23 March.

Reuters (1998) 15 April.

Riau Post (2000) 8 February.

Risse-Kappen, T. (ed.) (1995) *Bringing Transnational Relations Back In*, Cambridge: Cambridge University. Press.

Robison, R. (1996) 'Looking north: myths and strategies', in R. Robison (ed.) *Pathways to Asia: the Politics of Engagement*, Sydney: Allen and Unwin.

Rodan, G. (1997) 'Singapore in 1996: extended election fever', *Asian Survey*, 37, 2: 175–81.

Rose, N. (1996) 'Governing "advanced" liberal democracies', in A. Barry, T. Osborne and N. Rose (eds) *Foucault and Political Reason: Liberalism, Neo-liberalism and Rationalities of Government*, London: UCL Press.

Rose, N. and Miller, P. (1992) 'Political power beyond the state: problematics of government', *British Journal of Sociology*, 43, 2.

Rosenau, J. and Czempiel, E. (eds) (1992) *Governance without Government: Order and Change in World Politics*, Cambridge: Cambridge University Press.

Ross, M. (1996) 'Conditionality and logging reform in the tropics', in *Institutions for Environmental Aid*, Cambridge MA: MIT Press.

Ruwiastuti, M. (n.d.) 'Indigenous peoples' land rights in Indonesia: towards a bottom-up legal framework for the recognition and protection of *adat* land in the national context', unpublished manuscript (project proposal to Toyota Foundation).

Ruwiastuti, M., Fauzi, N. and Bachriadi, D. (1997) *Penghancuran Hak Masyarakat Adatatas Tanah* [Destruction of Community *Adat* Land Rights] Bandung: Konsorsium Pembaruan Agraria and INPI Pact.

Safitri, M. (1995) 'Hak dan akses masyarakat lokal pada sumberdaya hutan: kajian peraturan perundangan-undangan Indonesia' [Rights and access of local community to forest resources: evaluation of Indonesian regulations] *Ekonesia: A Journal of Indonesian Human Ecology*, 3: 1–24.

Salamon, L. M. (1987) 'Partners in public service: the scope and theory of government/non-profit relations', in W. W. Powell (ed.) *The Non-profit Sector: A Research Handbook*, New Haven: Yale University Press.

—— (1995) *Partners in Public Service: Government/Nonprofit Relations in the Modern Welfare State*, Baltimore: Johns Hopkins University Press.

Salamon, L. M. and Anheier, H. K. (1994) *The Emerging Sector: An Overview*, Baltimore: Johns Hopkins University Institute for Policy Studies.

Saludo, R. (1997) 'Crossroads for ASEAN', *Asiaweek*, 12 December.

Samson, M. (1998) 'Promoting conservation and forestation in Asia', *ADB Review*, 30: 3.

Samuelson, P. (1954) 'The pure theory of public expenditures', *Review of Economics and Statistics*, 36: 387–9.

Sandel, M. (1997) 'Anti-social security', *The New Republic*, 216: 3 February.

Sargeson, S. (1999) *Reworking China's Proletariat*, Houndmills: Macmillan.

Sargeson, S. and Zhang, J. (1999) 'Reassessing the role of the local state: a case study of local government interventions in property rights reform in a Hangzhou district', *The China Journal*, 42: 77–99.

Savage, V. (1992) 'Street culture in colonial Singapore', in B. Chua and N. Edwards (eds) *Public Space: Design, Use and Management*, Singapore: Singapore University Press.

Schindler, L. (1998) 'The Indonesian fires and SE Asian haze 1998/99: review, damages, causes and necessary steps', available online at *http//www.iffm.or.id/SIN-Paper.html*.

Schinz, A. (1989) *Cities in China*, Berlin: Gebrer Borntraeger.

Schipper, K. M. (1977) 'Neighborhood cult associations in traditional Tainan', in G. W. Skinner (ed.) *The City in Late Imperial China*, Stanford: Stanford University Press.

Schmidtz, D. (1991) *The Limits of Government: An Essay on the Public Goods Argument*, Boulder: Westview.

Selden, M. (1993) *The Political Economy of Chinese Development*, Armonk NY: M. E. Sharpe.

Sell, J. and Son, Y. (1997) 'Comparing public goods with common pool resources: three experiments', *Social Psychology Quarterly*, 60: 2.

Selvaratnam, V. (1994) *Innovations in Higher Education: Singapore at the Competitive Edge*, World Bank Technical Paper 222, Asia Technical Department Series, Washington DC: World Bank.

Serambi (1998) 17 September.

Shari, I. (1998) 'Economic growth and income inequality in Malaysia, 1971–1995', unpublished paper presented at International Conference on Economic Growth, Poverty and Income Inequality in the Asia Pacific Region, 19–20 March.

Shue, V. (1988) *The Reach of the State: Sketches of the Chinese Body Politic*, Stanford: Stanford University Press.

—— (1995) 'State sprawl: the regulatory state and social life in a small Chinese city', in D. S. Davis, R. Kraus, B. Naughton and E. J. Perry (eds) *Urban Spaces in Contemporary China*, New York: Cambridge University Press.

Siew, W. S. (1999) *Re-visioning a Barber's Tools: the Photographic Construction of Chinatown*, unpublished academic exercise, Department of Sociology, National University of Singapore.

Simon, P. D. I. H. (1998) 'Indonesian government must immediately implement just and democratic forest resource management', available online at *http://www.latin.or.id/diskusi_fkkm_jogja_english.htm*.

Skinner, G. W. (1977) 'Introduction: urban social structure in Ch'ing China', in G. W. Skinner (ed.) *The City in Late Imperial China*, Stanford: Stanford University Press.

Skinner, G. W. (ed.) (1977) *The City in Late Imperial China*, Stanford: Stanford University Press.

Skinner, S. (1998) 'Financing infrastructure: what it takes to get the big projects rolling', *Vietnam Economic Times*, November: 4.

Smillie, I. and Helmich, H. (ed.) (1993) *Non-Governmental Organizations and Governments: Stakeholders for Development*, Paris: OECD.

Smith, S. (ed.) (1996) *Public Policy for the Private Sector, Special Edition*, Washington DC: World Bank.

Smith, T. (1988) *Native Sources of Japanese Industrialization 1750–1920*, Berkeley: University of California Press.

Smyth, R. (1998) 'Recent developments in rural enterprise reform in China: achievements, problems and prospects', *Asian Survey*, 38, 8.

Snidal, D. (1985) 'The limits of hegemonic stability theory', *International Organization*, 39, 4: 579–614.

—— (1991) 'International cooperation among relative gains maximisers', *International Studies Quarterly*, 35.

Sodiki, H. A. (1996) 'Konflik pemilikan hak atas tanah perkebunan' [Conflict, property rights in plantation land] *Prisma*, 25, 9: 37–50.

Soesangobeng, H. (1988) 'Perkembangan konsepsi tanah dalam masyarakat desa: 25 tahun UUPA' [Developing conceptions of land in village society: 25 years since the Basic Agrarian Law] *Kabar Seberang*, 19/20: 59–83.

—— (1998) Notulen pertemuan LASA/ILAP, LSM, BPN Pusat, Bandung 2/7/98 [unpublished notes on the meeting of representatives of the Land Administration Project, Non-government organisations and the National Land Board].

Solinger, D. (1995) 'The floating population in the cities: chances for assimilation', in D. S. Davis, R. Kraus, B. Naughton and E. J. Perry (eds) *Urban Spaces in Contemporary China*, New York: Cambridge University Press.

Somboune, M. (1997) *An Overview of Hydropower Development in the Lao PDR*, Vientiane: Hydropower Office.

South China Morning Post (2001) 18 August.

Sonius, H. W. J. (1981) 'Introduction', in J. F. Holleman (ed.) *Van Vollenhoven on Indonesian Adat Law*, The Hague: Martinus Nijhoff.

Spiertz, J. and Wiber, M. G. (n.d.) 'The bull in the china shop: regulation, property rights and natural resource management: an introduction', in J. Spiertz and M. G. Wiber (eds) *The Role of Law in Natural Resource Management*, The Hague: VUGA.

Standing, G. (1996) 'Social protection in Central and Eastern Europe: a tale of slipping anchors and torn safety nets', in G. Esping-Andersen (ed.) *Welfare States in Transition, National Adaptations in Global Economies*, London: Sage.

Stanley (1994) *Seputar Kedung Ombo*, Jakarta: Lembaga Studi dan Advokasi Masyarakat.

Steinberg, R. (1987) 'Non-profit organizations and the market', in W. W. Powell (ed.) *The Non-profit Sector: A Research Handbook*, New Haven: Yale University Press.

Stern, N. H. (1991) 'Public policy and the economics of development', *European Economic Review*, 35: 241–71.

Stevens, R. (1996) 'Submission no. 25.1', in *Joint Standing Committee on Treaties: Inquiry into the Subsidiary agreement between the Government of Australian and the Government of Japan Concerning Japanese Tuna Longline Fishing*, Canberra: Australian Fisheries Management Authority.

Stiglitz, J. (1998a) 'Sound finance and sustainable development in Asia', keynote address to Asian Development Forum, Manila, 12 March.

—— (1998b) 'Remarks to Human Development Week', Arlington, 5 March.

Straits Times (1994) 3 December.

—— (1996) 4 November.

Strange, S. (1987) 'The persistent myth of lost hegemony', *International Organization*, 41, 4: 551–74.

—— (1994) *States and Markets*, London: Pinter.

—— (1995) 'Purposes of public action: provision of collective goods and redistribution of wealth: a European view', in R. Benjamin, C. R. Neu and D. D. Quigley (eds) *Balancing State Intervention: the Limits of Transatlantic Markets*, New York: St Martin's Press.

—— (1996) *The Retreat of the State: The Diffusion of Power in the World Economy*, Cambridge: Cambridge University Press.

Stretton, H. and Orchard, L. (1994) *Public Goods, Public Enterprise, Public Choice: Theoretical Foundations of the Contemporary Attack on Government*, New York: St Martin's Press.

Stuart-Fox, M. (1993) 'Prospects for democracy in Laos', *Asian Studies Review*, 17, 2: 121–8.

Stubbs, R. (2000) 'Signing on to liberalisation: AFTA and the politics of regional economic cooperation', *Pacific Review* 13,2: 297–318.

Suara Merdeka (1998) 19 July.

Suara Pembaruan (1998a) 27 November.

—— (1998b) 23 Nevember.

—— (1998c) 3 November.

—— (1998d) 14 November

—— (1998e) 26 December.

—— (1999a) 17 March.

—— (1999b) 15 April.

—— (2000a) 1 March.

—— (2000b) 6 February..

Suhendar, E. (1994) *Pemetaan pola-pola Sengketa Tanah di Jawa Barat*, Bandung: Yayasan AKATIGA.

Suhendar, E. and Kasim, I. (1996) *Tanah Sebagai Komoditas: Kajian Kritis atas Kebijakan Pertanahan Orde Baru* [Land as Commodity: A Critical Analysis of New Order Land Policy] Jakarta: ELSAM.

Suhendar, E. and Winarni, Y. B. (1998) *Petani dan Konflik Agrari* [Farmers and Agrarian Conflict] Bandung: AKATIGA.

Sunderlin, W. D. and Resosudarmo, I. A. P. (1997) 'Rate and causes of deforestation in Indonesia: towards a resolution of the ambiguities', available online at *http://www.cgiar.org/cifor/publications/occpaper/occpaper9.html*.

Sung, Ki-Young (1999) 'Regaining small shareholders' rights', *Sisa Journal*, 492: 74.

Suyanto, B. (1996) 'Pembangunan kota dan sengketa tanah' [City development and land cases] *Prisma*, 25, 9: 37–50.

Sylva Indonesia (1998) 'Petermuan menhutbun dengan mahasiswa fakultas kehutanan UGM Yogyakarta' [Meeting of the forestry minister with students from the forestry faculty UGM Yogyakarta] available online at *http://www. latin.or.id/info_bagi_kudeta.htm*.

Szelenyi, I. (1978) 'Social inequalities in state socialist redistributive economies', *International Journal of Comparative Sociology*, 19, 1–2: 63–87.

Tamar, M. A. and Walton, M. (1998) *Social Consequences of the East Asian Financial Crisis*, Washington DC: World Bank.

Tan, J. (1998) 'The marketisation of education in Singapore: policies and implications', *International Review of Education*, 44: 47–63.

Tang, W. (1994) 'Urban land development under socialism: China between 1949 and 1977', *International Journal of Urban and Regional Research*, 18, 3: 392–415.

Taylor, M. (1982) *Community, Anarchy and Liberty*, Cambridge: Cambridge University Press.

—— (1987) *The Possibility of Cooperation*, Cambridge: Cambridge University Press.

Taylor, M. and Singleton, S. (1993) 'The communal resource: transaction costs and the solution of collective action problems', *Politics and Society*, 21, 2.

Tempo (1999a) 5 April.

—— (1999b) 12 April.

—— (2000) 2 April.

Thayer, C. (1994) 'Vietnam's program of renovation', in G. H. Hassall and T. P. Truong (eds) *Infrastructural Development and Legal Change in Vietnam*, Melbourne: University of Melbourne.

THPC (Theun Hinboun Power Company) (2000) *Mitigation and Compensation Program*, Vientiane: Theun Hinboun Power Company.

Timber and Wood Products (1998) 'Indonesia's forest industry dogged by questions', 28 November.

Tjondronegoro, S. (1991) 'The utilization and management of land resources in Indonesia', in J. Hardjono (ed.) *Indonesia: Resources, Ecology and Environment*, Singapore: Oxford University Press.

Tsamenyi, M. and McIlgorm, A. (1995) *International Environmental Instruments: Their Effect on the Fishing Industry*, University of Wollongong and Australian Maritime College: Fisheries Research and Development Corporation Project.

Tsura, S. (1999) *Political Economy of the Environment: The Case of Japan*, London: Athlone Press.

Tuan, N. A. (1994) 'Foreign investment and infrastructure development', in G. H. Hassall and T. P. Truong (eds) *Infrastructural Development and Legal Change in Vietnam*, Melbourne: University of Melbourne.

Turner, I. M. and Yong, J. W. H. (1999) 'The coastal vegetation of Singapore', in C. Briffet and H. H. Chew (eds) *State of the Natural Environment in Singapore*, Singapore: Nature Society.

Underhill, G. (1995) 'Keeping governments out of politics: transnational securities markets, regulatory Cupertino, and political legitimacy', *Review of International Studies*, 21: 251–78.

UNESCO (1995) *Statistical Yearbook 1995*, Paris: UNESCO.

United Nations (1980) *Non-Governmental Organizations Associated with the Development of Public Information: NGO/DPI List, Information for NGO Representatives*, New York: United Nations.

—— (1999) *Human Development Report 1999: Globalization with a Human Face*, Oxford: Oxford University Press.

Usher, A. D. (1997) *Dams as Aid: A Political Anatomy of Nordic Development Thinking*, Routledge: London.

van de Walle, D. and Kimberley, N. (eds) (1996) *Public Spending and the Poor*, Baltimore: Johns Hopkins University Press.

Verdery, K. (1996) 'Wither "Nation" and "Nationalism"?', in G. Balakrishnan (ed.) *Mapping the Nation*, London: Verso.

Vermeer, E. B., Pieke, F. N. and Chong, W. L. (eds) (1998) *Cooperative and Collective in China's Rural Development: Between State and Private Interests*, New York: M. E. Sharpe.

Vietbid (1998) *BOT Investments in Power in Vietnam: Current Situation and Future Prospects*, Hanoi: Private Sector Development Programme, Royal Danish Embassy.

Vietnam (1996) *Public Investment Program 1996–2000*, Hanoi: Government of Vietnam.

Vietnam Economic Times (1996) 25 May.

Vietnam News Service (1999) 'Power price rise to fund much needed investment', *Vietnam News Service*, 10 September.

Viotti, P. R. and Kauppi, M. V. (1993) *International Relations Theory: Realism, Pluralism, Globalism*, New York: Macmillian.

Viraphonh, V. (1997) 'Country paper: Lao PDR', fourth meeting of the Subregional Power Forum, Asian Development Bank, 29–31 October.

Wade, R. (1990) *Governing the Market: Economic Theory and the Role of Government in East Asian Industrialization*, Princeton: Princeton University Press.

Walder, A. (1986) *Communist Neo-Traditionalism: Work and Authority in Chinese Industry*, Berkeley: University of California Press.

WALHI (1997) 'Sejuta bencana di proyek pengembangan lahan gambut satu juta hektar' [One million disasters regarding the one million hectare peat land project] unpublished manuscript.

Wang, C. (1995) 'Communities of "provincials" in the large cities: conflicts and integration', *China Perspectives*, 2: 17–21.

Wang, L. and Wu, C. (1993) 'Dui Guangzhou shi nongcun gufen hezuo jingji ruogan wenti de kanfa' [Opinions on several issues of the rural shareholding cooperative system in Guangzhou] *Zhongguo Nongcun Jingji* [Journal of Rural Economy] 3: 50–1.

Wang, M. (1995) 'Place, administration, and territorial cults in late imperial China: a case study from south Fujian', *Late Imperial China*, 16, 1: 33–78.

Warren, C. (1993) *Adat and Dinas: Balinese Communities in the Indonesian State*, Kuala Lumpur: Oxford University Press.

—— (1998a) 'Tanah Lot: the environmental and cultural politics of resort development in Bali', in P. Hirsch and C. Warren (eds) *The Politics of Environment in Southeast Asia*, London: Routledge.

—— (1998b) 'Whose tourism? Balinese fight back', *Inside Indonesia*, 54: 24–5.

Warren, C. and Elston, K. (1994) *Environmental Regulation in Indonesia*, Perth: Asia Research Centre Murdoch University and University of Western Australia Press.

Waspada (1998) 26 September.

Weaver, K. and Alden, D. (1999) 'Australia's oceans policy: a fisheries perspective', paper presented at the International Symposium on Society and Resource Management, Brisbane, 7–10 July.

Weber, M. (1997) 'Effects of Japanese government subsidies on distant water tuna fleets', in S. Burns (ed.) *Subsidies and Depletion of World Fisheries*, Washington DC: WorldWide Fund.

Weintraub, J. (1997) 'The theory and politics of the public/private distinction', in J. Weintraub and K. Kumar (eds) *Public and Private in Thought and Practice: Perspectives on a Grand Dichotomy*, Chicago: University of Chicago Press.

Weisbrod, B. (1977) *The Voluntary Non-profit Sector: An Economic Analysis*, Lexington: D. C. Heath.

Weiss, L. (1998) *The Myth of the Powerless State: Governing the Economy in a Global Era*, Ithaca NY: Cornell University Press.

—— (2000) 'Developmental states in transition: adapting, dismantling, innovating, not "normalising"', *Pacific Review*, 13, 1: 21–56.

Weiss, L. and Hobson, J. (1995) *States and Economic Development: A Comparative Historical Analysis*, London: Polity Press.

—— (2000) 'State power and economic strength revisited: what's so special about the Asian crisis?', in R. Robison, M. Beeson, K. Jayasuriya and H-R. Kimet (eds) *Politics and Markets in the Wake of the Asian Crisis*, London: Routledge.

Weiss, T. G. and Gordenker, L. (1996) *NGOs, the UN, and Global Governance*, Boulder: Lynne Reinner.

Weitzman, M. and Xu, C. (1994) 'Chinese township – village enterprises as vaguely defined cooperatives', *Journal of Comparative Economics*, 18, 2: 121–45.

White, G. (1993) *Riding the Tiger: The Politics of Reform in Post-Mao China*, London: Macmillan.

—— (1996) 'The dynamics of civil society in post-Mao China', in B. Hook (ed.) *The Individual and the State in China*, Oxford: Clarendon Press.

White, L. (1998) *Unstately Power*, Armonk NY: M. E. Sharpe.

Whyte, M. K. and Parish, W. L. (1984) *Urban Life in Contemporary China*, Chicago: University of Chicago Press.

Wigan, M. (1997) *The Last of the Hunter Gatherers: Fisheries Crisis at Sea*, Perth: Swan Hill Press.

Willets, P. (1982) *Pressure Groups in the Global System: The Transnational Relations of Issue-oriented Non-governmental Organizations*, New York: St Martin's Press.

Williams, D. and Young, T. (1994) 'Governance, the World Bank and liberal theory', *The Journal of Politics*, 55: 4.

Winters, J. (2000) 'The financial crisis in Southeast Asia', in R. Robison, M. Beeson, K. Jayasuriya and H-R. Kimet (eds) *Politics and Markets in the Wake of the Asian Crisis*, London: Routledge.

Wolch, J. (1990) *The Shadow State: Government and Voluntary Sector in Transition*, New York: The Foundation Center.

Wolf, A. P. (1996) 'The "new feudalism": a problem for sinologists', in L. Douw and P. Post (eds) *South China: State, Culture and Social Change during the 20th Century*, Amsterdam: North Holland.

Womack, B. (1991) 'An exchange of views about Chinese social organization: transfigured community: neo-traditionalism and work unit socialism in China', *The China Quarterly*, 126: 313–32.

Wong, A. K. and Yeh, S. (1985) *Housing a Nation: 25 Years of Public Housing in Singapore*, Singapore: Housing and Development Board.

Wong, L. (1994) 'Privatization of social welfare in post-Mao China', *Asian Survey*, 34, 4: 307–25.

—— (1998a) 'Unemployment', in J. Hebel and G. Schucher (eds) *Der Chinesische Arbeitsmarkt* [The Chinese Labor Market] Hamburg: Institute of Asian Affairs.

—— (1998b) *Marginalization and Social Welfare in China*, London and New York: Routledge and LSE.

—— (1999) 'Welfare policy reform', in L. Wong and N. Flynn (eds) *Marketizing Social Policy in China*, London: Macmillan.

Wong, L. and Ngok, K. (1997) 'Unemployment and policy responses in mainland China', *Issues and Studies*, 33, 1: 43–63.

Woo-Cumings, M. (1997) 'Slouching toward the market: the politics of financial liberalization in South Korea', in M. Loriaux (ed.) *Capital Ungoverned: Liberalizing Finance in Interventionist States*, Ithaca NY: Cornell University Press.

—— (ed.) (1999) *The Developmental State*, Ithaca NY: Cornell University Press.

World Bank (1990) *Indonesia: Sustainable Development of Forests, Land, and Water*, Washington DC: World Bank.

—— (1993) *The East Asian Miracle: Economic Growth and Public Policy*, World Bank Policy Research Report, Oxford: Oxford University Press.

—— (1994a) *Governance: the World Bank's Experience*, Washington DC: World Bank.

—— (1994b) *Indonesia Environment and Development: Challenges for the Future*, report no. 12083-IND, Jakarta: World Bank.

—— (1994c) *World Development Report 1994: Infrastructure for Development*, Washington DC: World Bank.

—— (1995a) 'Indonesia: land administration project' (unpublished internal document).

—— (1995b) *The Nam Theun II Hydroelectric Project Technical Mission: Aide-Memoire*, Washington DC: World Bank.

—— (1996a) *The Impact of Environmental Assessment: Second Environmental Assessment Review of Projects Financed by the World Bank*, Washington DC: World Bank.

—— (1996b) *Socialist Republic of Vietnam – Aide-Memoire of the World Bank: Mission to Support Private Investment in Infrastructure, July 5 1996*, Hanoi: World Bank.

—— (1997a) *Public Expenditure Review, Lao PDR*, Washington DC: World Bank.

—— (1997b) *World Development Indicators CD ROM*, Washington DC: World Bank.

—— (1997c) *China 2020. Financing Health Care: Issues and Options for China*, Washington DC: World Bank.

—— (1997d) *World Development Report: The State in a Changing World*, Washington DC: World Bank.

—— (1998a) *World Development Indicators CD ROM*, Washington DC: World Bank.

—— (1998b) *Social Crisis in East Asia*, www.worldbank.org/poverty/eacrisis/whatis.htm.

—— (1999) *Fueling Vietnam's Development: New Challenges for the Energy Sector*, Washington DC: World Bank.

—— (2000) 'Background on the forests: analysis of the existing situation', press release on Seminar on Indonesian Forestry for the Post-Consultative Group Meeting on Indonesia, Jakarta, 26 January 2000, lsalazar@worldbank.org.

World Health Organisation (1993) *Evaluation of Recent Changes in the Financing of Health Services*, Geneva: World Health Organisation.

Worley and Lahmeyer International (2000) *Hydropower Development Strategy for Lao PDR, Volume A, Draft Final Report*, Vientiane: Hydro Power Office.

Wu, F. (1995) 'Urban processes in the face of China's transition to a socialist market economy', *Environment and Planning C: Government and Policy*, 13: 159–77.

Wu, J. Y. (1994) 'Nation-state construction: social memory and monumental space: the construction of the 228 Monument', unpublished master's thesis, Graduate Institute of Building and Planning, National Taiwan University.

Wu, W. (1999) 'Temporary migrants in China's urban settings: housing and settlement patterns', paper presented at ISA RC21 international conference on 'The Future of Chinese Cities: A Research Agenda for the 21st Century', 28–31 July, Shanghai.

Wuthnow, R. (1991) 'The voluntary sector: legacy of the past, hope for the future', in R. Wuthnow (ed.) *Between States and Markets: The Voluntary Sector in Comparative Perspective*, Princeton: Princeton University Press.

Wyatt, A. (1996) 'The contested landscape of environmental assessment in a developing country: the case of Lao PDR', unpublished honours thesis, Division of Geography, University of Sydney.

Yee, A. H. and Lim, T. G. (1995) 'Educational supply and demand in East Asia: private higher education', in A. H. Yee (ed.) *East Asian Higher Education: Traditions and Transformations*, Oxford: Oxford University Press.

Yeh, A. G. O. and Wu, F. (1996) 'The new land development process and urban development in Chinese cities', *International Journal of Urban and Regional Research*, 20, 2: 330–53.

Yeh, S. H. K. (1985) 'The idea of the garden city', in K. S. Sandhu and P. Wheatley (eds) *Management of Success: The Moulding of Modern Singapore*, Singapore: Institute of Southeast Asian Studies.

Yin, Q. and White, G. (1994) 'The marketization of Chinese higher education: a critical assessment', *Comparative Education*, 30, 3: 217–37.

YLBHI (1998) 'Perampasan tanah dan sumber daya alami lain milik rakyat oleh negara akan terus berlanjut' [Seizure of land and other natural resources belonging to the people by the state will continue] unpublished report, Jakarta: Yayasan Lembaga Bantuan Hukum Indonesia, Divisi Tanah dan Lingkungan.

Yoshino, M. Y. and Lifson, T. B. (1986) *The Invisible Link: Japan's Sogo Shosha and the Organization of Trade*, Cambridge MA: MIT Press.

Young, O. (1983) 'Regime dynamics: the rise and fall of international regimes', in S. Krasner, (ed.) *International Regimes*, Ithaca NY: Cornell University Press.

—— (1994) *International Governance: Protecting the Environment in a Stateless Society*, Ithaca NY: Cornell University Press.

Yujia cun (Yujia village) (1994) 'Hangzhou shi xihu qu Gujia zhen Yujia cun cungui minyue' [The village code of Yujia village, Gujia town, Xihu district, Hangzhou] unpublished document of Yujia village.

Yujia cun dangzhongzhi (Yujia village party branch of CCP) (1995) 'Chuang wenming zuo gongxian: Yujia cun chuangjian wenming danwei gongzuo huibao' [Promoting civilization, making contributions: the report of Yujia village's effort to become a civilised organization] unpublished document of Yujia village.

Yujia VSC (1993) 'Gujia zhen Yujia cun gufen jingji hezuo she zhangcheng' [Regulations of Yujia shareholding cooperative, Gujia town] unpublished document of Yujia village.

—— (1996) 'Shenhua gaige zhuan jizhi, cujin jingji kuai fazhan' [Deepening the reform and transforming the mechanism, accelerating economic development] unpublished document of Yujia village.

Zarsky, L. (1997) 'Stuck in the mud? Nation-states, globalization and the environment', *Aprenet On-line Library*, available at *http://www.nautilus.org/aprenet/library/regional/mud.html*.

Zhang, D. (1990) 'Jiushi niandai Zhongguo shehui fuli shiye zhanwang' [Prospects of Chinese social welfare development in the 90s] keynote speech given at the 'China and Hong Kong in the Nineties: Social Welfare Development' conference, Beijing, 31 October.

Zhang, J. (1997) 'Informal construction in Beijing's old neighbourhoods', *Cities*, 14, 2: 85–94.

Zhang, X., Wang, D. and Pan, J. (1993) 'Qiangzhixing de zhidu bianqian yu nongdi zhengyongfei de shiyong yu quanshu' [Imposed institutional change and the disposal and ownership of the land requisition fee] *Zhongguo Nongcun Jingji* [Journal of Rural Economy] 2: 37–44.

Zhongguo Minzheng Tongji Nianjian [China Civil Affairs Statistical Handbook] (1998) Beijing: Zhongguo tongji chubanshe.

—— (1999) Beijing: Zhongguo tongji chubanshe.

Zhongguo Tongji Nianjian 1996 [China Statistical Yearbook 1996] (1996) Beijing: Zhongguo tongji chubanshe.

Zhou, J. and Wu, Y. (1992) 'Nongcun hezuozhi de xin fazhan' [New developments in the rural cooperative system] in *Zhongguo Nongcun Jingji* [Journal of Rural Economy] 8: 34–7.

Zhu, Q. (1999) '1998–1999 nian: zhongguo de renmin shenghuo zhuangkuang' [1998–1999: the Chinese people's livelihood], in Yu, X., Lu, X. Y. and Shan, T. L. (eds) *1999 Nian: Zhongguo Shehui Xingshi Fenxii Yu Yuce* [1999: An Analysis and Forecast of the Social Situation in China] Beijing: Shehui Kexue Wenxian Chubanshe.

Zhu, L. and Jiang, Z. (1993) 'From brigade to village community: the land tenure system and rural development in China', *Cambridge Journal of Economics*, 17, 4: 441–61.

Zhuang, G. (1996) 'The social impact on their home town of Jinjiang emigrants' activities during the 1930s', in L. Douw and P. Post (eds) *South China: State, Culture and Social Change during the 20th Century*, Amsterdam: North Holland.

Zhuang, Y. (1996) 'God cults and their credit associations in Taiwan', in L. Douw and P. Post (eds) *South China: State, Culture and Social Change during the 20th Century*, Amsterdam: North Holland.

INDEX OF AUTHORS

SUBJECT INDEX

NB. Bold numbers indicate a table.

For Product Safety Concerns and Information please contact our EU
representative GPSR@taylorandfrancis.com
Taylor & Francis Verlag GmbH, Kaufingerstraße 24, 80331 München, Germany

www.ingramcontent.com/pod-product-compliance
Ingram Content Group UK Ltd.
Pitfield, Milton Keynes, MK11 3LW, UK
UKHW021009180425
457613UK00019B/862